ECHOES OF ALL OUR CONVERSATIONS

The Actors - Bonus Book
2023 Annotated Edition

Interviews by
Joe Nazzaro

Edited and Annotated by
Jason Davis

Design, Production & Marketing: Jaclyn Easton, Publishing 180
Senior Editor: Jason Davis
Sr. Production Associate: Gretchen Brewer
Production Associate: Avery Devellis
Editor: Cynthia Davis
Archivist, Historian & Ombuds: Jan M. Schroeder
Proofreader: Gretchen Brewer

Echoes Of All Our Conversations - The Actors - 2023 Annotated Edition
Part 1: 978-1-63077-103-4
Part 2: 978-1-63077-104-1
Part 3: 978-1-63077-106-5
Bonus - Group Interviews: 978-1-63077-110-2

TABLE OF CONTENTS: The Group Interviews

Page 141
Apr 2001

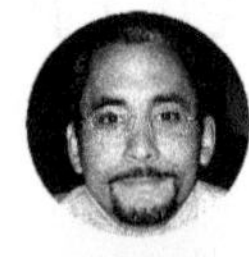
RICHARD BIGGS
Stephen Franklin

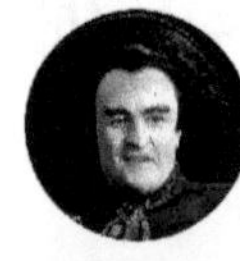
PETER JURASIK
Londo Mollari

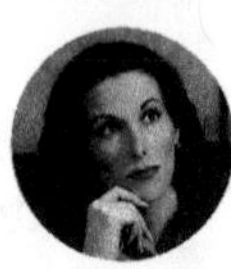
JULIE CAITLIN BROWN
Na'Toth & Guinevere Corey

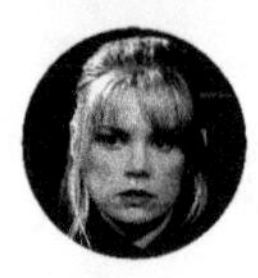
MARJORIE MONAGHAN
Tessa Halloran

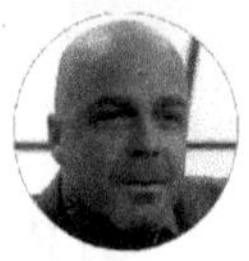
JERRY DOYLE
Michael Garibaldi

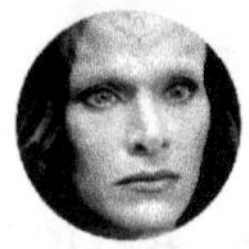
CARRIE DOBRO
Dureena Nafeel

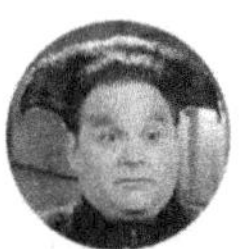

STEPHEN FURST
Vir Cotto

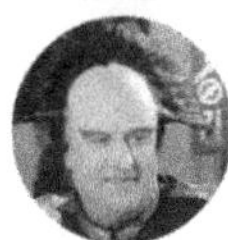

PETER JURASIK
Londo Mollari

6 February 1995, Babylonian Productions

Babylon 5 Timeline
In Production: "Knives" (216)
On the Air: "The Coming of Shadows" (209)

This interview was conducted by journalist Joe Nazzaro, with occasional input from his wife, British makeup designer Sheelagh Wells.

I was saying to [executive story editor] Larry [DiTillio], one of the nice things when you get to interview a couple of people together, is you get a different chemistry than if I talk to you, Stephen, on the phone. We'll talk about one thing. If I talk to Peter, you get another, but you don't get any sort of chemistry between other people.

I find when you're talking about a show like Babylon 5, certainly, that people tend to bounce off each other much more, because you say you remember this, you remember that. I think it makes for a nicer article sometimes.

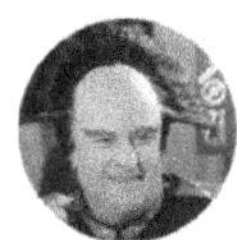

JURASIK
I think usually that's true. But Stephen, though, we don't really get along very well. There's not much chemistry. I don't have anything to bounce off a person like him. You got anything to bounce off someone like me?

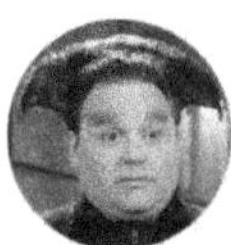

FURST
No.

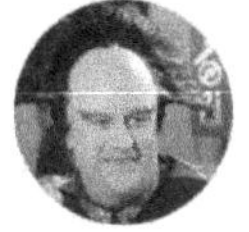

JURASIK
No. You know what I mean? I think your theory is right under usual circumstances, even though I think not.

I have been told—by no less than three people over the last two weeks—that the Centauri scenes that we see between the two of you are actually the tip of the iceberg. Most of the stuff that you guys do is actually cut out.

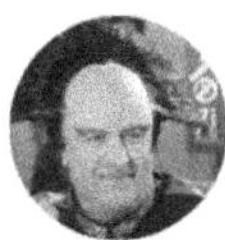

FURST
Yes, it's true. They don't like us, what we come up with. We would love to do the scenes the way we would like to do them, which are a lot more comedic, I think.

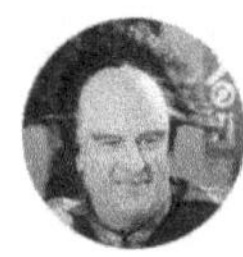

JURASIK
Maybe an exception for comedic actors, but Stephen and I both come from very very heavy acting-school drama background. The inner life and the background characters are very important to us. [A beat.] He's believing me. He's so serious! All we talk about is what Vir and Londo eat, what Vir cooks for him, right?

I think it should be pointed out that I have learned at an early age to keep an absolute straight face, so as to be polite.

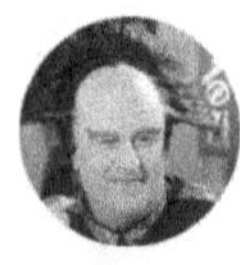

JURASIK
That's right.

I didn't wanna insult you by laughing in your face. I hope you realize that.

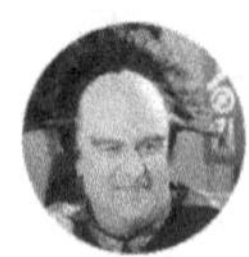

JURASIK
One of the things about this show is that you really don't have time to rehearse unless you actually say, "Let's go out for five minutes and do something."

Do you find that you actually try to get the chance to do that? Or do you just go out there and wing it, as far as the two of you are concerned?

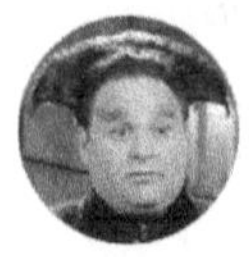

FURST
We actually do get a time to rehearse. By the time we do a blocking rehearsal and a lighting rehearsal—and then, while they're lighting—we run lines and come up with ideas and stuff. I think we do get time to rehearse.

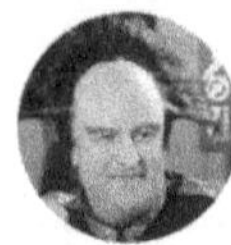

JURASIK
I need more rehearsal, generally speaking, than Stephen.

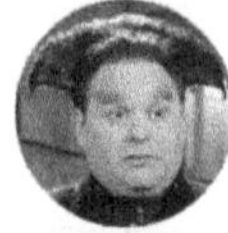

FURST
Because you have more lines!

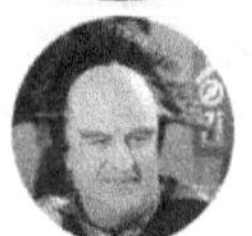

JURASIK
Why is that? I don't know. I like to go over things, and I really don't know what the reason is. I go over stuff and he's much more spontaneous actor. This is just pointing out the reality.

Yesterday, for instance, they were putting down marks, remember, marks on the floor, where to hit. Stephen said, "Don't put 'em down. I'll, I'll just hit wherever." He's just a looser actor, in some sense.

Have things changed from when you first started working on this series together? Looking at the episode that was just on last week ["The Coming of Shadows"], the characters' roles have changed considerably. Londo is now

changing into a character that you might not like very much. Vir is now becoming the person who's the last voice of sanity. Is there the same opportunity to be comedic about these things as there were in those first couple of episodes you were doing together?

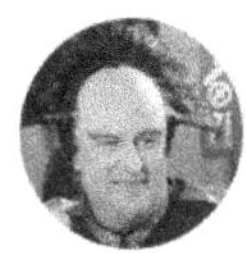

JURASIK
Moreso. The more serious it gets, the funnier behind-the-scenes Stephen and I get. Isn't that true? There's nowhere you'll laugh more than in church, as you know, or at a funeral. Once you start giggling at a funeral, you're gone. The more serious we get, the funnier behind the scenes. Is that true?

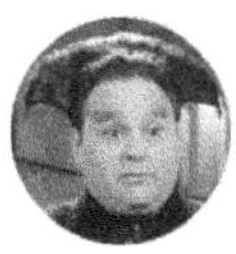

FURST
I think so, yeah. Very well put.

Even with this Centauri opera scene, in this episode ["Knives"] for example, it's still quite a serious one for Londo. Vir has the task of really pointing out to him again the faults that he's going through.

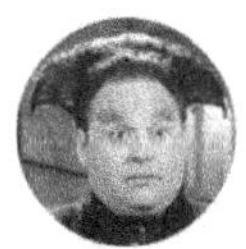

FURST
It's true.

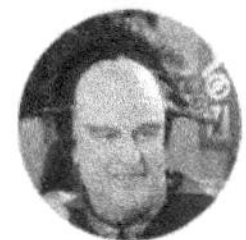

JURASIK
I guess we're not bouncing off each other are we? [Laughs.]

As the two characters, we have gone through a lot of changes. Vir really has become the conscience. Londo, in his inevitably weak-hearted style, has been seduced by power. So we've changed a great deal as two characters.

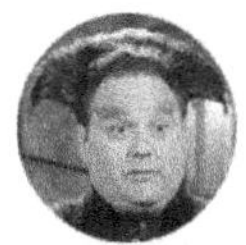

FURST
Yes, but you still have more costumes than I do. [Laughs.]

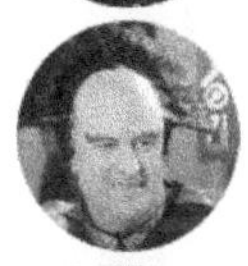

JURASIK
My hair is still bigger than his is.

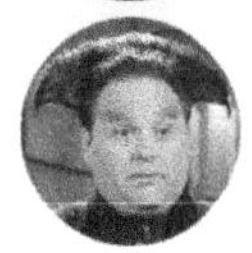

FURST
I have to have the same costume the entire season, and it doesn't make sense.

> While Londo Mollari changed coats mid-season and had a rotating selection of waistcoats, Vir Cotto got a complete wardrobe overhaul for year two, but wore the new costume in every scene.

Maybe that's why you need a raise.

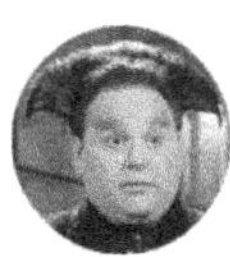

FURST
Well, that's for sure.

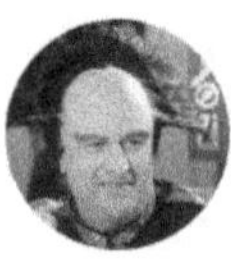

JURASIK
That's definitely true. For the most part, I'm sure everyone knows we work for a very meager salary, basically done out of love. Stephen, I don't think you get anything, right? You work for nothing.

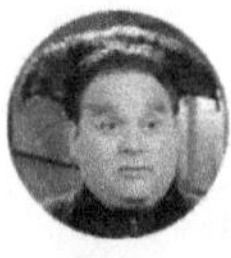

FURST
That's true.

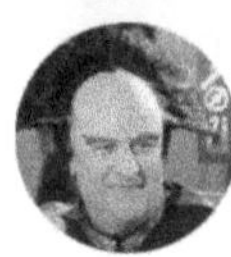

JURASIK
Well, some call it food.

That's a week's worth of things.

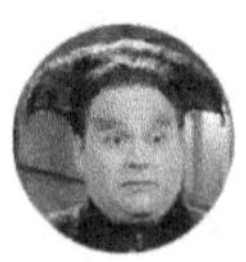

FURST
That's right.

Do the two of you sit down and watch these [shows] when they actually air? It's gotta be considerably different than when you're actually doing it on stage. Especially if you can't take it a hundred percent seriously, the stuff that is finally on the air.

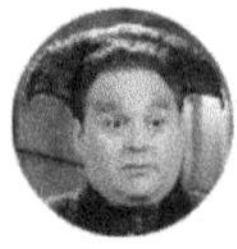

FURST
I'm just trying to find out the time slots. I keep channel surfing and cannot find the damn show.

> At the time of this interview, *Babylon 5* was broadcast on KCOP, channel 13 in the Los Angeles market, on Thursdays at 8:00pm, with a repeat Sunday at 10:00pm. While PTEN programming was formally scheduled for Wednesday nights, local programming directors could change it.

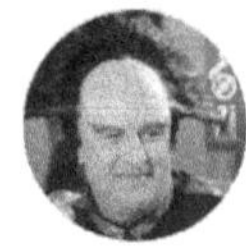

JURASIK
I know! I don't watch very much. I really don't. I'm looking forward to finding out who Kosh is, but no, I really don't. There are episodes from the first season that I was in that I haven't seen yet. It's for no other reason than in terms of interests.

I dunno if this sounds like an overly serious actor, but I was never an actor to watch dailies. Remember how when you were doing *St. Elsewhere*, and they used to show dailies down at the building at MTM? All the time, they said, "Come on down for dailies." He and I worked on the same lot when I was doing *Hill Street* [*Blues*], and I never went. I hated watching. I don't like to see them. What happens is vanity gets in the way, and you start looking at your own nose and saying, "Geez, my nose is that big? I don't like her nodding her head a lot about my nose being big."

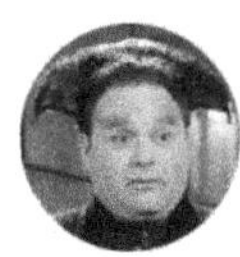

FURST
I don't like watching dailies either, unless I'm directing, and then you gotta watch dailies. But I don't like to watch dailies as an actor.

> Stephen Furst directed the 1994 movie *Magic Kid II*, and would go on to direct three episodes of *Babylon 5*, two episodes of *Crusade*, and many other projects.

It doesn't help you to adjust your performances, as far as each other? You've got it down now instinctively enough that you don't have to keep reevaluating it?

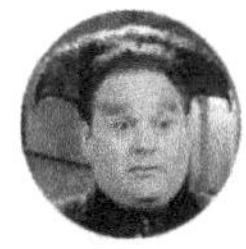

FURST
I don't think I reevaluate it, do you?

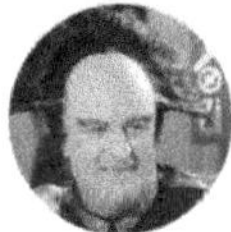

JURASIK
You know, Joe, when you were talking about joking—making people talk about us, joking around a lot—in a sense, that's how we grow together and make adjustments. Any adjustments are going on in our character. He and I joke a lot before we do stuff, but in a way, that keeps us really, really on top of how the characters relate.

In other words, we don't just have the scene to relate about. We talk about whether we're gonna get some smoked salmon and who's gonna pick up the bagels. Right? All the time. We do that all the time. Who's cooking dinner? Can Vir get my pants pressed, and stuff like that. That gives us an inner life.

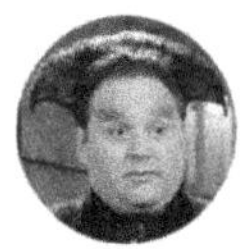

FURST
I think people get stuck, as an actor, when they take themselves in the character too seriously anyway. We can have very serious moments, but we're very light hearted in between the serious moments.

SHEELAGH WELLS: The danger of watching it in dailies all the time is it becomes a technical performance instead of an instinctive one.

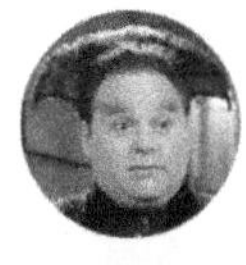

FURST
Mechanical, I think is the right word, right?

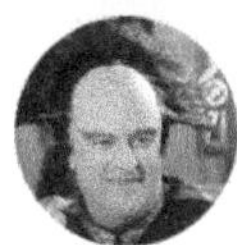

JURASIK
That's the joke of the day. That's very funny.

There isn't a temptation to direct him then, is there?

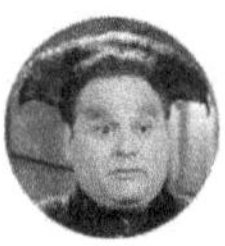

FURST
To direct Peter? He needs no director. He's great. He's one of my favorite people I've ever worked with, really. Seriously. I'm not just saying that because he's here...

Very close to you.

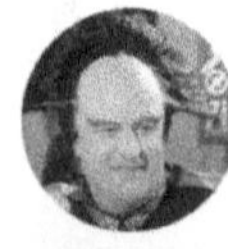

JURASIK
That's right.

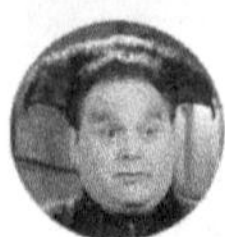

FURST
He's talented. He's funny.

This is probably unprofessional on my part. It's hard to act with somebody that you don't like. It's much harder. If I don't like the person, and I don't think they're a nice person, it's harder for me to act with them, especially if we're supposed to be close comrades and stuff.

Granted, you had known each other for years on a casual basis, how quickly did the two of you really link in together as far as your characters on this show? To the viewer, really from the start, there was this great chemistry, but there isn't always an instant chemistry between two people when you start working.

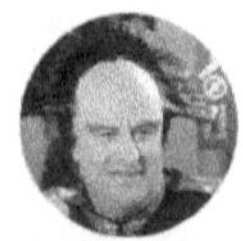

JURASIK
Well, should we tell him? People don't know that we are in fact distantly related. Seriously, Did you not know this? No.

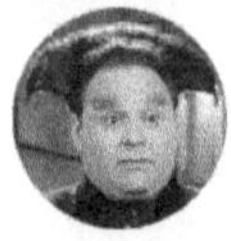

FURST
Yes. We started discussing it the first time we met each other.

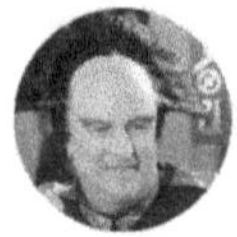

JURASIK
Here's the relationship. My father's brother—my uncle—married your father's half-sister. The first time we met, how old were we?

> Larry DiTillio integrated a relationship into his character sketches for Londo Mollari and Vir Cotto, giving the latter a Mollari mother.

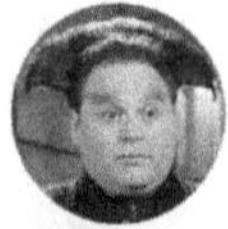

FURST
Oh, oh, oh. The very, very first time?

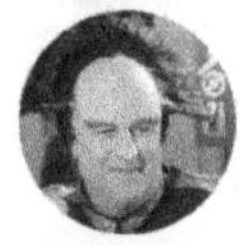

JURASIK
That's right.

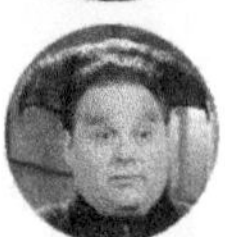

FURST
We were like four-years-old and I kind of blocked it out.

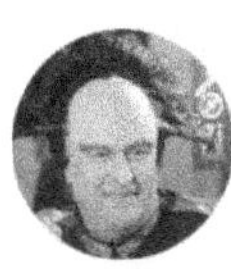
JURASIK
That half-sister was a circus performer, too, a Romanian circus performer. Right? A juggler?

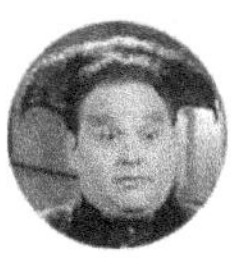
FURST
My last name is not really Furst, it's Fuerstein, which is German/Romanian.

Fuerstein?

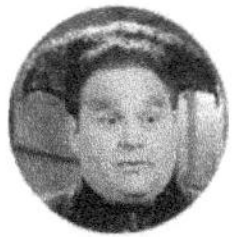
FURST
Fuerstein.

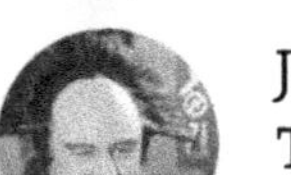
JURASIK
The tragic death of our aunt—

What happened to her?

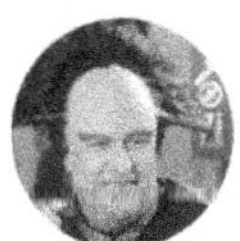
JURASIK
How was the story told?

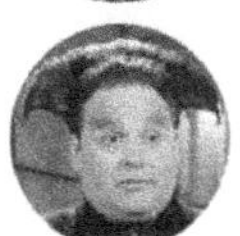
FURST
In Romania, the circus performers do more than one act. They don't do just one thing.

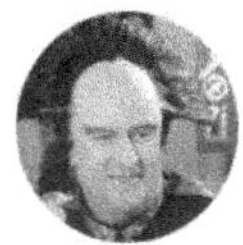
JURASIK
As you know about circus performers, in Romania, you gotta have a couple of gimmicks, or you ain't making a circus. That's the way Romanians are—what can I say?

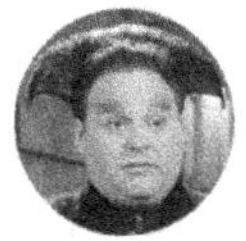
FURST
It's a very famous story within our family, and depending on which aunt or uncle is telling it to you, this aunt was killed by a different circus accident. [Laughs.] I always understood that she was juggling.

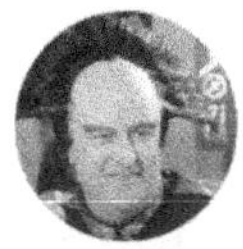
JURASIK
That's right.

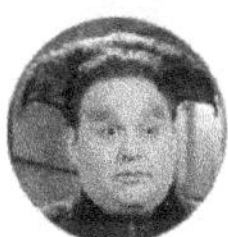
FURST
She got hit. It's not funny, but you can't help but laugh. You died getting hit by a juggling pin. Other people will say it's a high-wire or attacked by a circus bear, but I still believe the one about juggler. It had to be the juggler, because I saw pictures of her and she did have this mark—a permanent mark—on her head.

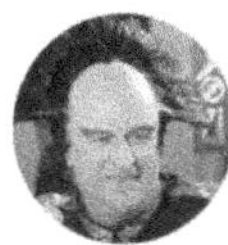
JURASIK
That wasn't a mark. That was her nose. That's no bump on my head; that's my nose. [Laughs.] He's three or four more episodes. I'm only kidding.

So this is just from sort of hanging out, talking to each other, that all of a sudden you realize that—

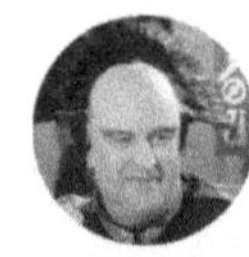

JURASIK
No, we met. We knew each other as kids!

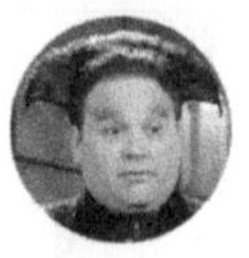

FURST
I barely remember. I barely remembered it. He brought it up to me and it kind of sparked my memory.

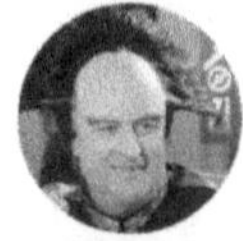

JURASIK
We met at two or three family gatherings in New Jersey. Your mother used to dress you as a girl for an inordinate amount of years.

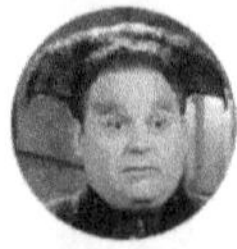

FURST
No, not as a girl.

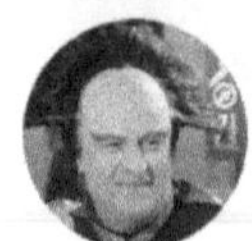

JURASIK
You wore a tam!

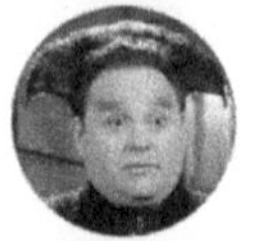

FURST
At party functions, my mother tended to dress me more feminine.

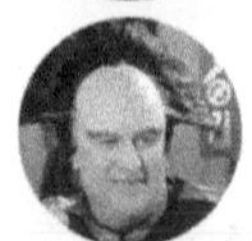

JURASIK
That's right. So that's why I remembered him.

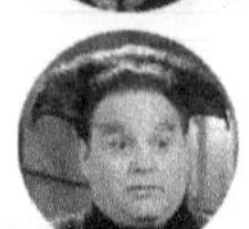

FURST
You know, little hats and things like that.

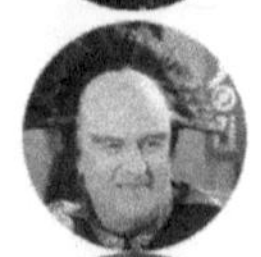

JURASIK
He was giving me the eyes across the room. Anyway, that's the family history.

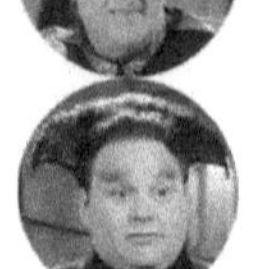

FURST
But we are related. I think we're second cousins.

I know there's always supposed to be subtext between the characters, but don't you think that's taking it just a bit too— So you said he's still overcompensating now, for all this, after all these— [Laughs.]

Has Joe really told the two of you—as far as both of your roles—where they're going to be over the next couple of years, or is he still sort of spoonfeeding information? I know it has been said that at some point Vir is really going to say, "Hold it. This is as much as I could possibly take."

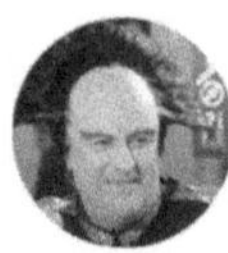

JURASIK
That's right. From what Joe has told me, Vir does that three or four episodes in, and then he's done, right? He's out of the series. That's what I understand. I guess

Furst was released from his contract in season three to star in the short-lived Fox comedy, *Misery Loves Company*, and Vir was briefly written out of the show, becoming diplomatic envoy to Minbar.

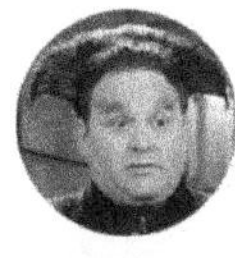

FURST
I know Joe has like a five-year plan, and I don't know where I fit into it.

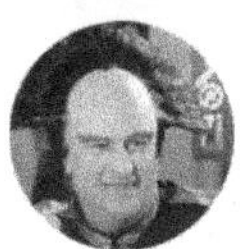

JURASIK
I don't know anything about the bible. I have no idea. Do you know? Does Vir eventually put his foot down with me?

A series bible is a document that outlines the premise of the show, details the characters, and sometimes provides clues to future story developments. *Babylon 5*'s bible was a revised version of the treatment originally used to pitch the series to Warner Bros., and wasn't updated after 20 May 1993, when the writing of the initial season one scripts began in earnest.

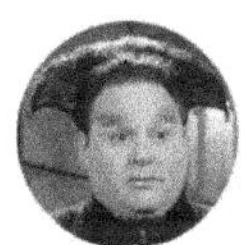

FURST
I don't know. I just heard that you're gonna become mean and meaner and that I think the Narns are gonna be taken over or something.

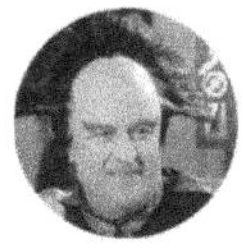

JURASIK
For the same reason that I don't watch dailies, I don't read the bible.

What Joe calls the bible, he's offered it to me, and I have no interest. I don't wanna know where the character is going, because then I start playing the arc. I don't wanna play the arc at all. You know when it's exciting and you're reading a novel and you start the new chapter—

Have the two of you sat down and done any sort of backstory, just to make the performances easier? I know Andreas [Katsulas, as G'Kar] and Caitlin [Brown as Na'Toth], last year, had sat down, figuring out the entire Narn culture.

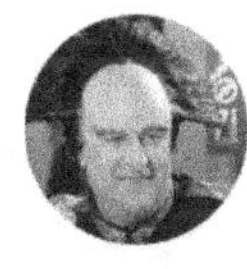

JURASIK
Once again, it gonna sound really boring, but we haven't, have we, Stephen? Did we do any backstory?

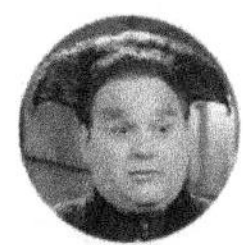

FURST
Just the fact that I know I was given this job as a token. He got it as a favor for me.

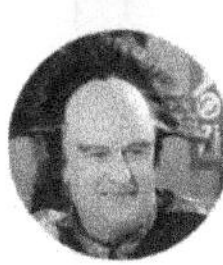

JURASIK
I think all the riffing we do on it, that's the base backstory we could do.

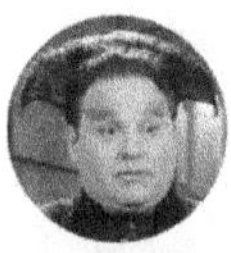

FURST
That's about it. We're very unartistic, aren't we?

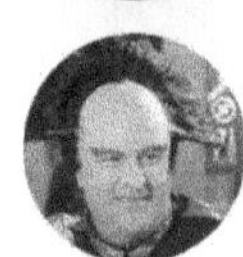

JURASIK
I don't know.

It's all in the perception, isn't it? I think you can be over-prepared, sometimes, for a character. If you're so mired in a backstory, then you might be afraid to break out of it.

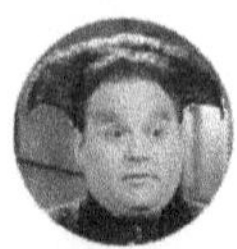

FURST
I never use, as an actor, the backstory. Only when I was forced to in school, and they told you to write back stories.

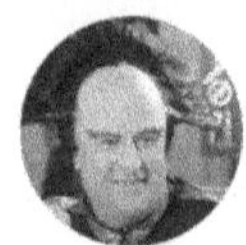

JURASIK
I've had horrible experiences with directors tying me down, making me do the backstory. Horrible.

Tell me about some of the scenes that have been cut out, that Babylon 5 viewers will never see—the guilty secrets of each other, the ones that have been cut.

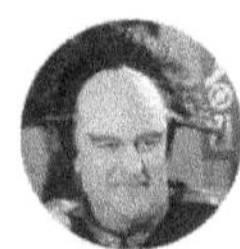

JURASIK
One of the most consistent riffs we do is with the character Refa. You know Lord Refa?

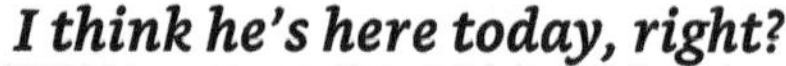

I think he's here today, right?

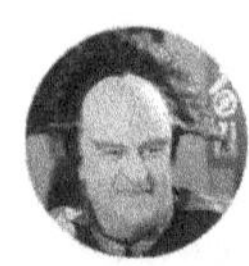

JURASIK
Stephen and I have our backstory on Refa. He's the guy who smuggles things onto Babylon 5. Thus the name: Refa. Right? So he can get you just about anything you want and he's always bringing us—what do we want him to bring?

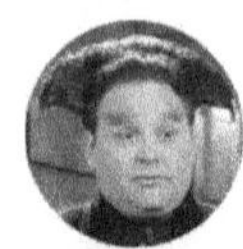

FURST
Gourmet-type foods that are illegal. [Laughs.]

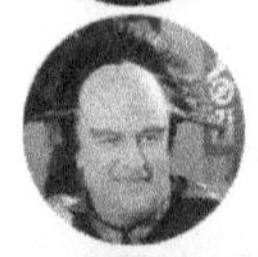

JURASIK
Like really good salmon, you know? Can you get us some bagels?

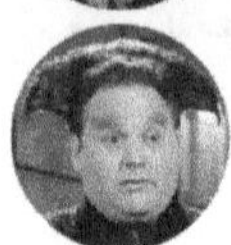

FURST
That's why Refa is so important to us.

> Jeanne Cavelos's third Babylon 5 novel, *The Passing of the Techno-Mages: Summoning Light*, established that the noble Refa family had suffered an economic decline that forced the current lord to engage in commercial ventures, including grain transport, so Jurasik and Furst's imaginings were retroactively semi-canonized in the tie-in novel.

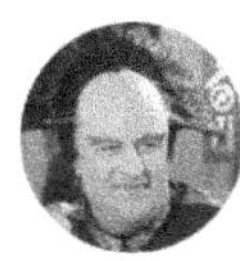

JURASIK
That's one of our big back stories. One about me doing the drink is one we always do.

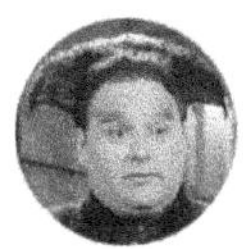

FURST
Every time he wants to drink—he doesn't even have to say it anymore—he just goes like this to me. It's like sign language, Centauri sign language. It means "Get me a drink." I always thought that we were romantically involved.

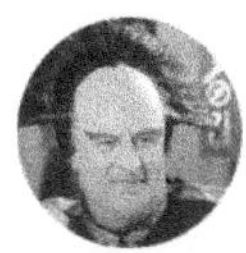

JURASIK
There's no question about that.

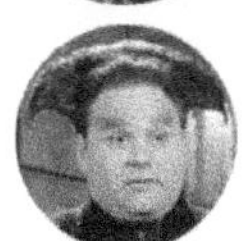

FURST
No, I did.

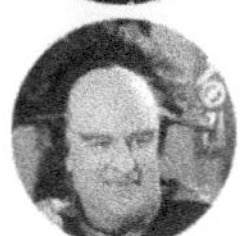

JURASIK
They dated for a little bit, but things didn't work out. He was not the dancer that Londo needed. He can't move well on his feet. I guess that's a war injury, right?

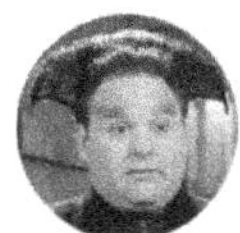

FURST
Oh yes, yes. I do let myself in for these things, don't I?

Have they cut scenes that you guys thought were just so good, for whatever reasons, but they just didn't fit in?

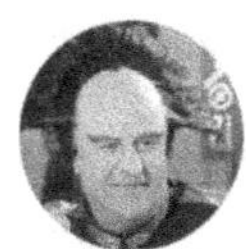

JURASIK
Do you know whether they have?

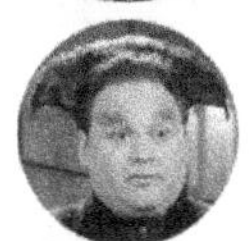

FURST
No, because we don't watch the show.

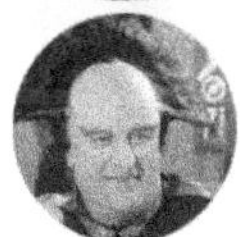

JURASIK
That's right.

So they could've cut 80% of your performance. You don't know.

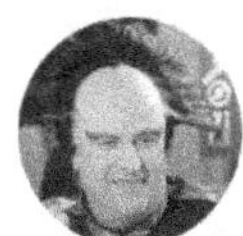

JURASIK
The bottom line on Stephen and I is: we just work here.

What have been some of the more enjoyable moments, as far as the two of you? Granted, you don't see these things, but you know when they print [a take], that scene worked really well between the two of [you].

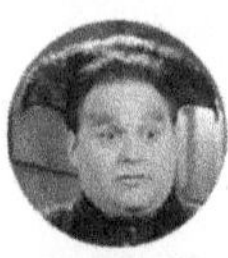

FURST
My favorite moments are when I have scenes with him. I don't mind doing things with other people, but—

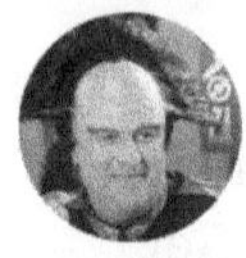

JURASIK
I didn't know you did scenes with other people! Do you?

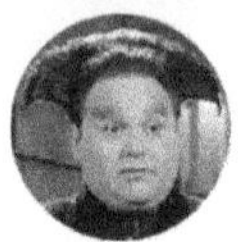

FURST
Very rarely. It's kinda like *St. Elsewhere*, where there's like two or three doctors that I did scenes with almost exclusively. Then, once in a while, I would—

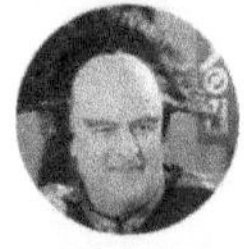

JURASIK
Do you have particular scenes you like that we did?

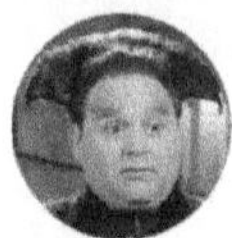

FURST
Oh. I like the scene we did a couple days ago when I was pouring my heart out to you. At the bar. I was drunk.

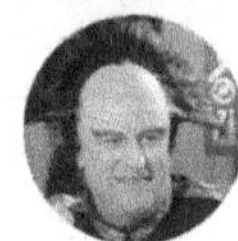

JURASIK
Oh, that was great. That was a great episode ["There All the Honor Lies"].

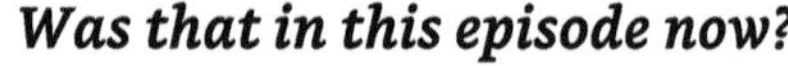

Was that in this episode now?

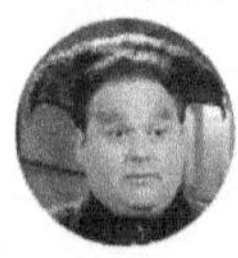

FURST
It was in the one before. Right? I'm drunk, and I'm telling all my problems because I feel like I'm getting replaced. I am actually getting replaced on the show.

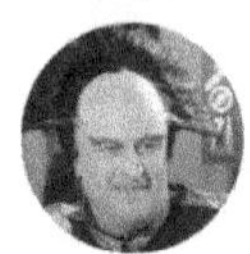

JURASIK
That's a great episode because, as I said, Vir's character's become my conscience a little bit in this second [season]. It sort of bubbles up to the top. It starts to grow on Vir, a little bit. You can't handle the fact that he has to be my moral touchstone.

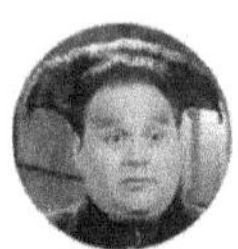

FURST
And keeping his secrets and stuff. He's gonna try to overthrow his own government [by replacing the emperor] and his own planet, and I have to keep that a secret because of my loyalty to him.

The one ["The Coming of Shadows"], that was on this past week, was a very good one for both characters. All of a sudden, as I was saying before, Londo isn't the kind of person that you will necessarily like. At the same time, Vir has this great scene where he is saying, "Well, I'm gonna have to remind you of this same conversation a couple of years from now."

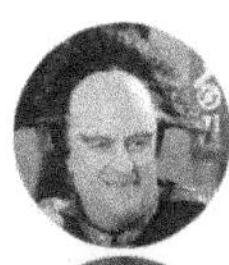
JURASIK
Oh, that was a good scene. Remember I told you a day ago about that scene?

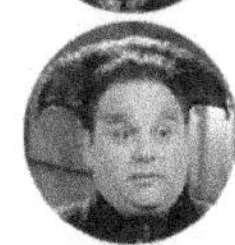
FURST
I didn't see the show. Did you see the show?

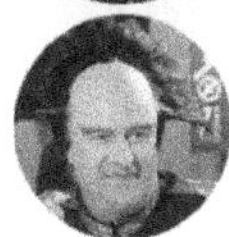
JURASIK
Yeah, I did see the show. I taped it. Yeah, that was a great scene.

That would pay it off really, really well. There's more meat to the characters now than there [was] a year ago. Most of the early stuff was really lighthearted, wasn't it? And now—

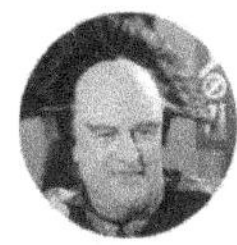
JURASIK
You know what, Joe? When you said my favorite moment, I bring this up all the time to [Stephen]. I say, "Remember that first scene [in "Midnight on the Firing Line"]—the very first day we had to work together—was really fun and really dangerous and interesting. It was just like stepping out on a high wire, or something.

There's the Romanian circus in us again. [Laughs.] But that's exactly how it felt, and I remember we were just winging it and—

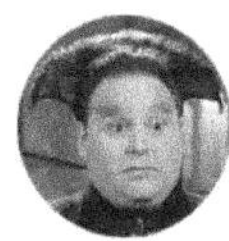
FURST
I had no idea where the character was; I was winging it. Then I was told—I think, at first by one of the directors—that I should not be as wimpy, but that turned out to be wrong and he never came back. I don't know.

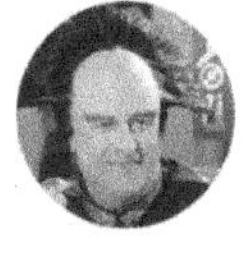
JURASIK
It's a little like Caitlin, a lot of good it did her. [Laughs.] She's gonna kill me. She's big, too.

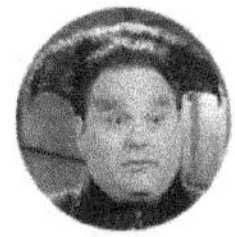
FURST
Our very first scene is me trying to help him, and him throwing things at me.

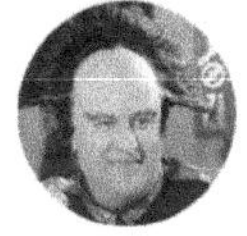
JURASIK
I was just drunk. We just had to go for it. I have such nice memories of that first day, because it just felt like we worked all day together. We had three or four scenes to do.

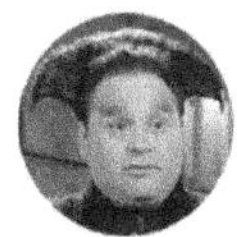
FURST
I said, "Do you think we're doing this too big?" and he goes, "I don't know." [Laughs.]

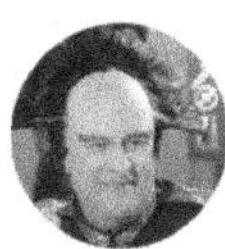
JURASIK
It's the first season. I don't know.

So—Just Keep Doing It.

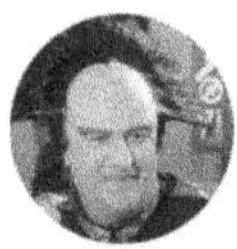

JURASIK
Yeah. Let's just go, let's just let it rip.

Do the directors more or less give you your head now, as far as how far you can take it? In an episodic—I'm sure you both know—the director will generally let the artists do their thing and concentrate on the technical performances and maybe work with the guest artists more, who don't know their characters. Do they pretty much let you guys just go about it? Then, when you've gone too far, they say, "Okay, that's it." They sort of trim off what they can't use?

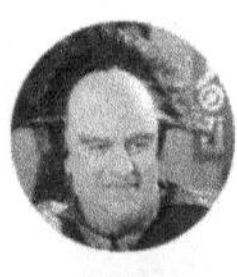

JURASIK
You're the director, you talk about the directors.

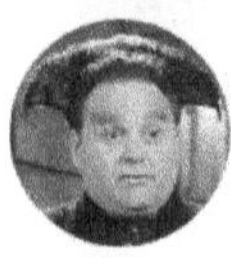

FURST
Each director is different, and I think some come in having their own ideas, even though they've seen the show. There are certain directors that I think both Peter and I enjoy working with more than others.

Give me an example.

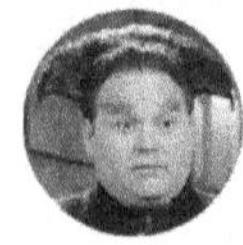

FURST
Names?

Yes.

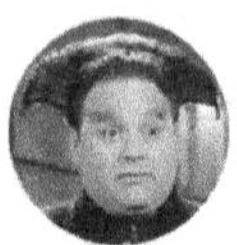

FURST
I think Janet Greek's one of our better directors.

That's who I was just going to say.

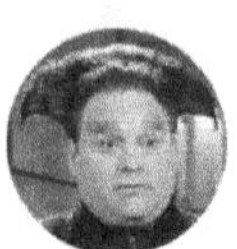

FURST
She did *St. Elsewhere*, so I knew her from there.

> *St. Elsewhere* was Janet Greek's first television directing assignment.

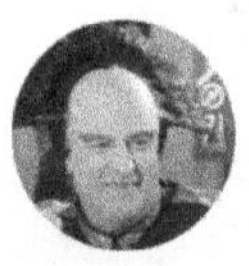

JURASIK
Oh, right. Yeah.

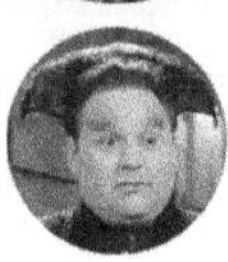

FURST
She was very good. I like Mike Vejar, the guy who did ["There All the Honor Lies"]. He's very good.

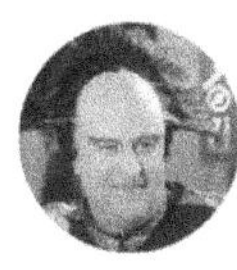

JURASIK
I like them too.

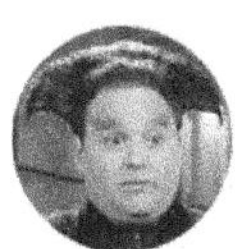

FURST
Not only is he expert with the technical stuff, but I think he talks to the actors very well. Learn how to communicate and get what you want from the actors without offending them. You know?

You did "Geometry of Shadows" with him earlier, as well, which is where you had to do that thing for this CGI [holo-demon] creature, where you do sometimes need a bit of direction.

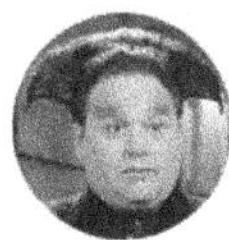

FURST
It's funny, because I had to do CGI with them on ["There All the Honor Lies"], the one he just directed. I was supposed to be falling through space and stuff. They hung me by a wire.

> Furst is referencing a deleted scene featuring a telepathic vision of Vir plunging into space that Talia perceived bumping into him in the Zócalo.

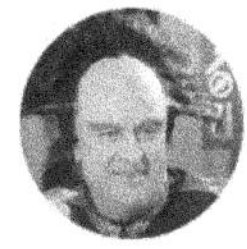

JURASIK
I have heard television directors say that one of their responsibilities is—especially in a series that's running for a while—to keep the lead actors happy, whatever that means. I think that attitude is one of the things that not only keeps the actors happy, but not be involved, really, in the process of making the scenes work, is the downfall of so much television, you know?

It's bad enough that it's gotta be done so fast and that we're under money and time restrictions. But the directors that don't take the risk of speaking up and telling you kind of leave you hanging out there.

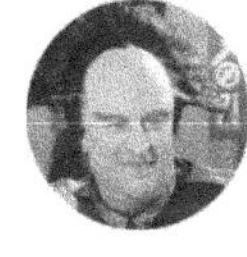

JURASIK
I like a man or a woman who will step up and say, "This ain't working." That's why everybody likes Janet. Janet would just say—I was thinking about the show that aired the other night ["The Coming of Shadows"]. Janet was saying to me, "Whatever you're doing, I'm not seeing it. It's just not playing."

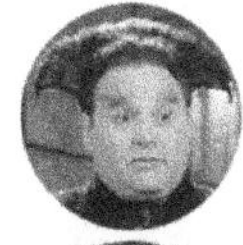

FURST
That's right. That's the kind of language she uses.

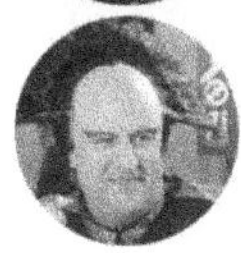

JURASIK
She's straight forward.

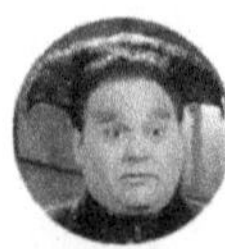
FURST
Exactly.

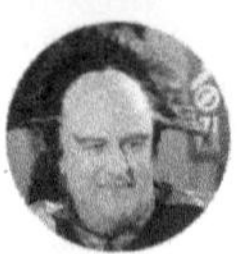
JURASIK
That's too much energy in that. It's too busy. It's too—you know what I mean? I like that, too.

Well that's the thing if you play it too broad. You don't necessarily wanna play it too broad, just keep going until somebody says take it back.

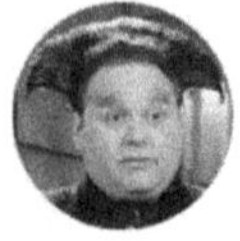
FURST
It's taking a stab in the dark.

I know [director] Jim Johnston was telling me that in one of the early episodes that you guys did together—"Parliament of Dreams"—the whole banquet scene was one where he just let it go for a while. Eventually, he knew he had what he wanted, and yet he wanted to keep the spontaneity of it because he said they just kept the camera on you and just let you do your thing.

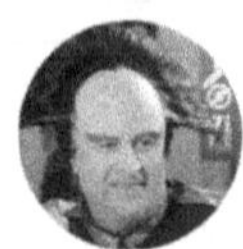
JURASIK
He let the line all the way out on that. I think that was a wise thing to do. Centauri banquet, you know. Excess. Let it run, let the line run.

It plays very well, although you haven't seen it obviously, so—

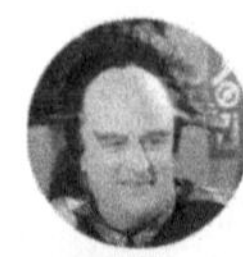
JURASIK
No, we've both seen that one, haven't you?

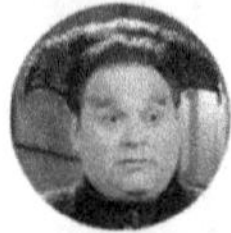
FURST
That's a funny scene, where he's crawling across the table.

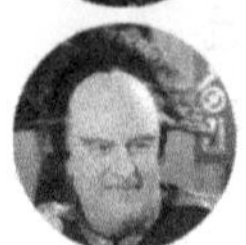
JURASIK
That's right.

But that's a good example. [Director of photography] John Flinn was just telling me last week—because he directed you on "Soul Mates," which was on a couple of weeks ago—he says, "My problem is when these two guys get going, I just wind up laughing so much, that I almost have to leave."

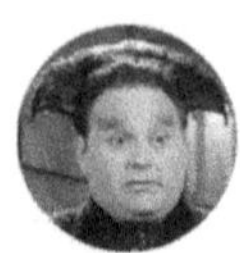
FURST
I always hear John going "hee hee," always trying to hide his laugh. He's very funny.

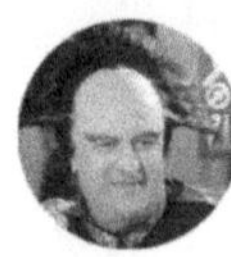
JURASIK
You know, wherever you can get fun in this process. People forget these crew people, every day back in this little box over here—the *Babylon 5* box. [If] we can get fun, yeah, inject it everywhere we can.

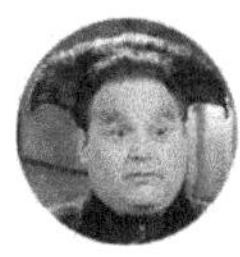

FURST
I've had crew members come up to us and say, "Thank god you're here today. I didn't think I get through the day." They like when Peter and I work together, because we keep things light on the set.

Like I said, actors tend to take themselves too seriously. I'm one of those that don't. I can get the same kind of performance joking around five minutes before I have to do it, than remaining in character and facing a wall. I've worked with actors like that.

WELLS: Yeah. That all comes together when you go to a director that you trust. If you do go too far, you know they're gonna pull you back.

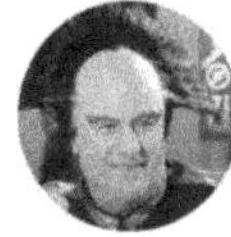

JURASIK
That's right.

WELLS: You can relax and just get on with it, knowing there is a caring eye watching.

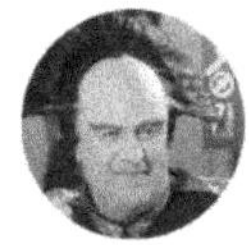

JURASIK
Stephen you're a very spontaneous actor that way. I know what you're talking about. The guys who turn and get into character and the people need to do that, that's fine and dandy. But even among people who don't, you're a pretty loose guy. You wing it. It's rolling, hop, off we go!

But you tend to prepare more then?

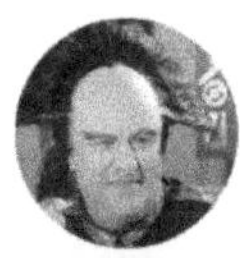

JURASIK
I think I do. I think I go over the stuff much more.

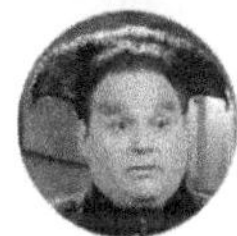

FURST
Oh, he does, yeah. But he knows his opera already, and I'm just starting to learn it.

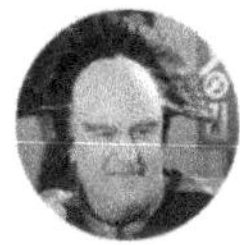

JURASIK
It kind of pisses him off that I do, you know? We were rehearsing the opera and I started singing a little of his part. He said, "How did you learn my part already?"

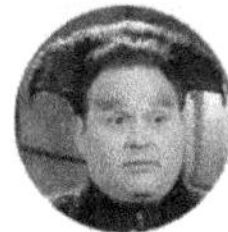

FURST
He already knows it.

At this moment 2nd Assistant Director Douglas Corring appears, to tell Jurasik that they want to rehearse the sword fight [with Urza Jaddo] Wednesday. "What's a good time or bad time?"

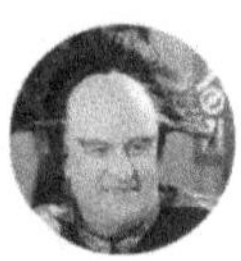

JURASIK
Any time is fine by me. No reason to do it at seven o'clock in the morning.

CORRING: Yeah. I don't think that would be the case.

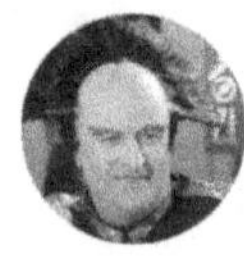

JURASIK
Doesn't matter. Any time is great. Thanks Doug. Will you gimme a call?

CORRING: Yeah, probably tomorrow.

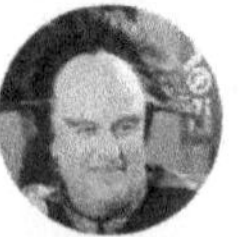

JURASIK
Thanks.

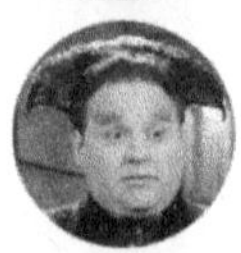

FURST
Ask Peter about all the science fiction conventions he's doing. [Laughs.]

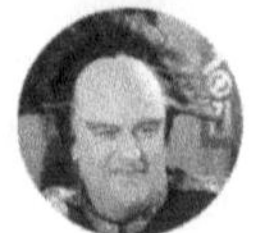

JURASIK
Do you wanna know something? I've taken a lot of shit for it. I have not done one science fiction convention. I did one free convention at the Burbank Hilton, which is about 12 minutes from my house. That's a pretty exotic location. I drove all the way down the hill. "You want me to pick something up on the way home, Honey?" [Laughs.]. Of course the money in that—what you got for that—well it was nothing. Absolutely zip.

So finally I accepted one convention. I got an invitation to a convention in Stratford, England. Of course I have taken a great deal of flack. People are just jealous. Oh, but, and you've been a zillion conventions already, haven't you?

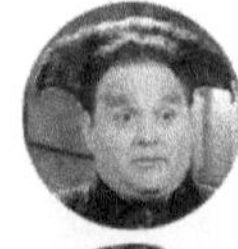

FURST
A zillion. I've been to one. One in St. Louis.

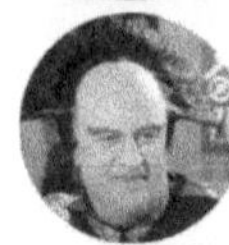

JURASIK
But you're going to Vegas.

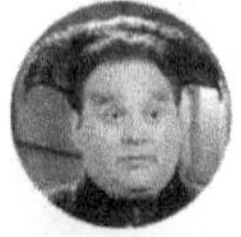

FURST
I'm going to Vegas and I don't know if I'm gonna get paid or not.

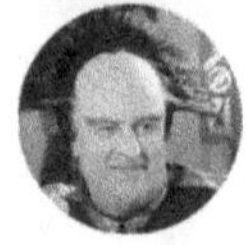

JURASIK
Oh, is that right? I asked them if you could come along. Do you what they said? Nope.

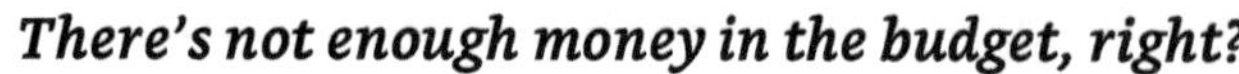

There's not enough money in the budget, right?

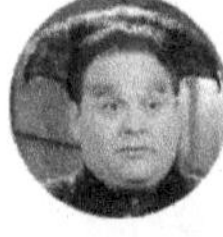

FURST
You didn't ask them?

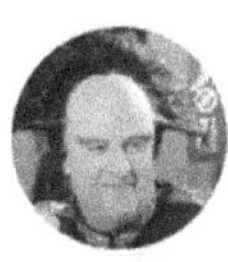

JURASIK
They said Vir? No thank you. Thank you very much.

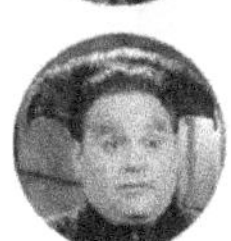

FURST
I'm not temperamental and I'm not jealous, but—like everything that says *Babylon 5*—it has his picture on it not mine.

I notice there's signs in this saying "get your own Londo doll."

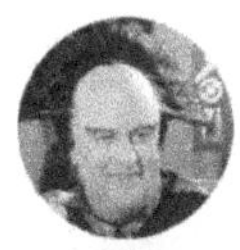

JURASIK
Now you wonder what the Vir and Londo backstory is, eh?

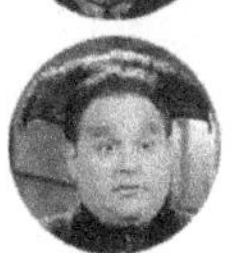

FURST
Every character's picture except mine.

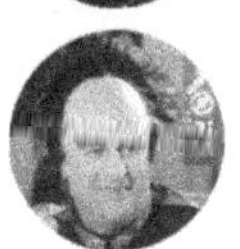

JURASIK
Vir is sitting in my bedroom, in Londo's bedroom, wringing his fingers, "When will I be ambassador?"

"Then I'll have my own action figure."

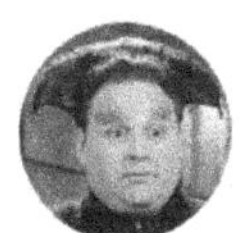

FURST
I want my own action figure.

That's gotta be a strange experience though, isn't it? When you see your own doll.

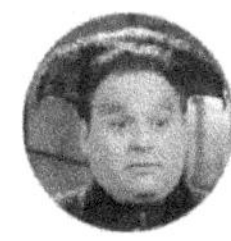

FURST
Oh, he's not sentimental. I would take a doll and keep it forever. He says, "What am I gonna do with a doll?"

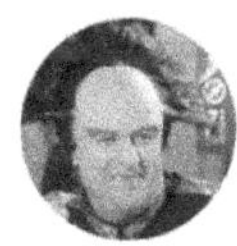

JURASIK
Yeah, that's true. What am I gonna do with it?

What I liked is the way Joe worked it into the story, which is making fun of merchandising and so, of course, Londo was outraged about it.

Joe told me two years ago—this is when the show was just getting started and we were talking about how the Star Trek guys are on QVC, hawking all the Star Trek merchandise—and I said, "I hope a couple years from now that I won't see you on QVC, hawking Babylon 5 action figures." This was at the pilot stage, right? He said —you could take my word for it—"If you ever see me like that, you can shoot me, because it'll never happen." It's been two years since then.

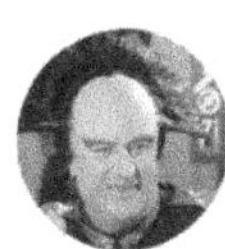

JURASIK
I have no interest, because I don't save memorabilia from my career, anything.

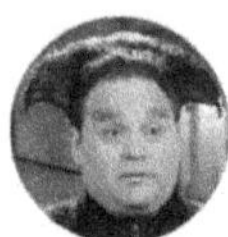

FURST
That's a weird thing.

Take my advice. Save the stuff, because if you're doing conventions, you'll be asked for things. The other thing, which is nice—a nicer part of doing conventions and public appearances—is that if it's a charity thing, you could use these things to make a little bit of extra money for charity, which is what I always do for Amnesty International and things like that. So you hold onto these things and you'd be sparing about them. If it's a good charity thing, it's putting your work into a good cause.

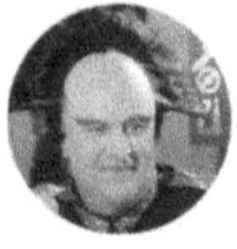

JURASIK
I always have a horrible feeling that I'm gonna be an old man sitting down in the cellar, going through a pile of junk, trying to show my niece and nephews, "This is when I was in the science fiction." They're like, "He's going on again...we're going upstairs for Ginger. He's talking to himself again." I mean "Now hold on, here, let me..." You know, you're babbling on by yourself.

Does that end of things get a bit overwhelming sometimes? Granted, there is a certain degree of prestige to doing a show like St. Elsewhere or Hill Street Blues, or whatever. Yet you don't have people stopping you on the streets and asking about things. You wouldn't have somebody inviting you to New York [to] talk about St. Elsewhere for the weekend? Is that whole end of things a bit strange?

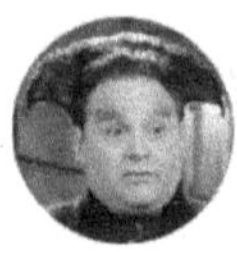

FURST
Personally, I love anonymity. I love that. I know, as a teenager, I wanted to be recognized all the time when I was doing local theater and stuff. Now it just gets in the way with my family and stuff. So I'm kind of glad. I've had people stop me at an amusement park. I was with my kids and she says, "Are you Stephen Furst?" I said, "Yes I am," and she says "No, really?" I said, "Yes, I am." She goes, "Do you mind if I see some I.D.?" I said, "Of course I mind."

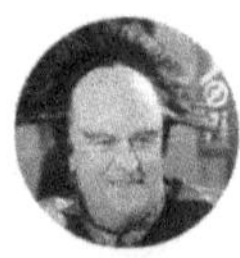

JURASIK
Do you mind if I see some I.D.? That's great.

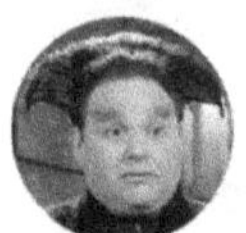

FURST
I learned my lesson. When someone came in and says, "I know you; you look familiar," and I said to them, "Well, I'm an actor," and they go, "No, that's not it." That kind of stuff.

I heard somebody asking you about that before, Peter, but do they recognize you? Does that happen?

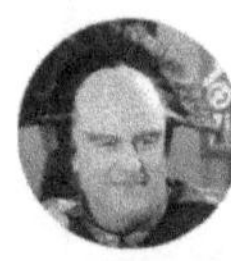

JURASIK
Not really that much, because of the amount of makeup—they get my

voice—compared to *Hill Street*, and maybe I'm speaking for you, Stephen, and it is not true. It's nice.

I had never had any experience with science fiction fans, and it's been a nice experience for me. I've been really surprised, you know? Because that kind of interest—as you said—you didn't get asked in *Hill Street* to go talk at a convention. They do take a great deal. I mean, they care about the show, that input stuff on internet. I dig it.

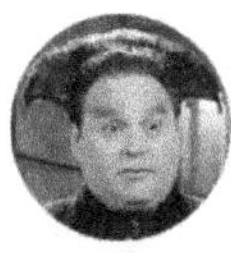

FURST
They're very into it. Science fiction people are very into it.

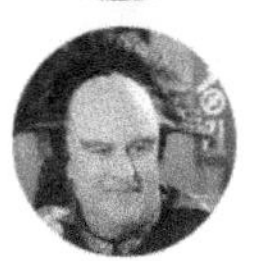

JURASIK
On the other hand, I echo your sentiments about fame and anonymity. Thank god we're character actors.

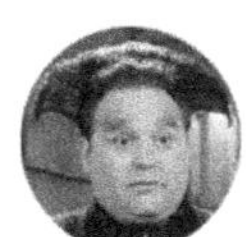

FURST
I just want to be able to work as an actor the rest of my life. I don't care if I'm recognized. I just wanna make a nice living doing what I love to do, and being recognized is so minuscule of a part of it. I don't even care.

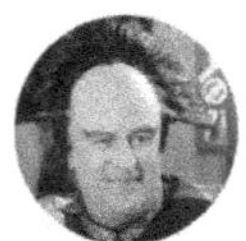

JURASIK
Well, it's a good thing you feel that way, because that's the way it's gonna go for you.

My father was reading Kirk Douglas's book while he was here, *The Ragman's Son*. He said Kirk Douglas had a thing called—in terms of being recognized—he had a thing they called a triple. He said a triple happened to him once he and Burt Lancaster were out together in a diner eating. Someone came over and sat down—didn't even recognize Burt Lancaster at all—sat down across from Kirk Douglas and said, "Mr. Mitchum, god, it's so nice to, to meet you. You're really wonderful in *Trapeze*," a film Burt Lancaster was in, they called that a triple. That's a great commentary on fame.

So you haven't gotten a triple yet?

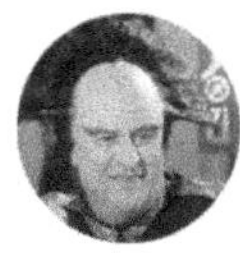

JURASIK
I don't know what that would be. That would someone sitting down, and saying to either of us, "Mr. Mostel"—thinking we were Josh Mostel—or saying to me, "I really liked you in *St. Elsewhere*." That would be a triple.

Are the two of you really comfortable with the show now? Could see yourself doing this for the next three-and-a-half years? Is it still fun?

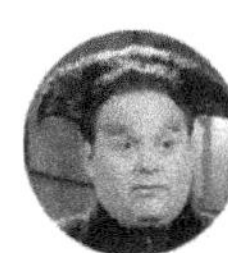

FURST
I am.

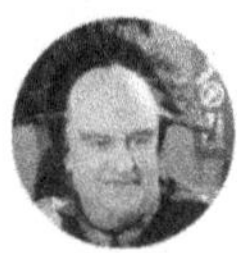

JURASIK
I'm still in a one-year [contract]. It's definitely still fun, in terms of interest level. That's great. Whether they make the deal or not—from a business point of view—is another thing.

> Due to budgetary constraints, Peter Jurasik nor Andreas Katsulas were hired on a year-by-year basis for the first two seasons, but signed three-year contracts at the beginning of season three for the remainder of the series.

So after this Centauri opera, maybe that might cancel this whole thing.

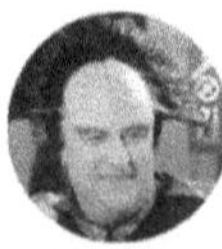

JURASIK
It could very well.

WELLS: You could have a whole new musical career.

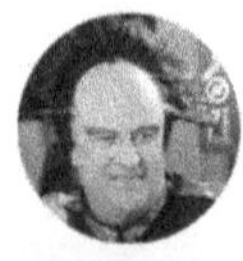

JURASIK
That's right. *Vir and Londo Sing Hits of the Seventies.* [Laughs.]

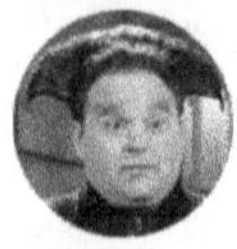

FURST
"Staying Alive."

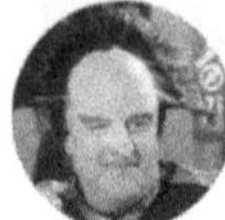

JURASIK
"Staying Alive." Exactly. Exactly. We'll make a bundle, Stephen. We'll cash in big.

It's probably just as well [this is] for print and not on audio or something.

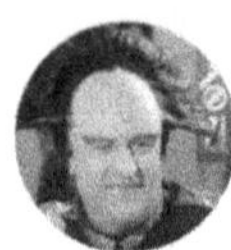

JURASIK
If you put it in print, let everyone know that they can mail in for that cassette sold out of the back of my car for $18.95. Mm-hmm.

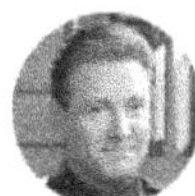
BRUCE BOXLEITNER
John Sheridan

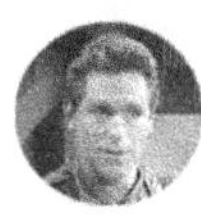
JEFF CONAWAY
Zack Allan

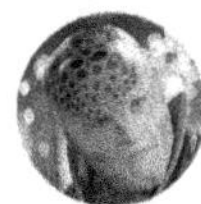
ANDREAS KATSULAS
G'Kar

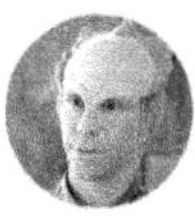
BILL MUMY
Lennier

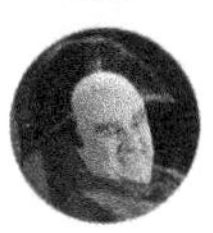
PETER JURASIK
Londo Mollari

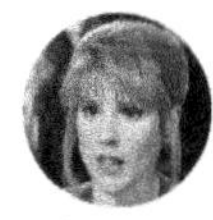
PATRICIA TALLMAN
Lyta Alexander

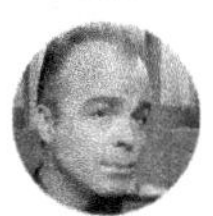
JERRY DOYLE
Michael Garibaldi

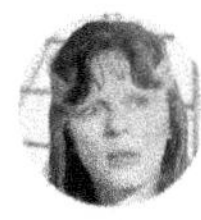
MIRA FURLAN
Delenn

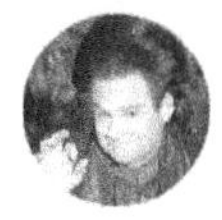
STEPHEN FURST
Vir Cotto

13 November 1996, Babylonian Productions

Babylon 5 Timeline
In Production: "The Illusion of Truth" (408)
On the Air: "Whatever Happened to Mr. Garibaldi?" (402)

JOE NAZZARO, INTERVIEWER
I want to tell you what exactly is going on, because I don't know what they told you in messages and faxes. This is—hopefully, if all goes well—going to be in the first issue of the new Babylon 5 Magazine, which will come out in the U.K. to coincide with when season four starts.

> Initially, *The Official Babylon 5 Magazine* published by Titan was a U.K.-only publication, so the features were keyed to U.K. broadcast dates, season four having already debuted in the U.S. After nine issues, the periodical would be relaunched, with U.S. distribution, to coincide with the show's move to TNT for season five.

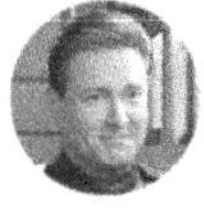
BRUCE BOXLEITNER
It's a magazine devoted entirely to...
A Gun, a Car, a Blonde.

Entirely to all you lot.

BOXLEITNER
Oh my god.

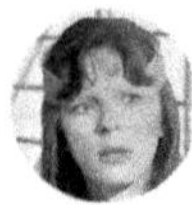

MIRA FURLAN
When will that be?

If it goes according to the past, it should be something like March or April.

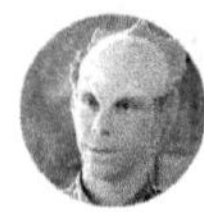

BILL MUMY
How indulgent, a whole magazine. We just babble on and babble on and babble on...

> Mumy would eventually write and record a song titled "Babble On" with his band, the Jenerators. It would appear on their 1998 album, *Hitting the Silk*.

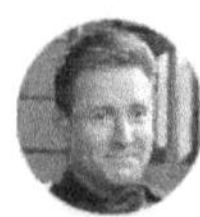

BOXLEITNER
You do.

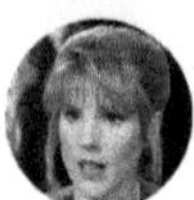

PATRICIA TALLMAN
[Laughs.]

That's going to be the job of some of us people, to knock things into a more coherent shape. But since this is going to coincide with season four, and people are going to be picking up not having seen too many episodes as far as the new season, maybe we can talk a little—

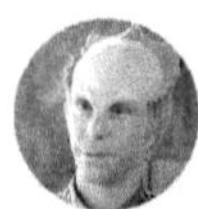

MUMY
We dare not give away too much of Joe's plots now.

Well, you generally can't anyway. That's the sort been a self-enforced rule for the last couple of seasons.

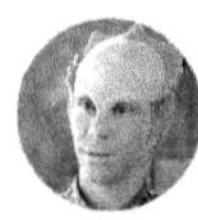

MUMY
In other words, you don't get [season four in the U.K.] 'til June, whereas we started them here [last week].

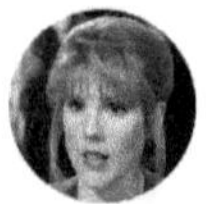

TALLMAN
But they're going to hear, on the Internet; they're going to hear it.

What sort of things have you folks noticed, as far as with the new season, in terms of the development of your characters?

When people in England tune in—come March or April—are they going to be slightly different versions of your characters than they've seen in season three?

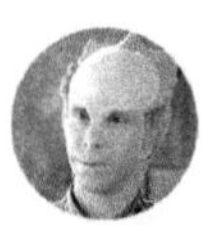

MUMY
Bruce's got a big haircut.

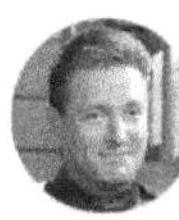

BOXLEITNER
Other than that, yes. I would say so.

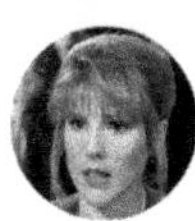

TALLMAN
Jerry has no hair.

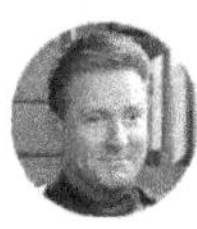

BOXLEITNER
That's true.

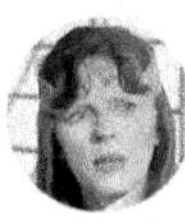

FURLAN
My hair is incredibly curly.

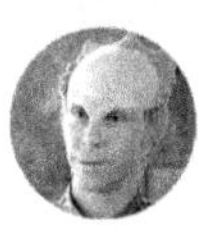

MUMY
I have no hair, but my bone is sprouted a little bit.

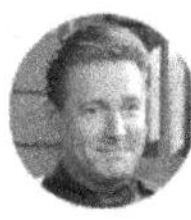

BOXLEITNER
It's a hair story.

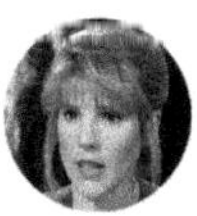

TALLMAN
My hair got a little longer.

So this would be a good show to watch, just in terms of hair.

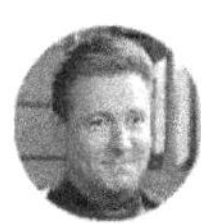

BOXLEITNER
For hair design.

> *Babylon 5*'s Tracy Smith was nominated for Outstanding Individual Achievement in Hairstyling for a Series at the 1995 Primetime Emmy Awards, but did not win.

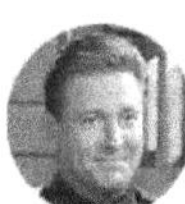

BOXLEITNER
No, I think every character has this tumultuous event. Events start coming a lot faster now, in this fourth season. You'll find there'll be very few intricate little side-character stories like this. Am I right?

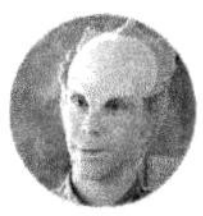

MUMY
You are right, sir.

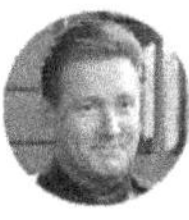

BOXLEITNER
Every story, every episode will be totally arc. We're gonna get to it instead of leading up to it.

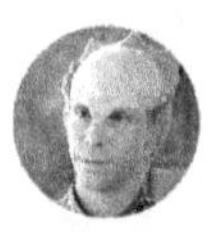
MUMY
Without giving too much away, I would say that one of the biggest surprises, I think, coming in the fourth season, will be from the Vorlons. That will be unexpected.

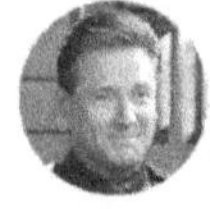
BOXLEITNER
Our Vorlons are major players in the early part of fourth season, and things are not what they seem. We've been saying that all along.

What can you say about some of your own particular characters as far as—

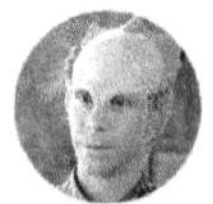
MUMY
I got a new dress.

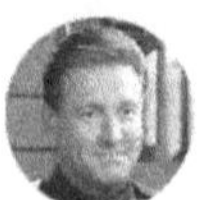
BOXLEITNER
Well, certainly Delenn and Sheridan take on a different thing than when last they were together. Right?

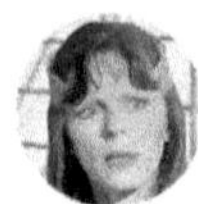
FURLAN
Different?

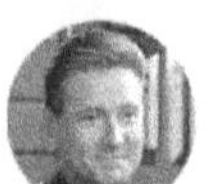
BOXLEITNER
Oh, I think so. I mean, we seem to be stronger couple afterwards—

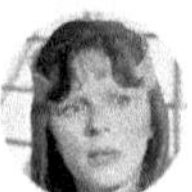
FURLAN
Yeah.

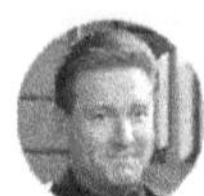
BOXLEITNER
—after the end of 322 ["Z'ha'dum"].

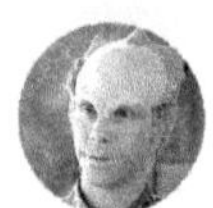
MUMY
I think we can give away enough to say that Sheridan didn't die [at Z'ha'dum]. [Laughs.]

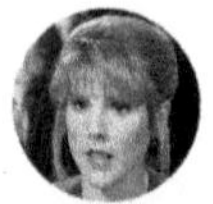
TALLMAN
I think they got that.

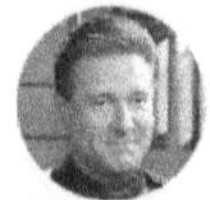
BOXLEITNER
When we get back, we're more united than ever.

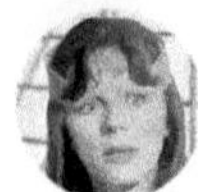
FURLAN
There's a war going on, and my character is kind of in this militaristic mood.

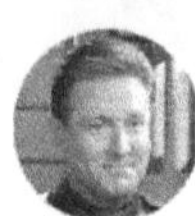
BOXLEITNER
She's gotten very strong.

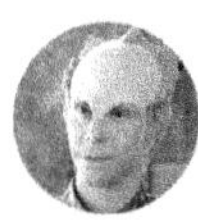
MUMY
Some major secrets about the Delenn's past will be revealed mid-season [in "Atonement"]. Absolutely.

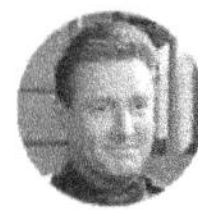
BOXLEITNER
That will probably shock few—

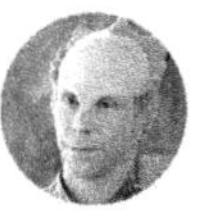
MUMY
Absolutely. It shocked me. Knock me right on my bone.

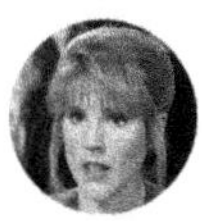
TALLMAN
[Laughs.] Look at you. [Laughs.]

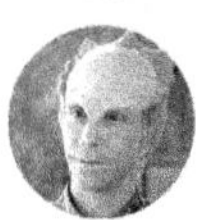
MUMY
Yeah.

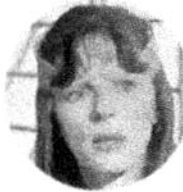
FURLAN
She used to run a brothel on Minbar.

> The Minbari term for "brothel" is "doxhouse," as established in "The War Prayer."

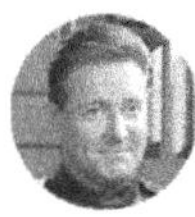
BOXLEITNER
She was a madam on Minbar. [Laughs.]

I don't think I want touch that with a ten-foot pole.

Pat, you've come in now as a regular on the show as well, and certainly—from the first couple of episodes—there's some big stuff coming up for your character.

> After guest appearances in the pilot and seasons two and three, Patricia Tallman was finally contracted as a series regular for year four, appearing in the opening titles with a guarantee of 13 episodes during the season.

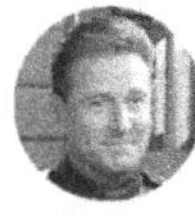
BOXLEITNER
Oh, certainly.

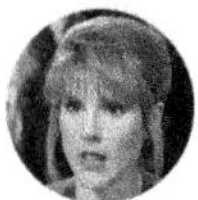
TALLMAN
Yeah the Vorlons keep me hopping. I sort of have to make some judgment calls between people that I care about and respect and the Vorlons, who've been my

mentors my whole life, and I'm completely giving myself over to them for now. Some interesting issues come up.

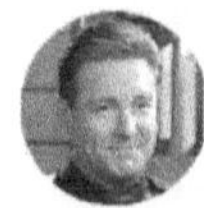
BOXLEITNER
She has to start—

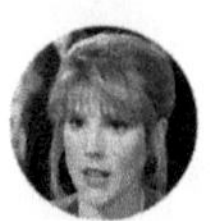
TALLMAN
Thinking on her own.

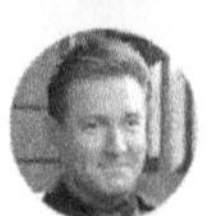
BOXLEITNER
—examining which side she wants to be on.

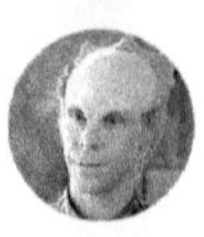
MUMY
It's great to have Pat with us, and we also have another character—

BOXLEITNER
I work her death in the fourth season. It's amazing.

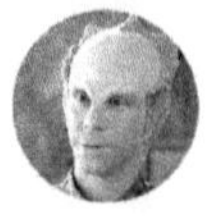
MUMY
The first part of this season there's another very important character that's new to this series named [mispronouncing the name] Lore-eye-un.

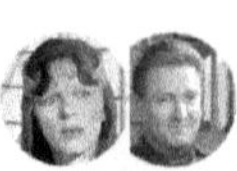
BOXLEITNER & FURLAN
Lorien!

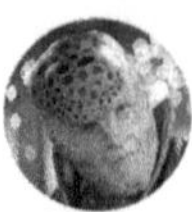
ANDREAS KATSULAS
Hey, everybody!

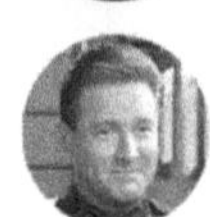
BOXLEITNER
There you are! Talk about somebody that goes through some changes. You can spend an all afternoon on his.

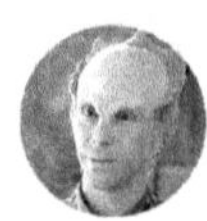
MUMY
Flok-sha, brother!

Thanks for coming and joining us, Andreas. Good to see you again. We saw each other in Blackpool [over the summer], and I was not doing any interviews that weekend. I was being a good boy, because, at the time, we knew this magazine may well be coming up, and that we'd come out here and talk to you all, more or less, in person. I know you're coming in on your day off, as are a lot of people—

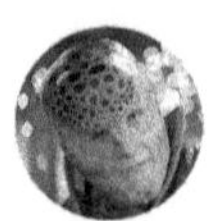
KATSULAS
Well, give us a free meal, and we'll be here all the time.

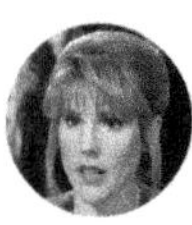

TALLMAN
Hi, sweetie, how are you?

We were saying when you walked in, Andreas, about how this magazine is going to come out in the U.K. to coincide with the beginning of season four, when it starts running in England. A lot of the viewers over there won't have seen too many episodes from the new season.

I'm just asking everybody what sort of changes their characters have in store with this new season. Certainly, as far as G'Kar is concerned, in those opening episodes, is there a good deal happening to him?

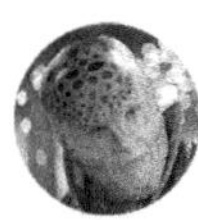

KATSULAS
I dunno, can we talk about season four?

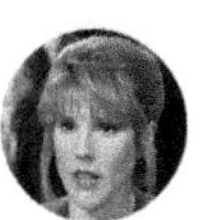

TALLMAN
You got better pieces [of food] than I got.

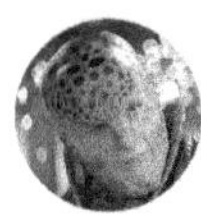

KATSULAS
I've got more pieces, too.

Joe [Straczynski] hates G'Kar, and so he's hurting G'Kar this season.

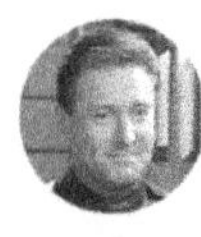

BOXLEITNER
I'll say. Talk about the martyr of Narn.

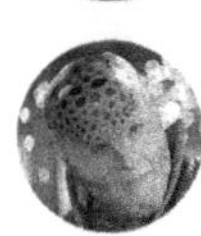

KATSULAS
Jesus.

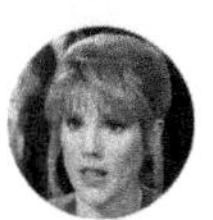

TALLMAN
Lyta will comfort you.

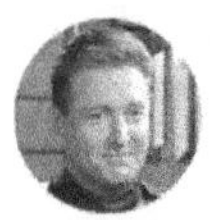

BOXLEITNER
He's going to come through the gate there with the cross of Jesus strapped to your—

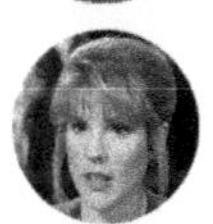

TALLMAN
Don't tell him!

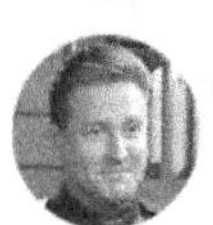

BOXLEITNER
Don't tell him? I gotta tell him something. We gotta give him something.

They gotta throw the British fans a bone, for goodness sake.

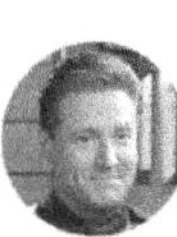

BOXLEITNER
You know how hard that was at the Blackpool convention, Andreas?

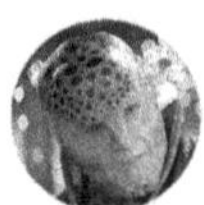
KATSULAS
Very difficult.

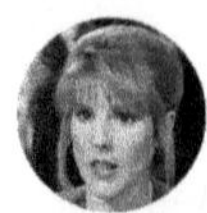
TALLMAN
What did you talk about?

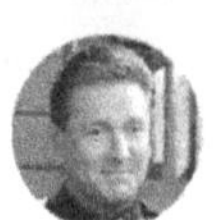
BOXLEITNER
We can't be specific?

For half of the convention, you didn't even know if the show was coming back [for season four]. Do you remember that?

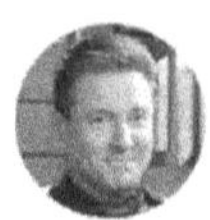
BOXLEITNER
That was rather dramatic.

Joe [Straczynski] said that night before we went on stage that afterwards, he calls us all together. We all looked at each other going, "Oh, Christ." Billy's jaw was clenching all over the place. Remember that? When he said, "I wanna meet everybody backstage afterwards."

> Warner Bros. formally renewed *Babylon 5* for its fourth season on Friday, 7 June 1996, as Straczynki, Boxleitner, Mumy, Furst, and Katsulas traveled to the U.K. for Wolf 359 "The Gathering."

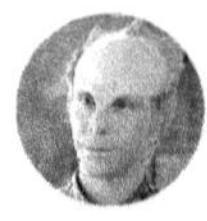
MUMY
Hey, Jeff!

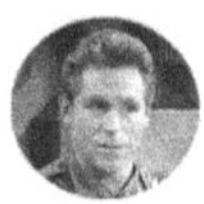
JEFF CONAWAY
How's everybody?

Good, how are you? We meet, finally! We keep being in different countries at different times. We went to your little convention in England and you weren't there.

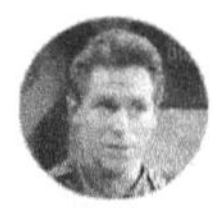
CONAWAY
I know. That was a little bit of a mixup.

Jeff, we were talking about how some of the various characters are going to change, as far as the beginning of the new season of Babylon 5. Is there anything in store, as far as Zack is concerned, in these early episodes?

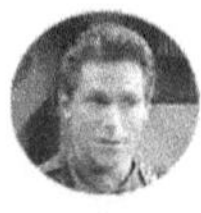
CONAWAY
Well, they just made me chief because Garibaldi goes off on some search of his own. But as far as anything else, I really don't know what [Joe Straczynski] has in his

mind. I think as far, as the character goes, more pressure. How's he gonna deal with it? And more responsibility, and things like that.

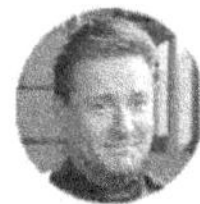
BOXLEITNER
Everybody goes through something.

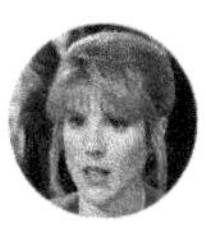
TALLMAN
He starts delivering pizzas.

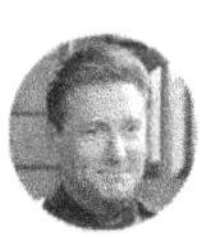
BOXLEITNER
He went from pizza man to head of security.

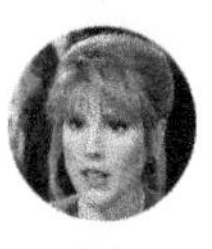
TALLMAN
It's true!

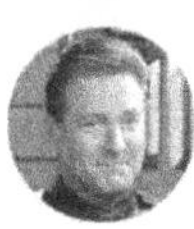
BOXLEITNER
We do an incredible lurch ahead here, and everybody has to assume something...

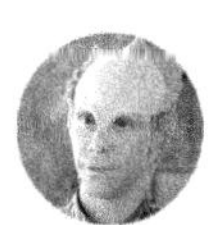
MUMY
Lennier opens up a little Flarns "R" Us place in the Zócalo.

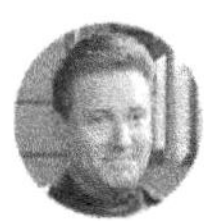
BOXLEITNER
Lennier is even more protective of [Delenn]. He's a little more militant himself, in fact, he starts lifting people off the floor.

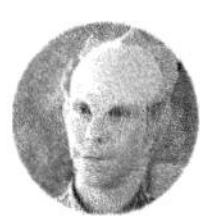
MUMY
Flexing the bone.

I know a lot of you have said over the years that, a good deal of the time, you don't know what's happening with your characters until you literally pick up the next script and say, "Oh, so that's what's going on!"

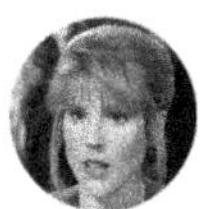
TALLMAN
That's especially been true this season, I think.

Yeah. What, what sort of revelations have come in these scripts that you've read them and just gone—and I'm not necessarily talking about season four, but the show in general—

What sort of events have you read for your characters that you just went in the next morning and said, "Joe..."

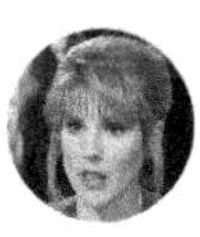
TALLMAN
Can we talk about it?

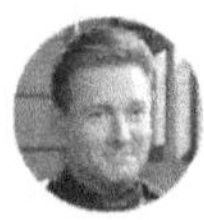
BOXLEITNER
You brought up the main thing. The Vorlons. All this time, ever since I came on the show, I've been thinking they've been Jesus and the Gospels on the right side of everything. We're gonna find out that possibly that's not the case, and every character—we've allied ourselves against these Shadows—

Well, who necessarily said the Shadows were wrong?

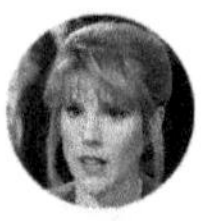
TALLMAN
Like Joe said, nothing's a hundred percent. It's just picking and choosing.

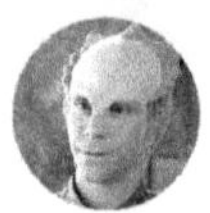
MUMY
So it's shaken Sheridan's very belief system, as to who was doing what.

[Stephen Furst enters.]

Are you wearing your director's hat or your actor's hat now?

BOXLEITNER
Vir Cotto.

But I mean—with Sheridan, for example—I remember you telling me this in the second season, when you found out he was there to investigate this whole thing [in "All Alone in the Night"]. Was it a revelation for you?

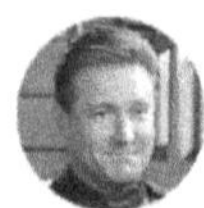
BOXLEITNER
Total revelation.

So your character pretty much been like that all along, hasn't he? You don't know what's happening.

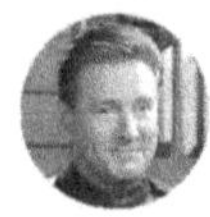
BOXLEITNER
I like that. I like when he bounces from one thing to another. The one thing is, with this woman here, that thing has—I would say—intensified and its going moreso. I think.

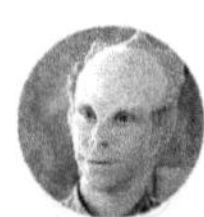
MUMY
Whoo-hoo.

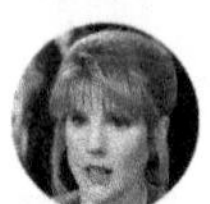
TALLMAN
It's finally some sort of love affair on B5.

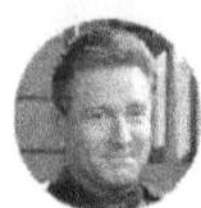
BOXLEITNER
Yeah, and our female demographics started to shoot up, by the way. This isn't just a male-oriented show. I guess where they're really surprised—Warner Bros. were

really surprised and they can't figure out why. We heard that the other day. "We can't figure out why." Well let me tell you why! Write some romance stuff in there and things happen.

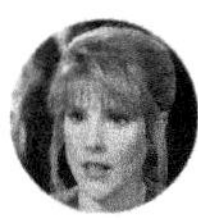

TALLMAN
Right. All of a sudden.

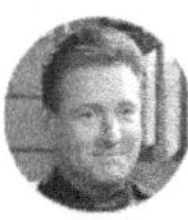

BOXLEITNER
Women like that kind of thing. Very appealing to female sensibilities.

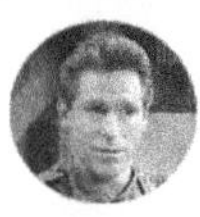

CONAWAY
Well I guess we're gonna go from pizza to dessert.

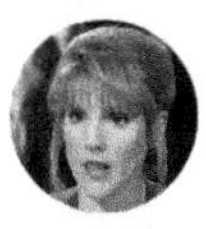

TALLMAN
I hope so.

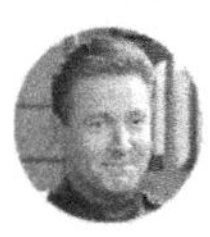

BOXLEITNER
Whoa.

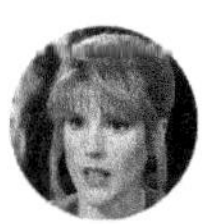

TALLMAN
Bada bing, bada boom!

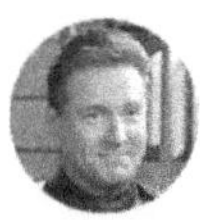

BOXLEITNER
But I find that funny when they say they can't understand; I think it's very obvious.

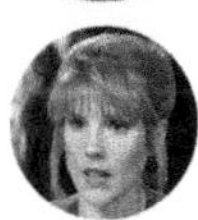

TALLMAN
Well, they don't watch the show.

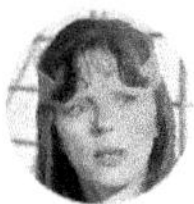

FURLAN
They don't watch the show.

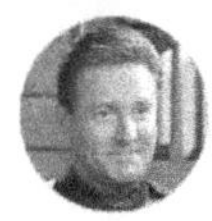

BOXLEITNER
No. They look at their computer.

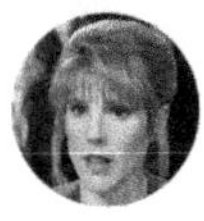

TALLMAN
That's it. They have no idea.

What sort of revelations have you all seen about your characters in the past, where when you pick up that script—it really surprises you because you, having played these characters for a while, you think you have a handle on them—and all of a sudden one of Joe's scripts comes in and sort of pulls the rug out from under you, in terms of the way you've been playing the character up until then.

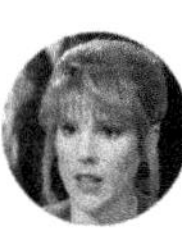

TALLMAN
Have there been any of those for any of you?

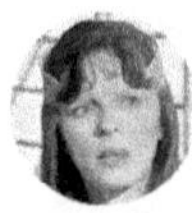
FURLAN
No.

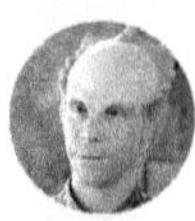
MUMY
[Laughs.] Just a severe haircut.

BOXLEITNER
Oh, cut the shit.

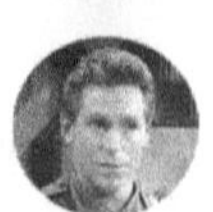
CONAWAY
Not really. Not for me.

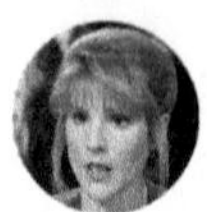
TALLMAN
Like every script in a row I got was like that. Because I thought I was going one way, and, oh my god. Oh no. Now what? It's just been like that.

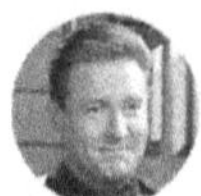
BOXLEITNER
Well, also the unpredictability is fun to play. Everybody here just seems to be, "Okay, I guess I'm going that direction now." He does keep it lively, as far as that. I can't tell where we're going with things two scripts away.

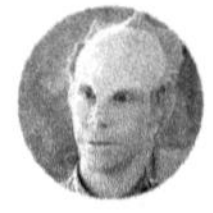
MUMY
Now that we're so far along into the novel, I think the characters tend to do their shifts a lot earlier.

The first season things were definitely planted and going into a direction that Joe definitely changed some time early in the second season when Bruce came aboard. Almost everyone did some sort of a 180, as we said a minute ago.

So far, in the fourth season, the biggest 180 like that comes with the Vorlons. As far as the cast here, our characters are pretty well defined by now into the arc. I don't think anybody's gonna turn around now and be too different from where we are.

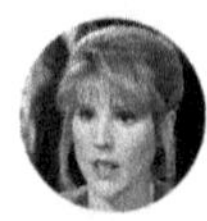
TALLMAN
Well, maybe this is the first string for Lyta, that's why these things are still happening to her.

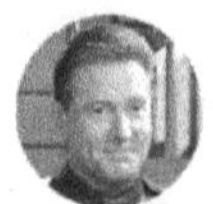
BOXLEITNER
Yeah and Zack as well.

Jerry's not here to say, but Garibaldi—he's been kind of not in for a while—and now suddenly he's coming to the forefront again in a whole twist that is about to happen with his character, which will then spin a number of us into a different direction, too. We've even started that in this episode ["The Illusion of Truth"].

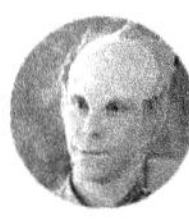
MUMY
Like with Andreas, in the first season, though, you got the impression that the Narn and G'Kar were going to be more or less antagonists and of more or less the bad guys. That definitely turned into this great nobility and it shifted. Those kind of shifts, I think.

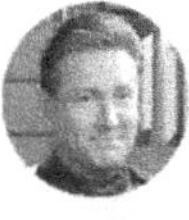
BOXLEITNER
But it switches around again this season, between Londo and G'Kar.

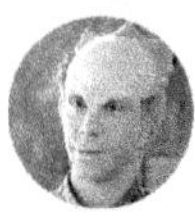
MUMY
G'Kar has some incredible stuff early [in the season].

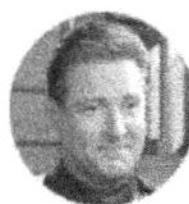
BOXLEITNER
But their friendship—we've been watching them battle it out at each other, just realizing that they really do care about each other.

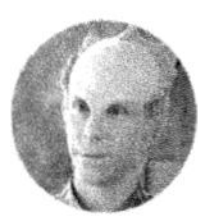
MUMY
They are Laverne and Shirley of the show.

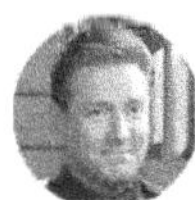
BOXLEITNER
They are Laverne and Shirley.

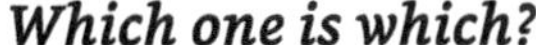
Which one is which?

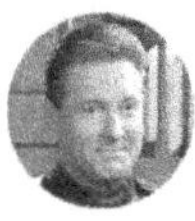
BOXLEITNER
Schlemiel! Schlimazel! Hasenpfeffer Incorporated! I want to see them do that down the hallway.

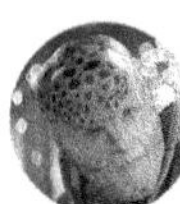
KATSULAS
I don't know, Bill, if you're right about the characters are pretty well set because Vir seems to be still evolving—

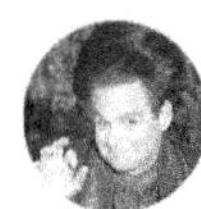
STEPHEN FURST
I'm still changing.

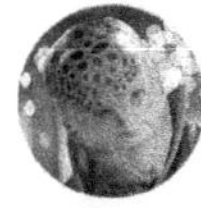
KATSULAS
—into I don't know what, and Londo's evolving.

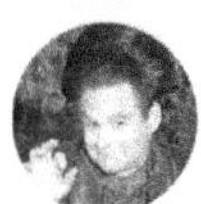
FURST
I think because of what happens with the emperor, I'm gonna have a total personality change.

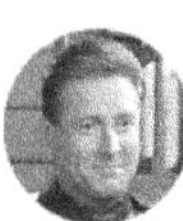
BOXLEITNER
Certainly. But look what's happened in his situation.

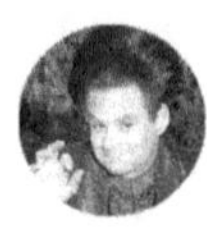
FURST
Do you know what we're not supposed to tell you or what?

Well, we're going to sort of keep things fairly cryptic. The way you're talking about it now, I think, is the sort of level we would probably keep.

[The interview is] going to come out in the U.K. when season four starts for them, so it won't start until March or April.

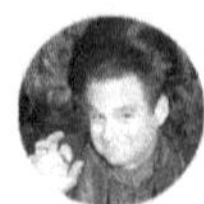
FURST
I thought they were ahead of us.

> Channel 4 in the U.K. broadcast the final four episodes of season two and the final five episodes of season three ahead of PTEN in the U.S.

They are, but then they take a break.

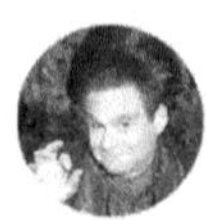
FURST
Since this is still going to be licensed with Warner Bros., Joe will still be able to look through it and say, "I think we should put this later."

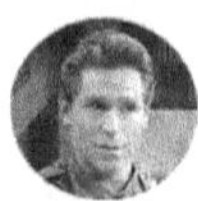
CONAWAY
When I was involved with Nightwatch, I thought I was a good guy. But apparently, maybe I wouldn't have been. I have no idea.

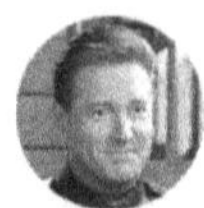
BOXLEITNER
You both were originally patriots for your worlds.

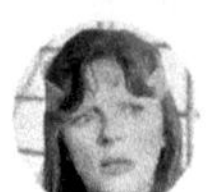
FURLAN
If you need me later, call me.

Bye.

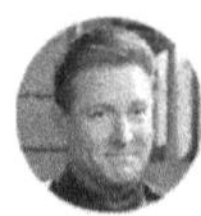
BOXLEITNER
What I see with you guys is that, eventually, even though you have more of a common enemy between you in Cartagia, and you actually allow yourself, in a way, to do what is needed to help Londo—even though you still have kind of a love-hate relationship—

I think you're being summoned there, young man.

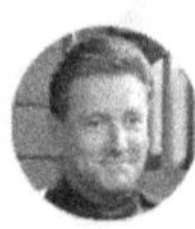
BOXLEITNER
There's hardly much to do with me in there, but I'll be there in a second. There's your new scripts.

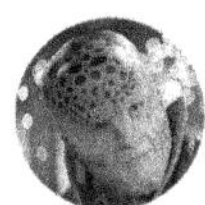

KATSULAS
So let me read 411 ["Lines of Communication"] to you and see what's going on.

What sort of changes are in store.

Bill said something on the Sci-Fi Channel last week, about being able to contribute a little idea to his character, where you told Joe [Straczynski] you'd like to maybe have this backstory where Lennier was secretly in love with Delenn.

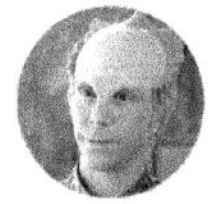

MUMY
That was early in second season. Yeah.

Well, the question I was leading up to is—because you guys well played your characters for a substantial amount of time now—have you been able to actually talk to Joe [Straczynski] and throw in some things that you would like to see for your characters yourself?

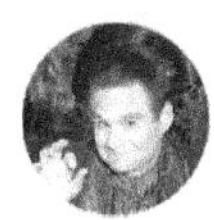

FURST
I haven't.

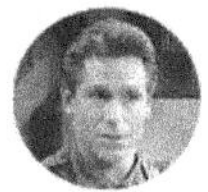

CONAWAY
I just told him I'd love to go into a Starfury sometime.

> Zack Allan would pilot a Starfury in *Thirdspace*, the first of two movies-of-the-week shot for TNT at the end of season four.

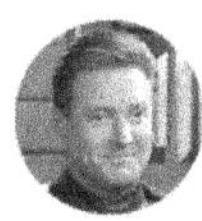

BOXLEITNER
Maybe not on a very simple level like that. I think what's wonderful with Joe, is you hear certain things come out of our mouths, and then a few weeks later, it's in the script.

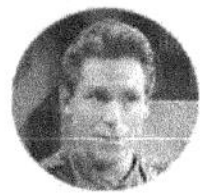

CONAWAY
It ends up in the script.

I was just going to ask you about that, because writers are very observant like that. We could be sitting here like this and something is being digested and you get the script and there's a little something in there.

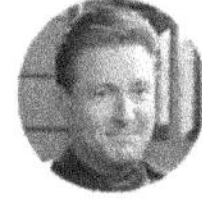

BOXLEITNER
Oh yeah. I think a classic example is Garibaldi's "sometimes makes me long for electric bleachers." [Jerry Doyle] was talking about capital punishment.

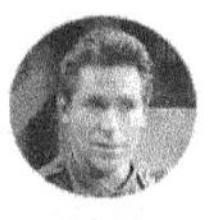
CONAWAY
I remember.

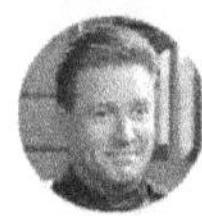
BOXLEITNER
He said that at lunch, weeks before. Suddenly there it was in the script [for "Passing Through Gethsemane"]. Garibaldi says, "Sometimes makes me long for electric bleachers."

But that's what's marvelous about Joe. He picks up these things. It hasn't been exact lines, but I've gathered, from various conversations and fights we've had at lunch, and debates, and, suddenly, I find myself with this similar attitude in a scene somewhere. I think that's what's wonderful about him. He listens to our speech patterns. He's definitely got a specific kind of dialogue for you, Jeff—much more a street type guy.

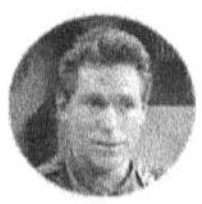
CONAWAY
More blue-collar.

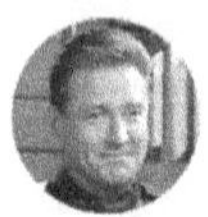
BOXLEITNER
A blue-collar type of guy, which is very much the way Jerry is, too. You're both cop-like guys. They're cops like we would recognize in a police department on Earth.

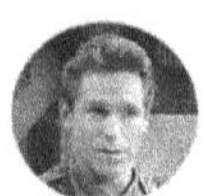
CONAWAY
The whole thing about my uniform last year, that was me complaining about—

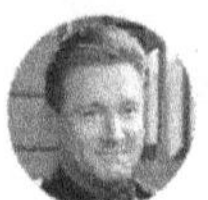
BOXLEITNER
Yes! He was complaining about the goddamn uniform.

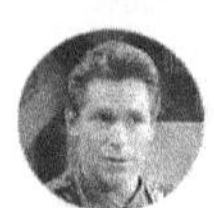
CONAWAY
Next thing you know it's in the show.

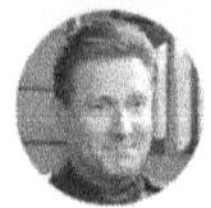
BOXLEITNER
It's a major issue in Zack's life, you know?

I think we use that in that Starlog piece that we did together. I think Harlan Ellison told me about that, and I said, "That's too good. I'm gonna throw that into the article."

> Harlan Ellison suggested proper tailoring should be a challenge for Zack Allan, an element that Straczynski wrote into the script for "Voices in Authority."

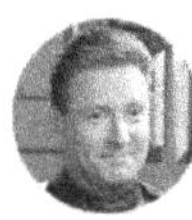

BOXLEITNER
Not every character's evolving at the same time.

But this show's a rarity in the sense that very few shows will the actors sit quietly and let the writers completely dictate what their characters are about.

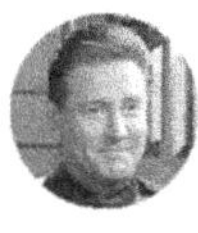

BOXLEITNER
I think we've been bullied into that. [Laughs.]

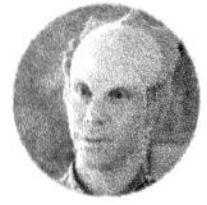

MUMY
Everyone came into his project with the understanding that this was a completely visualized novel by Joe, that he had pretty much outlined and completed before any one of us were cast. There's a great amount of respect from us to Joe, for that. In fact, that was the reason I stuck this out, because I thought this was such a great project to be involved with.

I think, because I write sci-fi tv and comic books and stuff, I've been a little more aggressive with going to him with ideas, and also, because I'm such a big fan of the show, that I see things now like, "Oh man, but hey, Joe, what if?" So I get into it from that perspective, and I do tease him about it a lot.

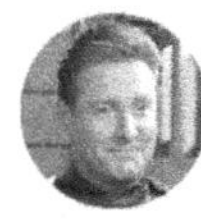

BOXLEITNER
He never lets Joe alone.

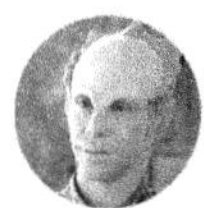

MUMY
It's true. It's true. I was in there yesterday. I was in there yesterday talking to him about an idea for the movie-of-the-week.

> After TNT purchased the syndication rights, two movies-of-the-week were commissioned to accompany the series repeats on the cable channel. The resulting movies were *Thirdspace* and *In the Beginning*, though they were broadcast in the reverse order.

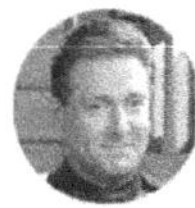

BOXLEITNER
It's good. I do know what you mean, when there are stars of shows, they literally throw out what the writers have written. I've been with that. I'm not of that school. I'm of the James Garner school. You hand me the scene. My job is to try to do that scene to the best of my ability. If it just can't work out, then it would certainly come to—

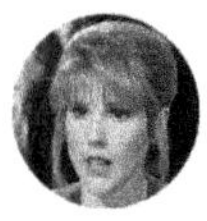

TALLMAN
Hey, Peter!

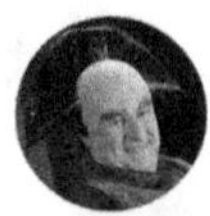
PETER JURASIK
I'll sit down at the Centauri end here.

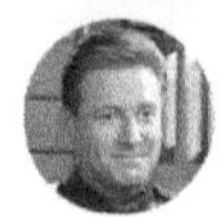
BOXLEITNER
Anyway. I think all of us have a different perspective. I think Joe has it very specifically in mind. I don't think anybody here argues with that. We don't have those kinda actors here.

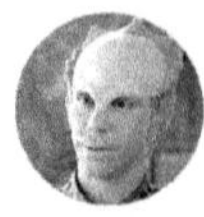
MUMY
I agree with you completely. But it is also very true—and it's again, a compliment to Joe—that we're not getting scripts that suck. We're not getting directions for characters that seem wrong. We get changes, we get surprises, but they're like, "Oh, wow. I would never have thought that. It fits very well." I think that if we were getting something that didn't feel right, we would go, "Wait a minute..."

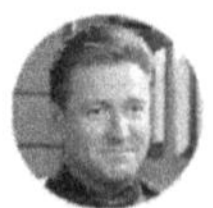
BOXLEITNER
It's also very open to it for him, we can go talk to him about this.

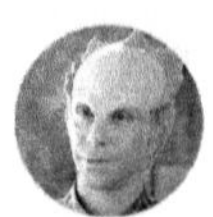
MUMY
He's definitely approachable.

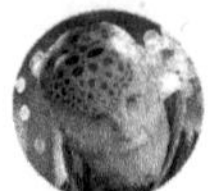
KATSULAS
You know, when we get our final draft like these? My lines have never changed in four years.

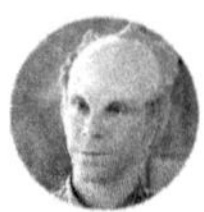
MUMY
Mine very rarely change.

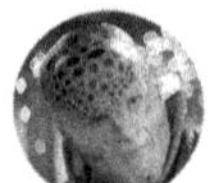
KATSULAS
From the final draft to the thing we put on the thing, there are never any changes for me. I find that remarkable.

> Though a given *Babylon 5* script might have one to three revisions after the final draft was published, they were often to relocate scenes or to deal with other production-oriented issues. The stories, scenes, and dialogue typically remained very close to the initial drafts seen by the actors.

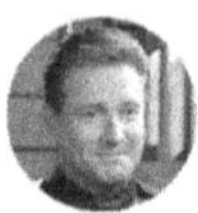
BOXLEITNER
I think all of us basically are handed some wonderful characters. I think he's the first one that's so—he's more in awe of us, in that way—that we take this stuff that he puts down on paper in the middle of the night on the computer, and make something out of it. I think, you guys [Peter and Andreas], we couldn't find two more

colorful characters—I'm just using you as example—anywhere on television today. I'm sorry. I mean, they're just not there unless you're a broad situation comedy guy.

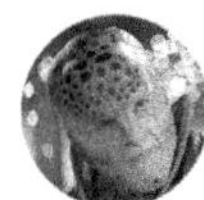
KATSULAS
"Executing the get the hell out of here maneuver." [Laughs.] He's colorful, too.

> Katsulas watched "The Hour of the Wolf" a week prior to this interview.

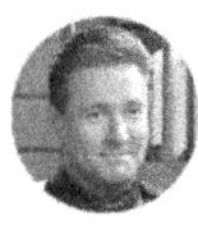
BOXLEITNER
Well, yes, but I mean everybody has got something, but I'm saying these two, in particular, are these larger-than-life guys.

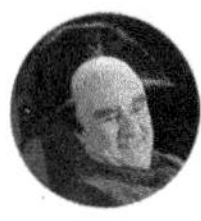
JURASIK
Let's not forget we have wonderful directors, too.

> Jurasik was sitting next to Furst, directing his first *Babylon 5* episode, "The Illusion of Truth," as this interview took place.

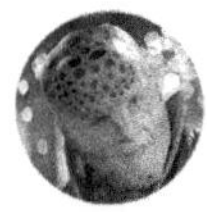
KATSULAS
Sucking up to the directors! [Laughs.]

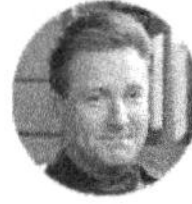
BOXLEITNER
What did he say today? Oh a classic today! Do you want to hear, here it is "Oooooh boy—*cut*!" He was out of the chair. I like, "Oh boy cut?"

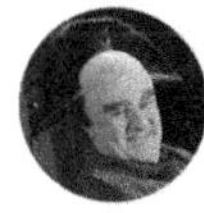
JURASIK
I like when it's a quiet scene. [Whispering.] "And action." Really gentle "Action." Did he say action?

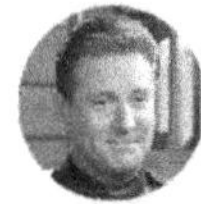
BOXLEITNER
So gentle, we went, "WHAT?" And then, "C-c-cut cut cut!" That was today. You got a three-cut. An oh-boy cut. I have to go. I have to work.

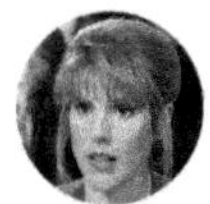
TALLMAN
See you, Bruce!

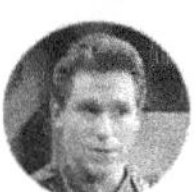
CONAWAY
See you later. Have a good afternoon!

Just to fill in the new dad [Peter Jurasik], on what's going. Congratulations, by the way. As I told everybody else, this interview's going to come out for the new Babylon 5 Magazine in the U.K. when—

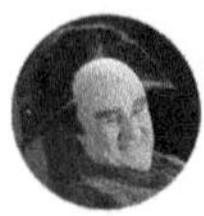

JURASIK
There's going to be a *Babylon 5* magazine?

Yeah. Pretty cool. Put it with your action figures and trading cards and everything.

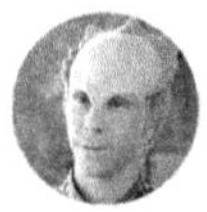

MUMY
Action figures? I want an action figure. Where are they?

So we're talking to the readers who will just be seeing season four, and it's just starting to come up. We've already talked about some of the big changes that are in store for the various characters, as far as the new season. Is there anything that you can talk about, in vague terms, as far as Londo—

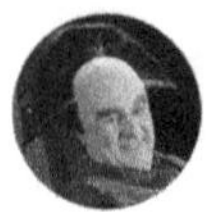

JURASIK
Will they have seen it or—

They will probably have seen the first couple [episodes of season four] and the other thing is—because this is gonna go through Warner Bros.—Warners and Joe will have a final cut on what is going to appear. If there's something that comes out where he thinks it's gonna spill the beans, I don't think we're going to have to worry about it.

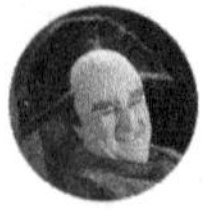

JURASIK
Without giving any spoilers, Londo and the Centauris have been dicking around with everybody else in the universe for a while, the Narns and all that. Now—especially at the beginning of the fourth season—they're putting things right at home. That's what the story is: getting things straight back on Centauri Prime, and, of course, finishing up and lining up the Shadow War relationship with Morden is straightened out.

I think G'Kar and Londo kind of have a culmination of their relationship. Right?

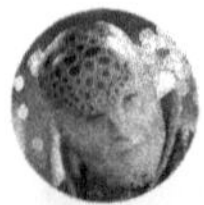

KATSULAS
Something still yet new for us.

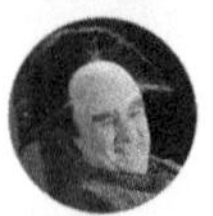

JURASIK
Uh huh.

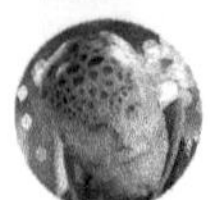

KATSULAS
Kind of a cooperation.

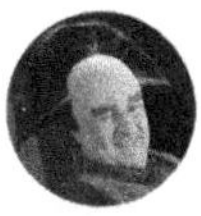

JURASIK
Brand new team. Right.

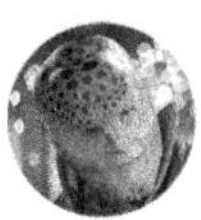

KATSULAS
Very sort of unexpected to see us in that position together.

But it seems to be a sort of a culmination every season for those characters, doesn't it?

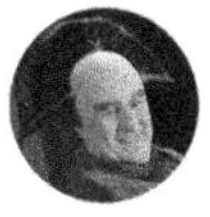

JURASIK
Joe's ready for cancellation at any moment. [Laughs.] They're gonna have a same-sex marriage eventually. [Laughs.]

> Jurasik's comment prefigures the relationship Londo and G'Kar would develop in the gag script Straczynski would write in retaliation for Jurasik and Katsulas playing a trick on him at a convention later in the month. The first draft of "The Exercise of Vital Powers" included a thread wherein G'Kar became a female Narn and mated with Londo.

The big news with the fourth season is Jeff and I actually have a scene together.

> The first interaction between Londo Mollari and Zack Allan occurred in "Epiphanies," more than two seasons after Jeff Conaway made his first guest appearance in season two's "Spider in the Web."

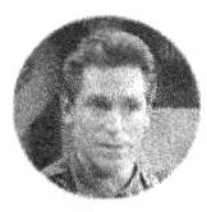

CONAWAY
Yeah.

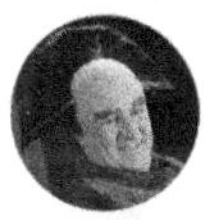

JURASIK
Which is long-awaited.

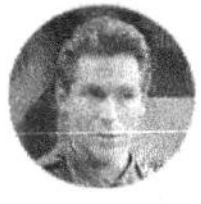

CONAWAY
I have a scene with you, and a scene with you. We have one coming up.

> Conaway is referring to his upcoming scene with Bill Mumy, in "Atonement," another first encounter for two of the series's regular characters.

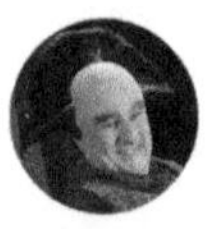

JURASIK
You're getting around.

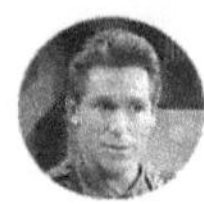

CONAWAY
I'm getting around.

That's something I was actually going to ask, because when I talk to people individually, everybody always says, "I wish I had a scene with X or Y. We see each other, maybe for a drink or something, but we haven't worked together yet."

Do you find that's still true sometimes? That there are people you would love to do a scene with?

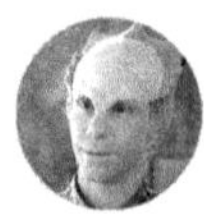

MUMY
Sure, to an extent. In the four years that I've been here, I've had scenes with everybody, but Londo and Lennier really only had one show where they were together.

> Mumy is referring to Lennier and Londo's adventures in "The Quality of Mercy." While the two characters shared screen time in "Convictions," only Jurasik was present for much of their medlab shoot, Mumy having been released to mourn his father.

I've never really had good moments with Lennier and G'Kar together. We've chatted, briefly, in the hallways and things like that, but we haven't really had our time together. That would be fun. I'd love to do that.

> A shot-but-deleted scene from "Day of the Dead" would have featured G'Kar wondering if he'd just seen Lennier in a corridor.

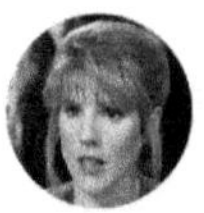

TALLMAN
I'd love to have some sort of resolution from the pilot. I told Joe—

The pleasure thing?

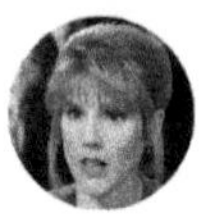

TALLMAN
—we could take my two-year-old son, put a little Narn head on him, have him run down the hallway saying, "Mommy!" and just never explain…

G'Kar would once again address Lyta Alexander's pleasure threshold in season five's "Darkness Ascending."

Now you've both got the gills, I suppose.

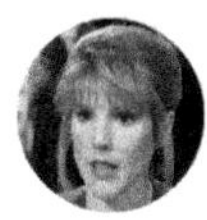

TALLMAN
Now that we both have gills some amazing things could happen.

G'Kar's gill implants were displayed in *The Gathering*, but never referenced subsequently. Lyta Alexander received gill implants from the Vorlons prior to her reappearance in "Passing Through Gethsemane."

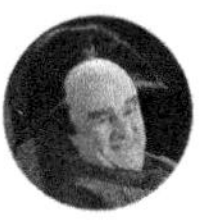

JURASIK
One of the down sides, if there are any, to this long story arc is that the stories are already plotted out and kind of run in lines. It's hard for Joe [Straczynski], I think, to cross us over in another serious situation. I mean, they can start to mix if they think, "Well, it'd be interesting to mix this character with this character."

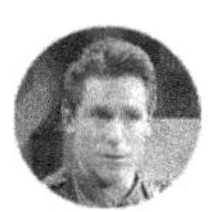

CONAWAY
Other shows figure it out as they go. Other series, they'll have some bible, but it means nothing. They throw that out as soon as they get picked up and they go from there.

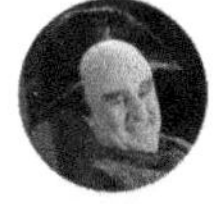

JURASIK
And in this, I feel like they gotta stay true. It's hard to mix characters.

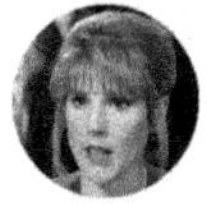

TALLMAN
You're mixing species, not just characters.

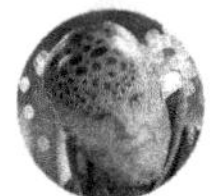

KATSULAS
You know, one thing we're set up for—it'll never happen—but because of this long-standing conflict between Centauri and Narn, a love story—Romeo and Juliet, a Narn boy and Centauri girl—because I know the fans are really into those two races. So to see them struggle through all the hatred and everything—

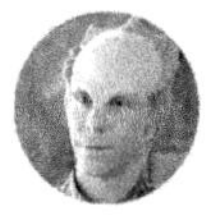

MUMY
I think he's doing that so up front, with Sheridan and Delenn—with the Minbari and the Human—that it might be a little close to that.

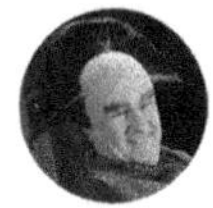

JURASIK
That's right.

I was thinking of something you just said to me not too long ago, Peter, when we were doing that interview for Starlog. You said, "I don't really think that London's gonna make it through the whole five years of this, this whole thing."

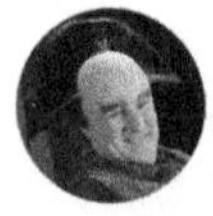

JURASIK
I'm just curious, do any of you have thoughts about that for yourselves? Do you think your characters are gonna make it through to the bitter end?

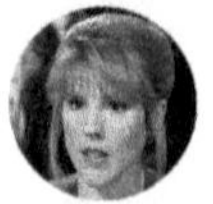

TALLMAN
Oh, don't even look at me and start that conversation. That's unbelievable.

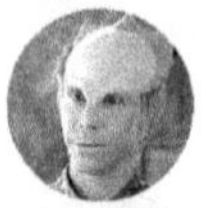

MUMY
I'm not giving Joe the ammunition.

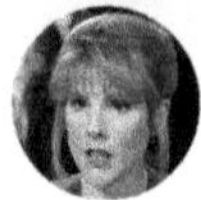

TALLMAN
Oh my god.

Neither Lennier nor Lyta Alexander were alive by the time of the series finale, "Sleeping in Light." A scene written for the *Crusade* episode "The Path of Sorrows" would have established that the two died side-by-side during the Telepath War, but the scene was rewritten when Tallman declined to appear in the spin-off series.

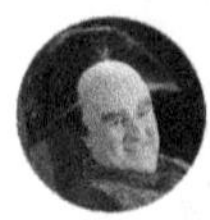

JURASIK
The interesting way Joe is, there's all just inklings. There are good guys and bad guys sitting around this table, but we don't know who's good and who's bad. Joe doesn't tell us. So we don't know who's gonna get knocked up, and who's gonna make it. [Laughs.]

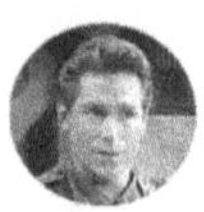

CONAWAY
We don't like to think about those things, really.

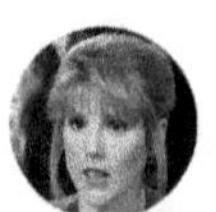

TALLMAN
No.

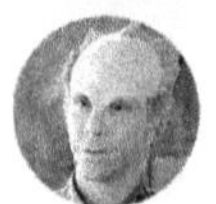

MUMY
It's true.

That's, that's a writer asking an actor the ultimate nightmarish question. Let me get my contract...well I'm in here for five years, so...

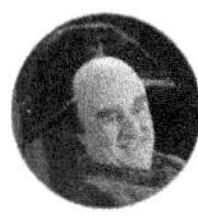

JURASIK
So it must be a shocking thing when Bill Forward found out about Refa [being killed in "And the Rock Cried Out, No Hiding Place"]. I was blown away. I couldn't believe it.

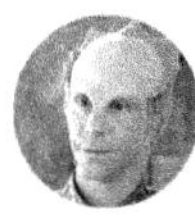

MUMY
But we've seen some major surprises along the way so far in our four seasons. I mean, people that we certainly expected to stay left—

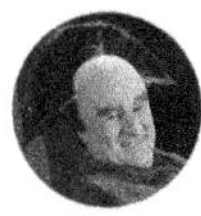

JURASIK
That's right.

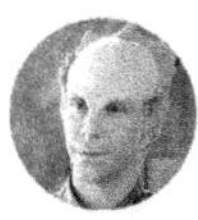

MUMY
—so as firm as the novel is, it's still somewhat liquid.

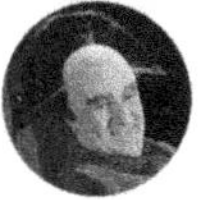

JURASIK
Like the whole security thing. Jerry's character, he's going and [Jeff's] moving up—

> Garibaldi's resignation and Allan's promotion were recent surprises, having taken place in the just-filmed "Epiphanies."

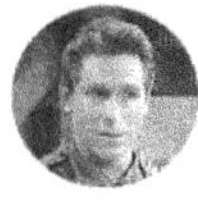

CONAWAY
I like it that way. I really like the surprise and what's coming up. Just like in life, I don't know what's happening tomorrow.

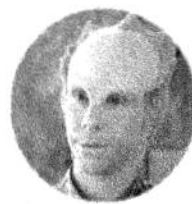

MUMY
Joe has an extreme amount of pressure on him, writing every episode again this season. Last season, when he finished writing the twenty-second script, I think we were starting to film 17 or 18 and it was like the weight of the world was released from his shoulders. I said, "Hey, it's an amazing accomplishment. Congratulations." His response was "Never again." But, nonetheless, he's gone back for more this season.

> The final draft of "Z'ha'dum" was published to the cast and crew on 4 March 1996, while the eighteenth episode of the season, "Grey 17 Is Missing," was in production.

You're looking at script what, number 11?

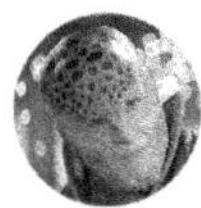

KATSULAS
Eleven ["Lines of Communication"] and 12 ["Conflicts of Interest"].

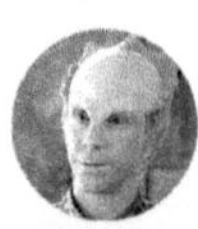
MUMY
He's more than halfway through.

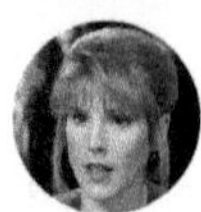
TALLMAN
With a movie at the end of it to do!

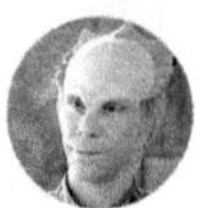
MUMY
So, in terms of going to Joe and saying, "Hey, what's gonna happen? Hey, what's gonna happen?" It's a dangerous thing. It's a dangerous place to go to right now, because he's not sure. He's got this map, but he's not necessarily positive.

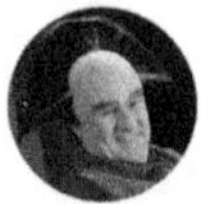
JURASIK
Hey, Jerry!

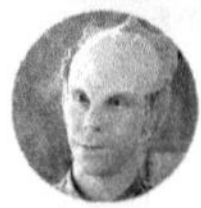
MUMY
Mr. Doyle, how are you?

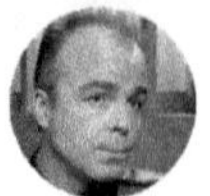
JERRY DOYLE
You must be the guy, because I don't recognize you. [Laughs.]

I'm the guy. Yeah. I'm the writer guy.

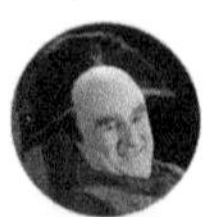
JURASIK
Coming in or going out, Jerry.

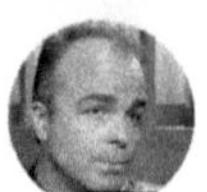
DOYLE
What's your name again, sir?

Nazzaro. Joseph. Joe.

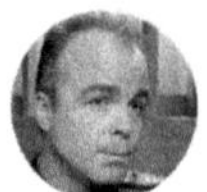
DOYLE
Is the tape on?

Yeah, but we take all the "fucks" out.

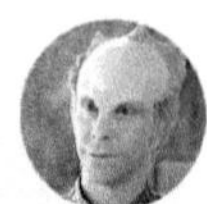
MUMY
How was the premier, the screening?

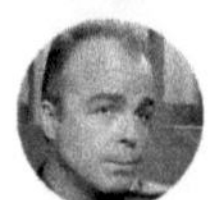
DOYLE
I thought [Andrea Thompson] just rocked it.

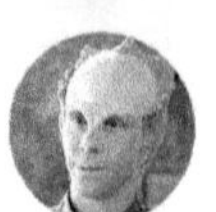
MUMY
Great.

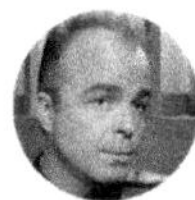
DOYLE
It was good. Yeah, it's good.

Glad to hear it.

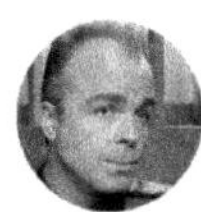
DOYLE
Sorry to interrupt.

That's alright. Running late. Yeah, they screened it last night.

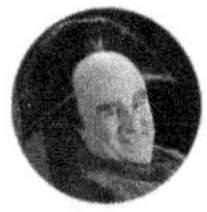
JURASIK
What is it?

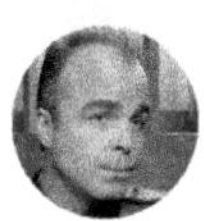
DOYLE
A Gun, a Car, a Blonde. She plays the gun.

> Doyle is referring to a new movie released in 1997, starring his then-wife, Andrea Thompson, formerly Talia Winters on *Babylon 5*. Stephen Furst, meanwhile, is watching dailies on the conference room television.

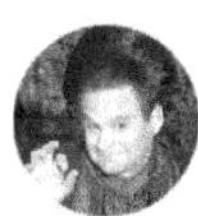
FURST
I just saw your scene.

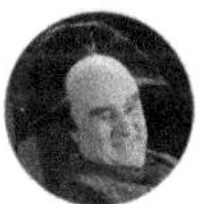
JURASIK
Oh, no kidding. Yes, good?

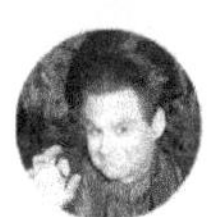
FURST
Really fine.

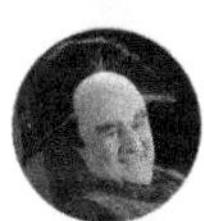
JURASIK
Good!

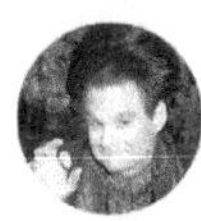
FURST
Very funny. You're on there.

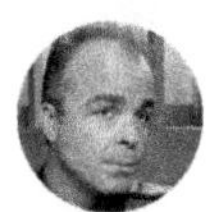
DOYLE
Huh?

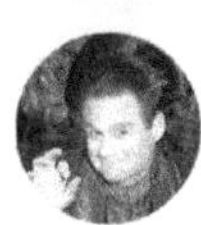
FURST
We're watching your stuff [from "The Illusion of Truth"] now.

I know most of you watch the show as a fan—which is also unusual—because a lot of people don't like to watch the show because they work in it. What sort of moments in the show have really interested you that didn't concern your own characters?

For example, Peter, you might be interested in something that was going on with some of the other characters that doesn't have anything to do with Londo. I'm giving you all the benefit of the doubt.

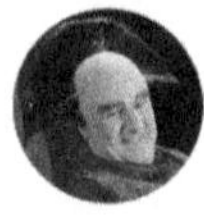

JURASIK
I, particularly, don't find the other rest of the show interesting. [Laughs.] No. We were talking about all the twists and turns in the plot Bill was talking about. We don't see them. We get the scripts and we don't know where they're coming from, so it's wonderful to see stuff turn out where your character—not giving the spoilers away—but the changes in Garibaldi—his storyline, that's a particularly interesting one. Who knows where that's headed?

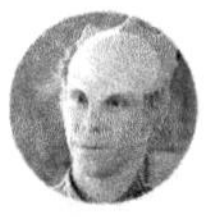

MUMY
I was blown away with the G'Kar stuff this season. I thought that that was just the greatest stuff I've read in the series.

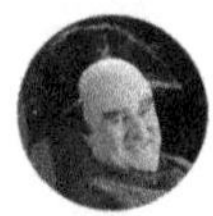

JURASIK
I think now that Pat's back on the show, her relationship with Kosh is very interesting. Those scenes have been great.

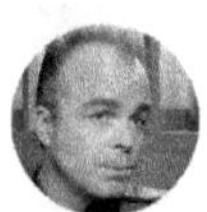

DOYLE
Ask Peter about his baby.

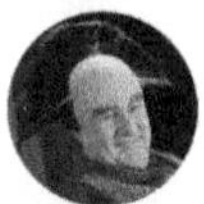

JURASIK
We covered that.

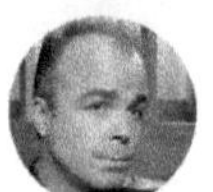

DOYLE
Did you tell him about the poop?

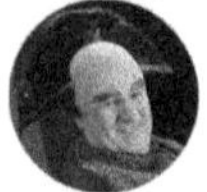

JURASIK
I've already pulled the peanut butter gag on [my wife] Barbara already. When we got a clean diaper, [I] put chunky peanut butter in it, [and] said, "Oh, I love this boy. Oh. Oh, it smells—it actually tastes good!" [Laughs.] You should see Barbara's face—Barbara was like, "Oh, we gotta get him to sleep! The man needs sleep."

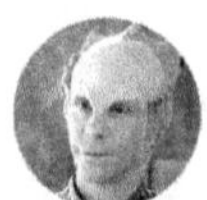

MUMY
That's funny.

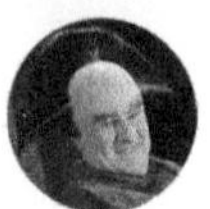

JURASIK
Just a little scoop, you know? It just works for newborns.

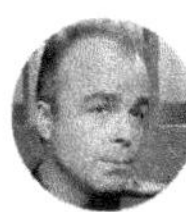

DOYLE
[First assistant camera] Wally [Sweeterman] did it on the set one day, [Laughs.] We were on [Stage] A, and while we were shooting something in a Docking Bay, [Wally] goes, "What the hell?" A little while later he goes, "There's dog shit on the set here. I know that's dog shit." He starts looking around, went out to craft service and got a blob of peanut butter and mixed it in with some chocolate and stuff like that and he goes, "Yeah, right." [Takes a taste.] "Yep. Oh yeah, that's dog shit." [Laughs.] And people were just like—

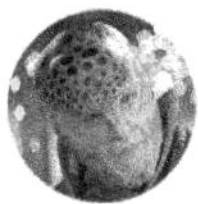

KATSULAS
I love that.

So much for the joys of impending fatherhood.

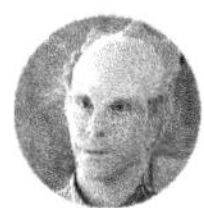

MUMY
You want deep thoughts on *Babylon 5*? This is more true to how it is.

That's as deep as it gets.

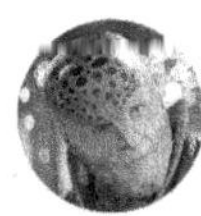

KATSULAS
Thank god I didn't step in it.

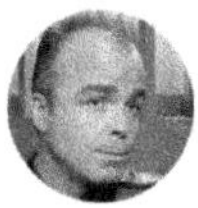

DOYLE
Aren't you glad I showed up. [Laughs.]

We just went right through the roof in terms of quality conversation here.

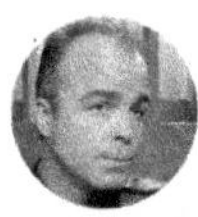

DOYLE
I go where I feel comfortable.

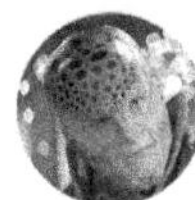

KATSULAS
This is different than anything else I've done. I don't know about you guys, but because I know you guys so well, when I watch the show, it's like watching home movies. I pass no judgment. I don't look at the show for quality. I don't look at anything objective at all. I just watch the show. I say, "Oh, look at Peter; he's funny."

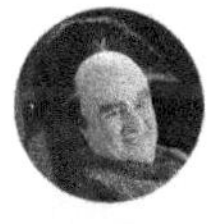

JURASIK
I can relate to that.

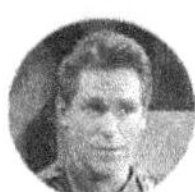

CONAWAY
I get lost in the whole fantasy of it. I'm a fan. I love it. I just get totally excited about the whole thing.

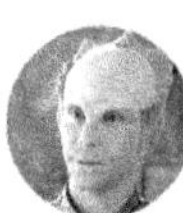

MUMY
I'll tell you, the CGI is so great.

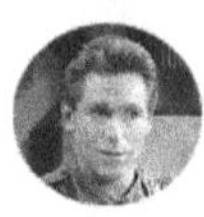

CONAWAY
It is.

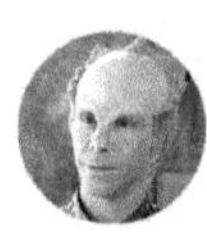

MUMY
There's nothing better, that's for sure, CGI-wise on television.

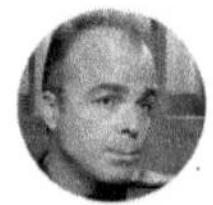

DOYLE
Not even [Mumy's series] *Space Cases*?

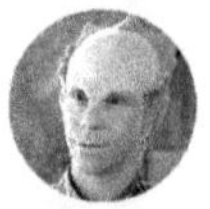

MUMY
We're close. If I just sit there and see the CGI, it just draws me into that world.

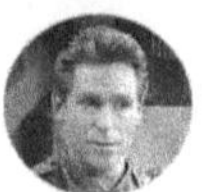

CONAWAY
All that stuff in "Shadow Dancing" was amazing.

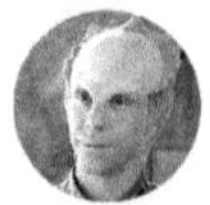

MUMY
Yeah. I always liked Andy Gibb.

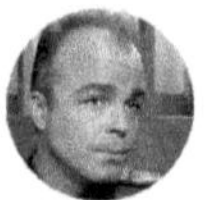

DOYLE
I like *Flashdance* better.

> While Conaway is referring to "Shadow Dancing," the penultimate episode of *Babylon 5*'s third season, Mumy is referencing Andy Gibb's 1978 single and/or album of the same title. Doyle is referring to the 1983 movie, *Flashdance*, released by Paramount Pictures.

I know this is an easy trap to fall into when you say, "Is there a particular favorite episode that people have?" but is there an episode that's aired that you guys can look at as the benchmark of quality of the show to date?

A couple of years ago it was "Coming of Shadows" and that was the one everybody said, "We're gonna be hard put to beat that." Is there now a sort of a high-water mark on this show that you guys look at? That's gonna be a tough one to beat?

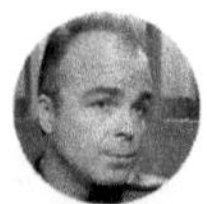

DOYLE
I think, in this business, the next one is always the high-water mark.

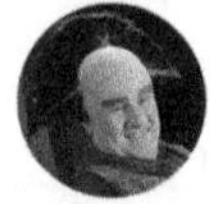

JURASIK
It's true.

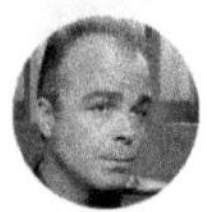

DOYLE
You know you're still on the air. I watched CBS cancel *Public Morals*, *EZ Streets* and *Almost Perfect*. There's a bunch of guys sitting around in suits who put actors

through fucking hell to decide who's gonna get the role. Then they hire all these people who spend all this money on rewrites and all of this money to shoot it, all this money to promote it, to figure out what slot to do the big announcement. One week later, they pull it off the air.

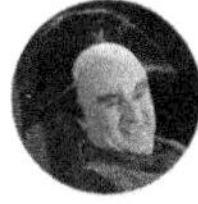

JURASIK
Horrible. One week?

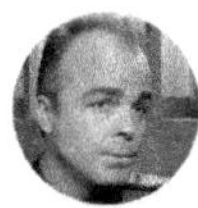

DOYLE
If we all sat here with a keg of beer, got all fucked up and came up with a story idea, shot it the same day, edited and sent it to CBS and got canceled after a week. You would expect that, right? That's what they should do.

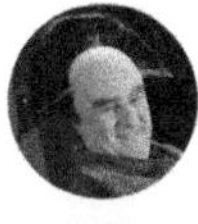

JURASIK
Almost Perfect was on for two years.

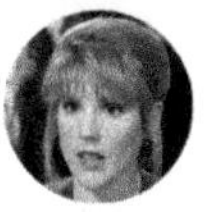

TALLMAN
Almost Perfect was halfway through the season.

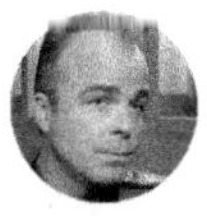

DOYLE
So the fact that we're still on the air, I think is, is a testimony to—

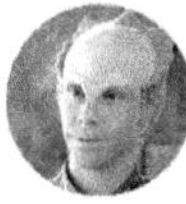

MUMY
It's the blessing and the curse of syndication. Because if we were network, we wouldn't get 22; we'd get six or 13.

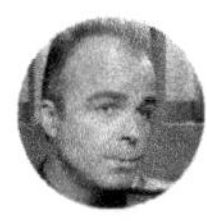

DOYLE
If we were network, we wouldn't be here.

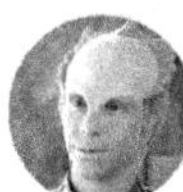

MUMY
We'd be living half-a-dozen to half-a-dozen. On one hand, the curse of syndication is you're on at 1:00 AM on Sunday night in Des Moines and you're on at 10 in the morning in Florida on Saturday afternoon, and you can't get that regular locked-down time slot. But the blessing is you get 22 [episodes] at a time.

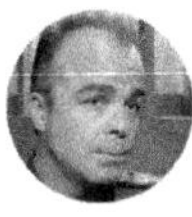

DOYLE
Well, the slot is a problem with the show at times. I think another problem is the critics and the writers—not science fiction writers, because obviously that's your genre—but I think most critics don't have any creativity. If they were good at something, they'd be doing it instead being critical of other people's ideas and work. They separate science fiction from overall television because of their own short sightedness. We are a one-hour drama that happens to be a science fiction genre instead of just being science fiction, 'cause if you're relying just on science fiction, you'd be gone like all the shows that are already gone.

But that's sort of manifests itself, doesn't it, when it comes time for Emmy nominations and things like that? Those things are usually few and far between when it comes to anything to do with science fiction. Maybe something for special effects, and that's their acknowledgment of your efforts. But you don't see anybody being nominated from anything that has any sort of science fiction cred.

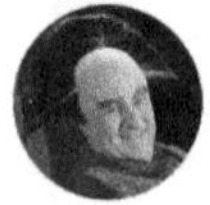

JURASIK
It's always hair or special effects, and—on our show—John Flinn has gotten nominated every season for us.

> Director of photography John C. Flinn, III, ASC was nominated for the Primetime Emmy Award for Outstanding Cinematography for a Single-Camera Series (One Hour) in 1995 and 1996, for the episodes "The Geometry of Shadows" and "Comes the Inquisitor." He lost to Tim Suhrstedt of *Chicago Hope* and John Bartley of *The X-Files*.

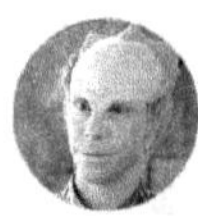

MUMY
But it's just the whole nominations, competitions, awards. It's so bizarre to begin with anyway. Who cares about awards?

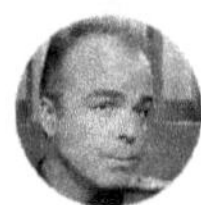

DOYLE
It's all a giant stroke. Every year it's the same fucking comedy. It's the same fucking dramas. The same people get nominated, same people win. In the end, you're not sending out tapes like you are with the academy. It's name recognition. "Oh, Jerry Seinfeld up for the funniest guy on TV." Is it? Why? Because he was funny last year? Funny this year? Yeah. He's a funny guy, but there are funnier people out there, occasionally. There are more guest stars that should be nominated. There are people on this show that should be nominated that aren't, and won't be, because of the system.

The flip side of this, because you're working in a science fiction series, is that it brings you in touch with this whole different area that most television doesn't, with going to science fiction conventions.

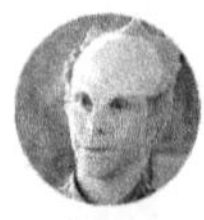

MUMY
Yeah. You don't see sitcom conventions.

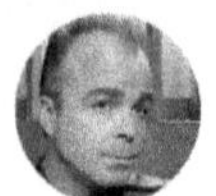

DOYLE
No.

Or the fan mail, and things like that, which, I'm sure for some of you, is a completely different phenomena when you came on Babylon 5 and faced some of that for the first time. Is that a strange thing to get used to?

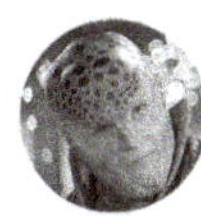
KATSULAS
Yeah, it is.

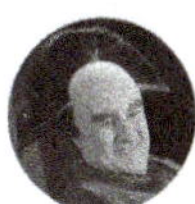
JURASIK
Just as a footnote to what Jerry was talking about
Creativity really is creativity no matter what you're on, of what you're doing. It all basically feels the same. Right? If you're at home editing your album, Bill, or [Jeff is] in an off-Broadway play, and you work, it all feels creative. The process is the process. All that other stuff is—I dunno—business stuff. That's right. The actual creative work. When we're doing our scene, we're doing our scene.

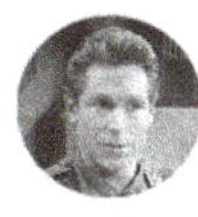
CONAWAY
Doesn't make a difference where you are.

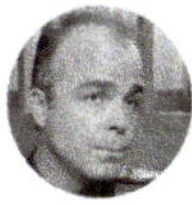
DOYLE
It'd be great for the show to get recognized. It would be great for people on the show to get nominations. It only helps, personally and collectively. But you can't go out on the stage thinking this is an Emmy scene. We always joke around out there. You have five-page scene where somebody has one line. They say the line and somebody goes—

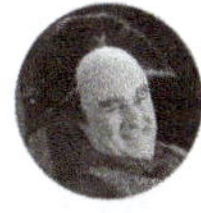
JURASIK
"I smell an Emmy!"

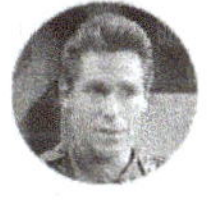
CONAWAY
"That's an Emmy line right there."

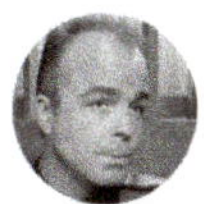
DOYLE
"That's it. baby, That's it."

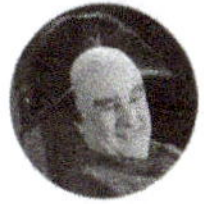
JURASIK
When it comes to this fan stuff. I don't even know why it is restricted almost exclusively to science fiction and fantasy. I don't even know why.

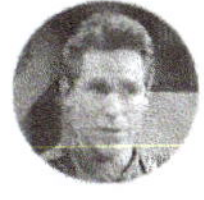
CONAWAY
And soap operas. They're that fanatical kind of fan.

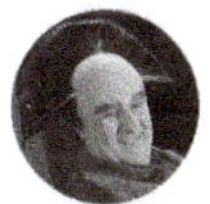
JURASIK
I don't know why that fandom is that way.

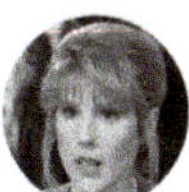
TALLMAN
The incredible thing about the science fiction fandom, I think, is that I'm meeting neurosurgeons.

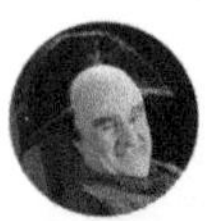

JURASIK
Yeah, right.

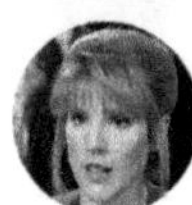

TALLMAN
I'm meeting some people who run the country but are fans of the genre and of our show. It's different than ladies watching a soap opera on an afternoon and have nothing else to do. It's an incredible cross section. It blows my mind.

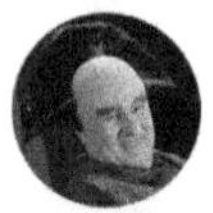

JURASIK
I just don't know why they're so vocal and so out there.

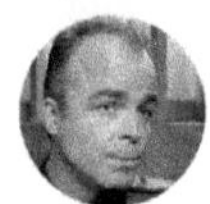

DOYLE
Can I help you answer that? I'll give you a little bit of an acid trip.

I went down to the Cape last week to watch the shuttle go. It was gonna be the three-hour tour with Gilligan, the Skipper, Mary Ann and the professor. Then it got scrubbed. So we got to do what we wouldn't have been able to do had it gone because it would've left. [Laughs.]

The culmination was putting on the space suit, going up the gantry, out the walkway into the white room, into the space shuttle on launch pad 39B, strapped to the boosters and the mains that's gonna fly Saturday. I can't tell you; it was religious.

It ended up 15 hours a day for four days, a working tour of NASA. I went into every room, talked to all the people, asked them what they did. They wanted to talk to me. They wanted to touch me. They wanted to know what I did. What I told them was, "You don't understand how wrong this is."

For four days, 15 hours a day, no one talked about themselves. They talked about It. They talked about the collective vision. They talked about where they wanted to go, what their dreams were, what could be done, what the possibilities were. It was so humbling. It was so life altering to be around people with double degrees from MIT that speak four languages, that are licensed pilots, SCUBA divers, and just happen to be astronauts. They do the stuff that most people do in life—for life—as a hobby.

Story Musgrave, flying this Saturday, 61 years old. He's got six degrees. He's currently getting two more. Right. He's got 17,500 flight hours. He's got 500 skydives. He's an underwater demolition expert. He's got five missions so far. This is his sixth. Gonna tie him with John Young.

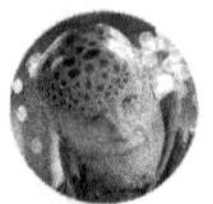

KATSULAS
They don't ever wanna stop.

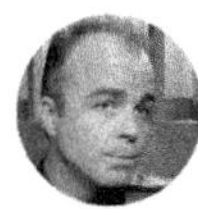
DOYLE
People tell me, "I was too busy to—" This guy's 61, but they were saying—and this was three o'clock in the morning at the astronauts' beach house, drinking tequila out of a bottle with Mike [Baker], the best looking man in aviation, who he's like 28 years old. I figured, "Yeah, he's just something like kinda whacko." But later I get his business card. He's an astronaut, plasma engineer, mechanical engineer, graduated MIT, speaks fluent Japanese, Chinese and Russian.

They think that what we do is possible. They see beyond what the critics can't. The critics are so today. These people are so tomorrow.

This one girl that we got friendly with, Marsha Ivins, is flying on STS-81 in January. It's a night launch. Mike [Baker], the commander; Brent Jett, the pilot; she; and some of the others, we sat there and I just said, "Tell me what you do." They fucking blew me away. I was like that scene where they took the top of the crypt off in *Raiders of the Lost Ark.*

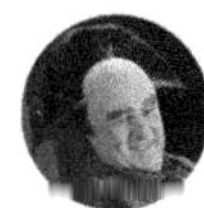
JURASIK
Like Pandora's box.

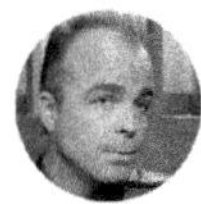
DOYLE
I got back to the hotel room at 3:30 in the morning and I'm still sitting in a room going "Woooooooooow." For an hour. Just like coming down from a rock concert. But they think that what we do is so cool. They think it's possible and they think we inspire young physicists.

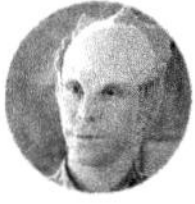
MUMY
Yeah. Well, they grew up watching *Star Trek* and *Lost in Space* and all that stuff.

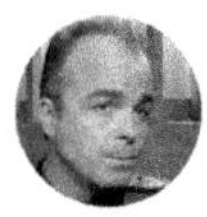
DOYLE
The first black woman astronaut [was] because of *Star Trek.*

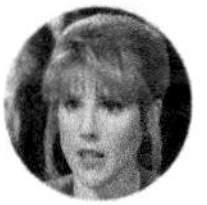
TALLMAN
Because of Uhura.

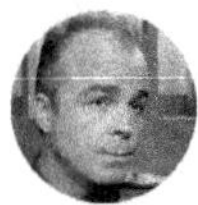
DOYLE
And Uhura stayed on *Star Trek* because of Martin Luther King. Because he wanted her to be the black face that you see on *Star Trek.* She said, "All I do is say comm-link open," and he said, "But you are a black woman, and every time they turn on the show you're gonna see a black woman. That's important." So she stayed and then she inspired, Mae [Jemison], the first black woman astronaut. Think about that, man. The first black woman astronaut. That's unbelievable.

We, in whatever way, inspire these people every day. [Andrea Thompson and I] were mobbed at NASA and I'm just going, "No, you people got it all backwards." They wanna shake hands, and, finally, one of the astronauts just went, "Oh fuck, just gotta touch you." [Laughs.] It was religious man.

We walked into the orbit-processing facility, came around a turn, and I looked up and I'm like, "Oh man." It was the belly of *Discovery*. Andrea started weeping. We put on the bunny suits and went in it. This thing had been in outer space 21 times and we got to touch it. It was like you said, "You could sit there and watch your baby for hours and hours and hours." I sat there in the shuttle and just was like, "This is so incredible and so humbling. 'Cause we're such fucking frauds." [Laughs.]

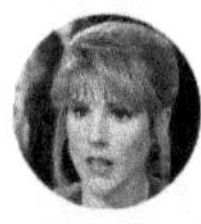

TALLMAN
We make believe in space.

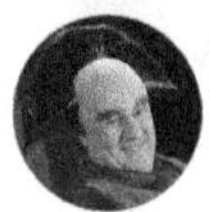

JURASIK
I never heard that point of view, especially from the real thing. I love you said, "Critics are so today and this is fucking tomorrow."

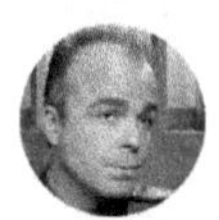

DOYLE
They are so tomorrow.

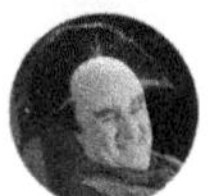

JURASIK
That's great.

But you bring an interesting point, Jerry. You're saying to people that are watching this, that may grow up to become a rocket scientist or almost anything, but doesn't that put an unnecessary pressure on you sometimes? Certainly, as far as Bruce would be concerned, I would think this, where people are watching you and maybe emulating you or looking at you as some sort of a role model.

Does that ever factor into things?

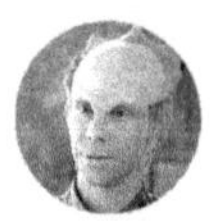

MUMY
No, it's our job to believe our lines when we deliver 'em.

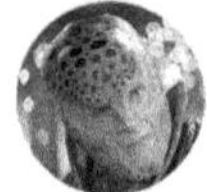

KATSULAS
I think that the admiration circle goes full cycle because then Joe—he gets off on what NASA does, and what they do and where they go—and it inspires him to write this, which in turn inspires them. It's this pendulum that turns.

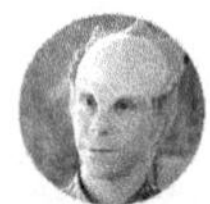

MUMY
In terms of pressure or responsibility to be a role model, I don't accept that.

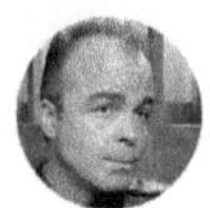

DOYLE
I agree and disagree. I agree with you mostly and I disagree in certain areas. I remember Bruce had something where his lines were, "There's no Santa Claus,

there's no Easter Bunny, there's no blah, blah, blah, blah, blah." The only thing that there is, is boom. He said, "I'm not gonna say there no Santa Claus. What if there's some kid watching [that] believes in Santa Claus?"

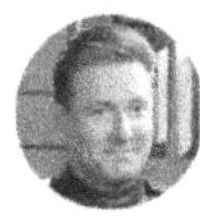

BOXLEITNER
It's not gonna be outta my mouth. If I'm really sincere about it, they'll believe me.

> Sheridan's speech about the departure of the techno-mages in "The Geometry of Shadows" was written and filmed to include a catalogue of imaginary things: "No Santa Claus, no Tooth Fairy; no such thing as elves, genies, sprites, spirits..." The scene was cut in editing.

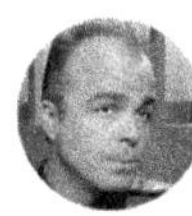

DOYLE
In one episode they wanted me to hit a woman. I said, I'm not gonna hit a woman. Don't do it in life. Don't do it on TV. 'Cause there's somebody thinks Garibaldi is cool, and I crack somebody, then they may think it's okay. If it's just one person, then it's wrong.

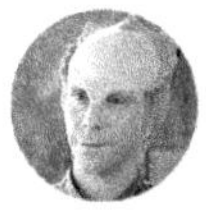

MUMY
But if you go up for an *NYPD Blue*, and you play the rapist/murderer...

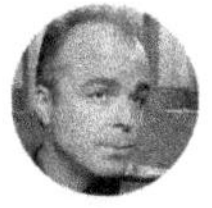

DOYLE
I wouldn't do it.

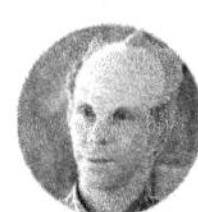

MUMY
I'm just talking about acting.

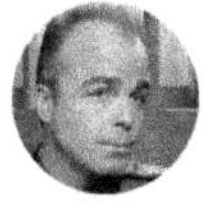

DOYLE
I don't think I'm enough of an actor to overcome what I am so adamant against in life.

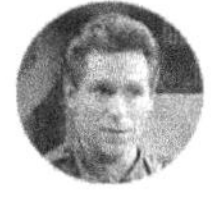

CONAWAY
Well, sometimes if you show what's wrong in life, you can enlighten people. I mean, everything can't be the Easter bunny.

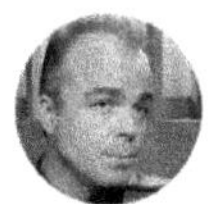

DOYLE
Wanna play a child molester?

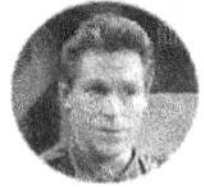

CONAWAY
If I could stop child molesting, yeah.

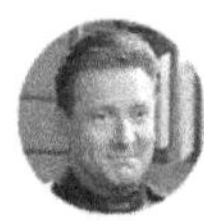
BOXLEITNER
I wouldn't do it. I don't care if they say this one will get me the Academy Award. I would say, "You are a sick bunch of motherfuckers if you think a child molester, or even understanding a child molester— If you're playing a great role where a community thinks you're a child molester and you overcome that and you're not—but you've been falsely accused—that may be a great role. But to actually play somebody that does it—

I've played killers. Ironically, people don't like *me* playing killers. They want me to be the guy where I'm doing this.

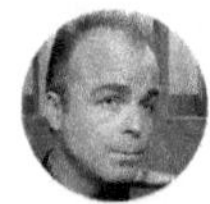
DOYLE
Andreas, what's your story on this, 'cause you played a real bad guy this summer.

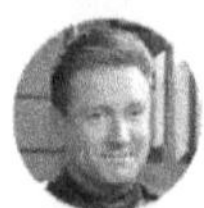
BOXLEITNER
You were a marvelous bad guy, in that huge-budget film, *The Fugitive.*

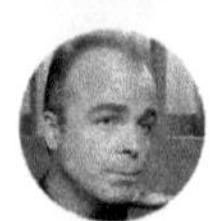
DOYLE
He played the blind sheikh [in *Executive Decision*].

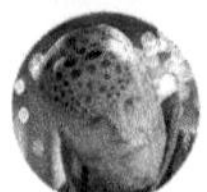
KATSULAS
I've said no to a couple parts that I could not have played because I felt the character was being glorified. I don't care that they're bad, but when they come off as cool—

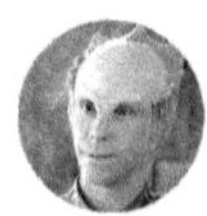
MUMY
Yes. Very bad.

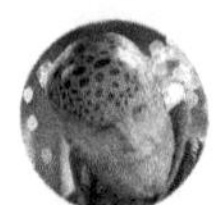
KATSULAS
—that some twisted guy's gonna wanna be like him, then I say no.

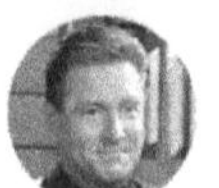
BOXLEITNER
That's what I was saying.

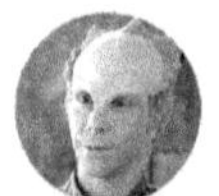
MUMY
I've turned down a million hack-up-naked-women movies from the '70s, *The Re-Animator* and all that naked—

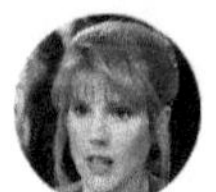
TALLMAN
I turned down being those naked women. [Laughs.]

You could have been hacked up by him!

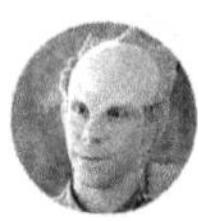
MUMY
I agree with you that if it glorifies violence or things like that, it's the right choice not to do it. But ultimately somebody will do it. Somebody will play those parts.

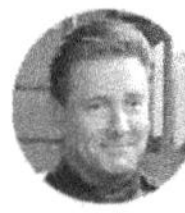
BOXLEITNER
Robert De Niro, and he'll get tremendous kudos for it. He plays every twisted form of humanity there is. And so well.

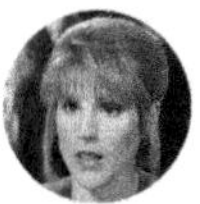
TALLMAN
So does John Malkovich.

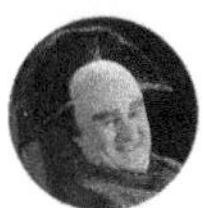
JURASIK
I get to play Londo, who's corrupting all you.

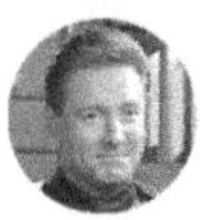
BOXLEITNER
But you have this incredible sense of honor, though.

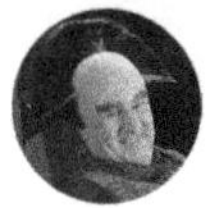
JURASIK
My take on this is that you know what the flip side of this is. It's a dangerous thing to play excellent people, and excellent beings. I think that it's not nearly as dangerous as playing some who smacks women.

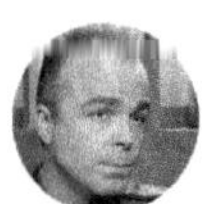
DOYLE
My character is a recovering alcoholic.

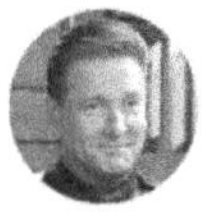
BOXLEITNER
That's a marvelous relationship. We all have problems.

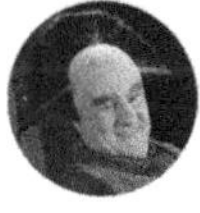
JURASIK
That's an excellent example of excellent people who have flaws. You don't want perfect people; that I think is dangerous.

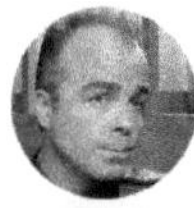
DOYLE
I think good people striving for greatness is better than great people doing good.

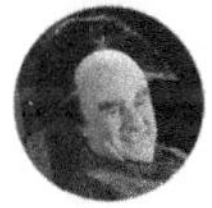
JURASIK
Or flawed people striving.

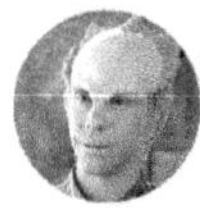
MUMY
But you don't want us all to be Mr. Rogers.

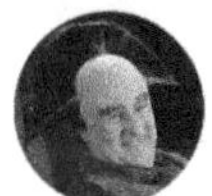
JURASIK
No, as I said, I think that's bad for excellence.

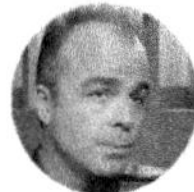
DOYLE
If we didn't have a Jeffrey Dahmer, we wouldn't realize we wouldn't have a benchmark of just how fucked up, fucked up is.

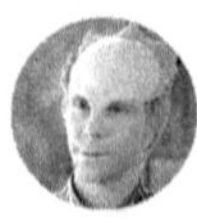

MUMY
Going way back to where you were a little while earlier, Joe, talking about the uniqueness of the science fiction genre and fans and conventions. One of the things that—being the old man of sci-fi here—

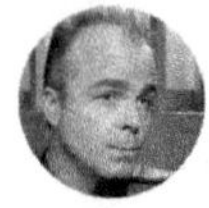

DOYLE
SAG member, 37 years.

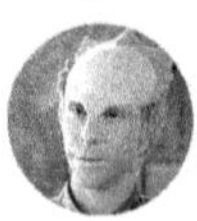

MUMY
—I find that the science fiction community, in general, are a group of people who very much are pro-space program, who are very pro-environmental conscious. They know the dangers that can happen to nature and want to take care of the planet Earth. They're not racist. They're not prejudiced against other life forms, or tribal. They think like humans, which is a really good thing.

The science fiction community, in general, are really good people. They just tend to forget that it's only a TV show. You know, there's a small percentage of them that take it too seriously. Those kind of people need to remember that it is just pretend.

> In 1998, Mumy would release the album *Trying to Forget* by the Be Five, consisting of Mumy, Andreas Katsulas, Mira Furlan, Peter Jurasik and Claudia Christian, with Patricia Tallman on back-up vocals. The final track, written by Mumy and performed by the ensemble, was titled "It's Just a TV Show."

The thing sometimes—and it goes back to what we were talking about role models—is that if you go to a science fiction convention, it's very easy for some people to identify you with the character, and therefore think that you possess some of those same traits as the character.

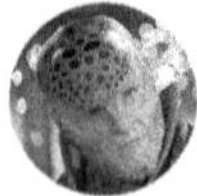

KATSULAS
Right. I try to make that clear in interviews, that that is not the case. I should *be* a tenth of what G'Kar is, or a hundredth. I feel about G'Kar the way [Jerry feels] about these NASA guys. This guy never rests in a quest for his people. He's got energy, resources all ready to go and, and I'm a couch potato. [Laughs.] It's true, you know.

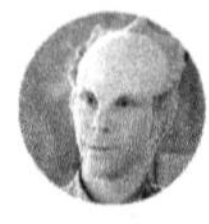

MUMY
I feel the exact same way about Lennier.

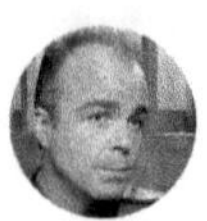

DOYLE
I think it's what you put out there to the audience, too. If you are what you do, that's so obvious. I think you have to put some of who you are into what you do and as little or none of what you do into who you are. If you give that out to the fans, that's

what they're gonna perceive. If you walk out on stage at a convention—or if you meet people in an airport—you wanna draw a crowd, get six bodygaurds.

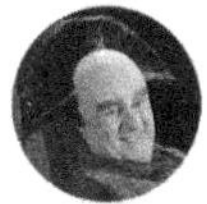

JURASIK
That's right.

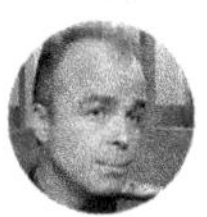

DOYLE
You gotta do it, but I think they know us for us. In any group, there's always gonna be one guy who has way too many drinks and drops his pants in the middle of a birthday party. You know? Same thing at a science fiction convention. There's always gonna be one person who has no grasp on reality, who's gonna—

I'm standing in the bathroom, taking a leak. I got my crank in my hand and some guy's standing next to me, staring at me and starts asking me about the show. I said, "Do you find this odd?" [Laughs.] I said, "I'm standing here taking a leak and you asking me about..."

How many people have been asked for their autograph in those situations?

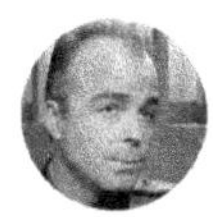

DOYLE
They're asking me about a TV show. I said, "How would you like it if I came up to you while you were standing in the bathroom taking a leak with your crank in your hand, and asked you what you did?" And he was like, "Yeah."

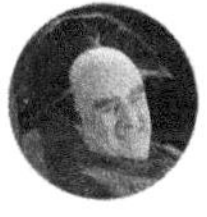

JURASIK
Unbelievable, right?

Do you get interesting feedback from the fans, in terms of fan letters and other stuff?

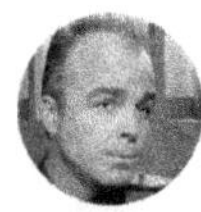

DOYLE
I think Andreas had a very interesting fan letter you can share.

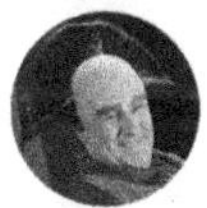

JURASIK
Oh, he certainly did. I read that one.

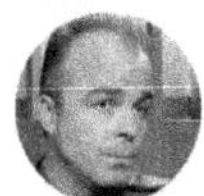

DOYLE
Did you read it?

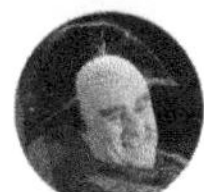

JURASIK
That was a good one.

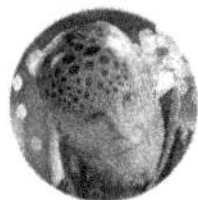

KATSULAS
Sometimes they're a little too interesting. [Laughs.]

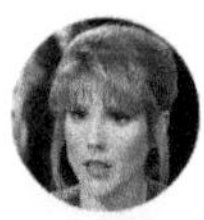

TALLMAN
How interesting?

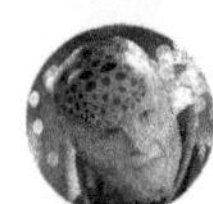

KATSULAS
Oh, very interesting. You could touch it, and it burns your hands, you know?

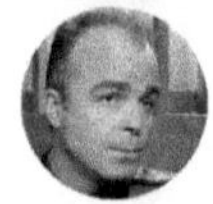

DOYLE
She had fantasies—sexual encounters—with G'Kar.

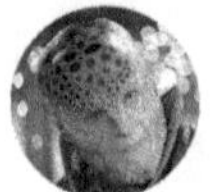

KATSULAS
Yeah. There were like three of 'em in a row. When it rains, at pours. I had never gotten anything like that. Suddenly, there were three. They all had basically the same fantasy. They saw themselves somehow getting connected, being in this show, and that the character they play would fall in love with G'Kar and have a love affair with him.

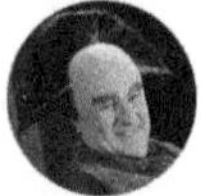

JURASIK
Isn't that great?

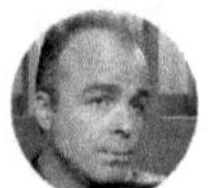

DOYLE
I think it's so cool.

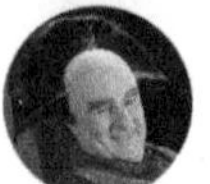

JURASIK
No one wants to get in the bed with Londo, unfortunately.

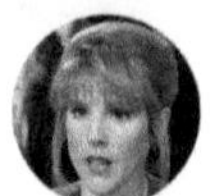

TALLMAN
They've heard about your equipment.

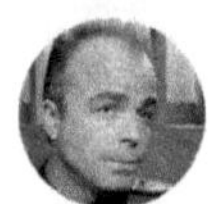

DOYLE
Six penises! You could kill her! [Laughs.]

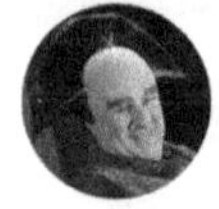

JURASIK
Do you get those? Hot little letters? Anybody want Garibaldi?

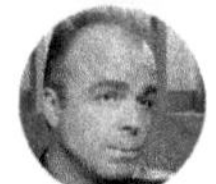

DOYLE
We all get the same stuff, you know, "I love your character, you're the sexiest man," and that they've seen all your other work, which—right there—is a lie because there is really nothing else. [Laughs.]

Mostly it's just, "Thanks for what you do." That's the bulk of letters. I think it is a little off-putting to get fan mail. I think teachers should get fan mail and cops and firemen. They should get fan mail 'cause they're really doing the day-to-day.

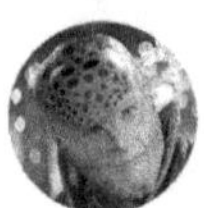

KATSULAS
That's right.

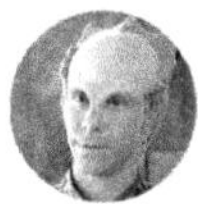

MUMY
Absolutely.

But you get fan mail from teachers and cops and people like that.

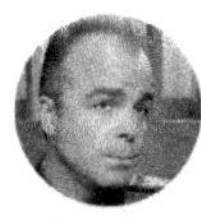

DOYLE
But it's so fucking twisted, man.

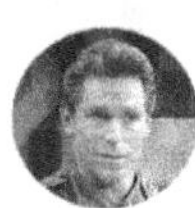

CONAWAY
You're an escape for people. They like to get away from being a fireman or a cop or whatever they do in life, and fantasize with that they're us. We provide that.

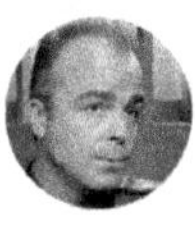

DOYLE
This will piss on a fellow thespian, but who cares?

I'm standing in the shuttle bay, the orbiter processing facility. As I'm walking out, they have this giant poster—a night shot [of a launch]—and all the signature are on there, like John Glenn, Neil Armstrong. They said, "Would you sign the picture?" I go, "No, I can't." They said, "No, really. You've been here. You're like one of us now. Sign the thing." I said, "No, I can't sign the thing. It's irreverent. I'm putting a mustache on a *Mona Lisa*. You don't get it." Somebody says, "What if I give you a good reason?" So he drags me over and says, "Look at the bottom." I look at the bottom. It says "[L.A. Law star] Corbin Bernsen." I said, "Give me the fucking pen."

That's not the piss on Corbin, but across the top I wrote, "Wow, Jerry Doyle." We provide a wow to them that other people in life provide to us.

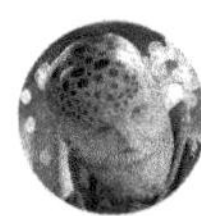

KATSULAS
It's good that we're not sitting here thinking we do provide a big wow for them. That's where we should be. We should be here not realizing it.

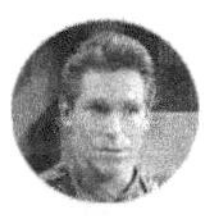

CONAWAY
We're doing our job. They're doing their job.

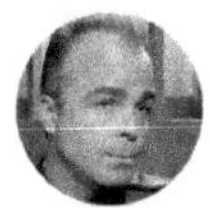

DOYLE
If they didn't do their job, we wouldn't have Velcro. [Laughs.]

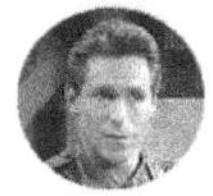

CONAWAY
Hey, if the plumber didn't do his job, we couldn't take a shit.

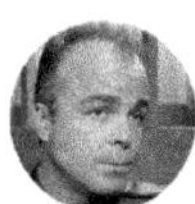

DOYLE
Well, we could. We could take a few, but then we'd have a problem.

Do any of you guys go on the internet to see the sort of thing that's on there?

> The recording of this group interview suddenly stops and then resumes.

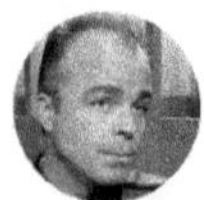

DOYLE
Are we rolling?

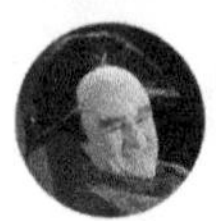

JURASIK
I've lurked in the *Babylon 5* chat room and I always remain stupid and quiet in the corner. [Laughs.] Occasionally, I say stuff like that. "How do you spell G'Kar? How do you spell Garibaldi?"

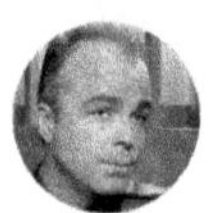

DOYLE
I can't get online. I bought the computer. I downloaded Netscape. It said I need Netscape Chat. I downloaded like the blueprints for— I can't. I got like $9,000 in it.

So it's not a case of not wanting to, you just don't know how.

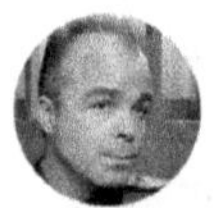

DOYLE
I got a $9000 calculator.

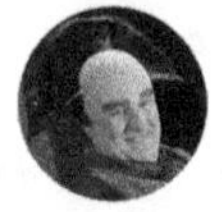

JURASIK
You're not worthy of signing that poster!

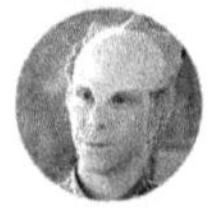

MUMY
I was here from six o'clock in the morning yesterday till eight o'clock at night. When I go home, the last thing I want to do is go surf the internet to talk about *Babylon 5*.

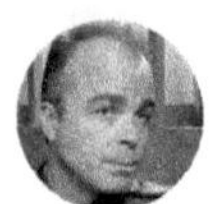

DOYLE
Some people say, "Did you see the show?" Last week I said, "No, I didn't watch it." They said, "You didn't watch the show?" I'll get tapes from here and watch it or catch from time to time. I don't catch all the shows.

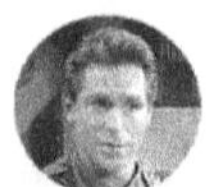

CONAWAY
I gotta go. You got my number?

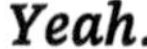

Yeah.

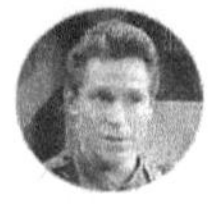

CONAWAY
Give me a buzz. It was nice seeing all you lovely people. Bye.

I'll try to wrap this up, so you guys can get back to your days off, because I cut into that quite significantly, and I apologize for that.

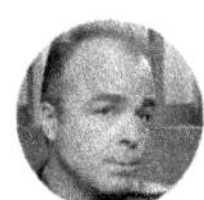

DOYLE
I think the fact that you've got all these people talking to you is a testimony to the enthusiasm that we all have for what we do. We, collectively, can only do so much to put out a quality product. Once it's on the reels and it's heading off to wherever it's going to—or it's getting uplinked—it's out of our hands. Then it's up to marketing and distribution and PR and promotion. It's up to all those people to do all those things that haven't collectively been done well enough to push the show.

We can only do so much, but to have everybody come in here on their day off to talk to you—not that you're not a nice guy—but it's a half an hour here, half an hour home. What is this one article gonna do? Is it gonna make the show any more popular or widespread? I'm not trying to knock what you're doing, but the fact that you did get everybody here, tells you that we all like what we do. We enjoy the process and we're trying to put out the best product we can and we're excited about it.

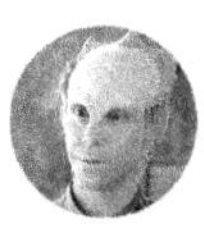

MUMY
I concur with your astute observation, man.

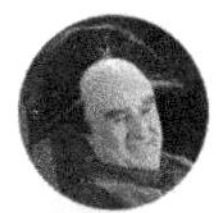

JURASIK
I do too, man. It's true.

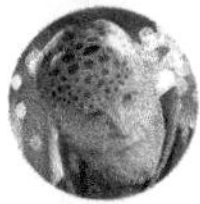

KATSULAS
I just came for the lunch. [Laughs.]

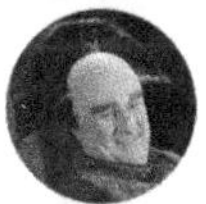

JURASIK
That's true, too. We know that's true also.

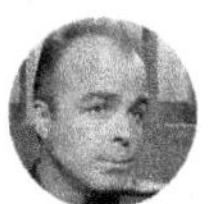

DOYLE
Spoken from a true couch potato.

How do you feel about the future of Babylon 5? There's the possibility of this spin-off, a possibility of a TV movie or whatever. How do you guys feel about all this stuff? Are you happy to do more Babylon 5?

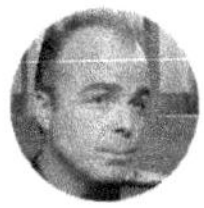

DOYLE
Do you want the arty answer or a capitalist answer?

You can give any answer you want.

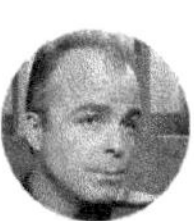

DOYLE
The arty answer is "Yeah, that'd be kind of cool to see where this is going." The show is now starting to build momentum and I think it deserves a better, bigger audience. That will happen if the show goes on. The current show will be appreciated much more, later, down the road than it is now.

From a capitalist standpoint, spin-offs sound great, movies sound great, features sound great. All sounds great. Make me an offer.

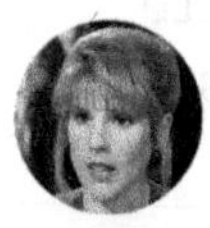
TALLMAN
Yeah.

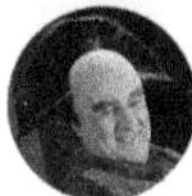
JURASIK
What worries me about it going on, I've been in the back years of a couple of series already—the sixth, seventh, eight seasons. I always said if I was ever a producer of the show, what I would do was take the whole cast, fire them all, and bring on a whole new cast.

I worry about it getting stale, not only from the actor point of view, but Joe originally set out to make a five-year show. God knows, Joe's had enough creativity that I shouldn't underestimate him. He can probably write another five years, but let's hope that he doesn't take it and water it down. When we're talking about these wonderful characters getting washed out and there's nothing new to say. That's a worrisome factor.

On the capitalist answer, I'm with Jerry. Make me a deal.

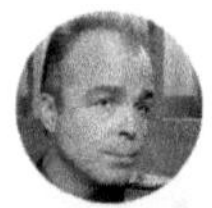
DOYLE
What's the deal?

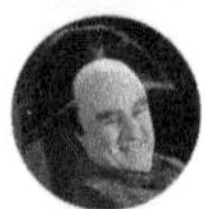
JURASIK
"Slide a contract toward me." I'll say, "What are the numbers? I'll consider it."

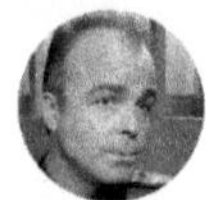
DOYLE
On the capitalist side, in this business, when you're working, you're blessed. So many people in this business don't work. It's obviously not a talent contest because a lot of people who are working wouldn't be, and a lot of people who aren't would be.

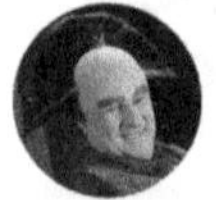
JURASIK
Let's just see what do they want Garibaldi to do in the eighth season?

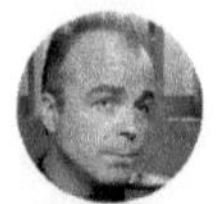
DOYLE
I heard it's impressionistic dance.

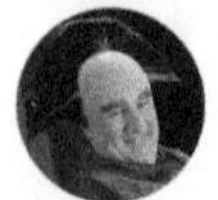
JURASIK
That's what I'm worried about.

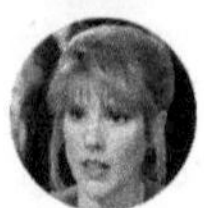
TALLMAN
[Laughs.]

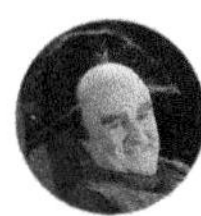

JURASIK
Londo goes to McDonald's. [Laughs.] Oh god no. I don't know. We'll see.

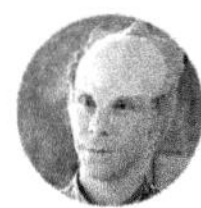

MUMY
I think the idea of returning to these characters on an annual or biannual reality—to do a couple of movies of the week like the *Alien Nation* people have been doing—is great. That's very appealing to me. I would be happy to see Lennier be a part of those projects.

As far as the spin-off series goes, it's just wind in sails.

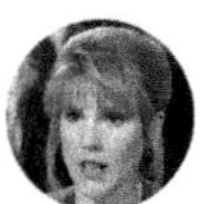

TALLMAN
We really haven't heard anything serious.

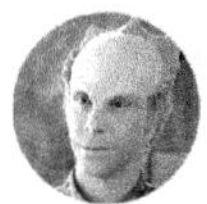

MUMY
I'd have to sit down and I'd have to read something and I'd have to know what kind of—

That's a whole other ball game. That's five years of staying in one location.

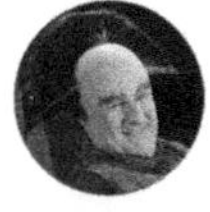

JURASIK
The most exciting thing I've heard is "prequel." That would be fun.

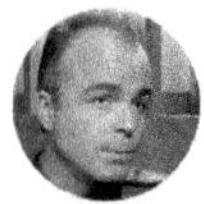

DOYLE
I've heard prequel. I've heard "What was everybody doing, individually, before?"

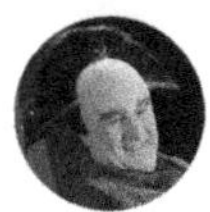

JURASIK
That would be fun.

> Though there were rumors regarding the content of the two TNT movies-of-the-week, the premises would not be formally announced to the cast and crew until February 1997.

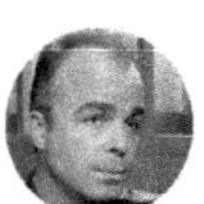

DOYLE
I've heard there's gonna be a spin-off to *Space Rangers*.

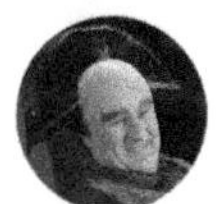

JURASIK
That's right.

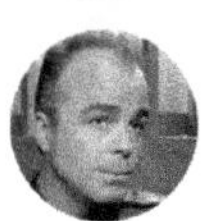

DOYLE
Rangers in Action—solving crime at every turn.

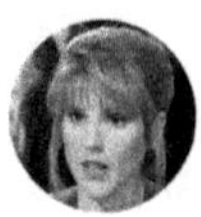
TALLMAN
[Laughs.]

Doyle is referencing *Space Rangers*, a short-lived series that debuted on CBS on 6 January 1993, roughly 6 weeks before the *Babylon 5* pilot was broadcast. It was cancelled twenty days later, just under a month before the pilot screened. Straczynski's plan for a *Babylon 5* spin-off, at this point, was a premise called *Babylon 5: Rangers*, about the Anla-Shok enforcing the laws of the Interstellar Alliance to be established at the close of season four.

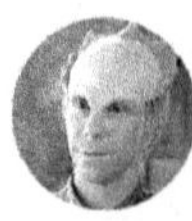
MUMY
The Ranger thing, though, from the little I've heard from Joe, is more or less knights of the round table in space.

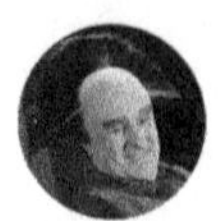
JURASIK
That's rights.

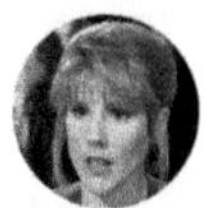
TALLMAN
That's a great idea.

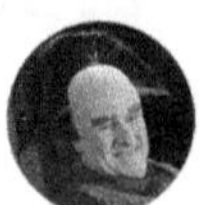
JURASIK
That is a good idea.

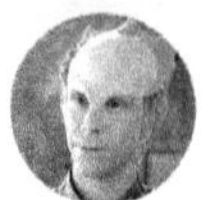
MUMY
The whole Camelot in space—

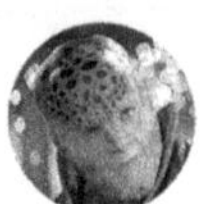
KATSULAS
I'm already Sir G'Kar, you know.

G'Kar was knighted by David McIntyre, believing himself to be King Arthur, in "A Late Delivery from Avalon."

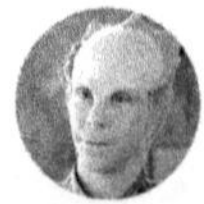
MUMY
The concept could be very cool.

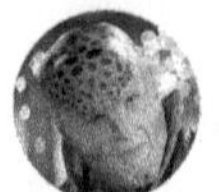
KATSULAS
Michael York knighted me.

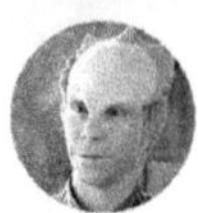
MUMY
The first movie-of-the-week supposedly is the Earth-Minbari War—

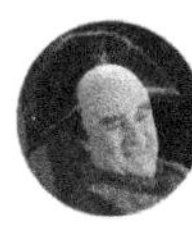
JURASIK
So it is a prequel? Far out.

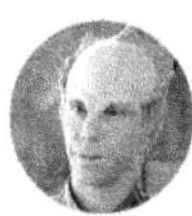
MUMY
—that's led up to so much of where our foundation rests.

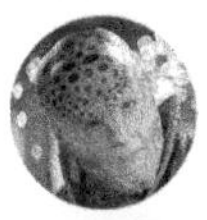
KATSULAS
We're not in it.

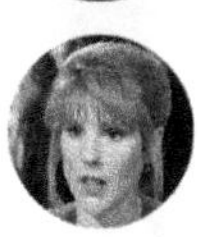
TALLMAN
It's where you are.

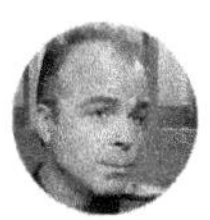
DOYLE
They said, "Yeah, we're gonna do a couple of movies. How much will you work for?" Well, that's good. Let me start negotiating against myself right off the bat.

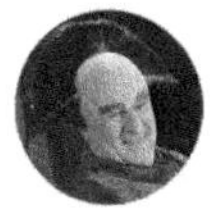
JURASIK
Wasn't that classic? Classic negotiation.

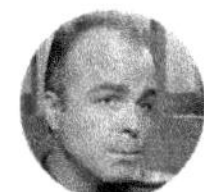
DOYLE
I say, "What's the budget?" They said, "Well, it might be three, four million." I said, "Alright, $500,000." They said, "That's absurd." I go, "So was your question."

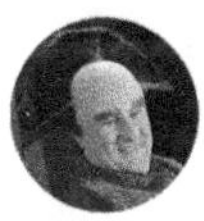
JURASIK
Can I see a script? How long do I work?

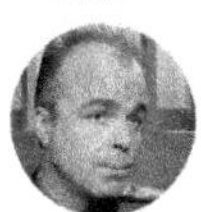
DOYLE
Does it shoot in Kuala Lumpur, or here? Is it the same caterer?

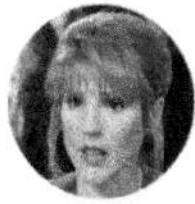
TALLMAN
Is it a three-week shoot?

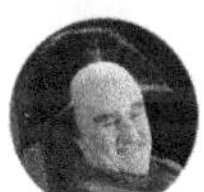
JURASIK
Or in Nicaragua, during the revolution?

> Doyle did not appear in either *In the Beginning* or *Thirdspace*. Though Garibaldi appeared in the first-draft script for the latter, it was re-written to feature Allan instead.

To close this up, do you folks have any words for your fans back in Britain, who seem to be extremely loyal?

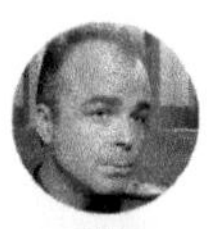
DOYLE
Yeah, thanks for the fucking food poisoning.

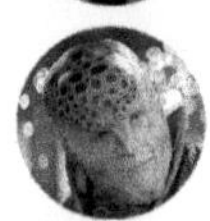
KATSULAS
Keep those sexy letters coming.

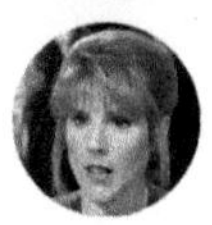
TALLMAN
See you in July!

Tallman is referencing Wolf 359 "The Alliance," a convention that most of the Babylon 5 cast would attend between 11–14 July 1997, at Norbreck Castle Hotel, Blackpool, England. The convention would become infamous due to the last-minute contract negotiations for Babylon 5's eleventh-hour renewal by TNT, Claudia Christian's failure to re-sign for the fifth season, and the loss of J. Michael Straczynski's fifth-season notes due to a housekeeping mishap.

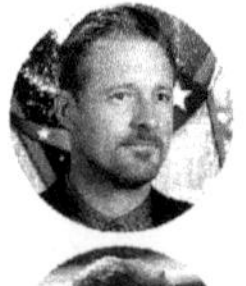

BRUCE BOXLEITNER
John Sheridan

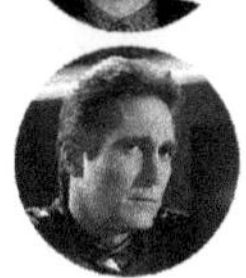

MICHAEL O'HARE
Jeffrey Sinclair

13 July 1997, Norbreck Castle Hotel in Blackpool, U.K.

Babylon 5 Timeline
Last In Production
In the Beginning (MOW2)
Last on the Air
"Intersections in Real Time" (418)

This interview was conducted by journalist Joe Nazzaro, with occasional input from his wife, British makeup designer Sheelagh Wells.

What I thought would be interesting to maybe start with was something that I know we both talked about separately on different occasions, which was the whole concept of being a role model. I know, Michael, you had had some thoughts on this a couple of years ago, when we talked, and Bruce has certainly said it, but once you've become a role model of sorts, does that stay with you? Regardless of whether you've left a part, whether you're on stage or in a film or whatever, once you've become a role model, does that sort of stick with you afterwards?

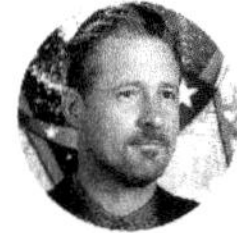

BRUCE BOXLEITNER
Well, I think most actors would prefer it wouldn't, but I think it's part of the stock in trade that comes with it. You know, everyone would, ideally in their personal life, [want] to be left alone, I think, and be able to do what you want to do and not have that responsibility of a role model. But I think it comes, and I think you just have to be aware of it and go accordingly. I think it's there with you. I don't know how you try to dog it. It's there.

There are a lot of people that try to play that, "I'm gonna play the bad boy" or what have you—you know what I'm saying—in their private life and tabloids, and that's fine. But, I, myself, I think there is a certain responsibility in which to try to keep a good profile out there.

SHEELAGH WELLS
You sort of live with it maybe, don't you? It's just part of what it is.

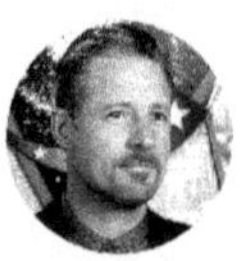

BOXLEITNER
I really do believe it is. It comes with the territory, that clichéd statement, but this is so true, and I am very good at clichés. [Laughs.]

Did you find that that happened to you, though, Michael, that people will still expect a certain attitude from you?

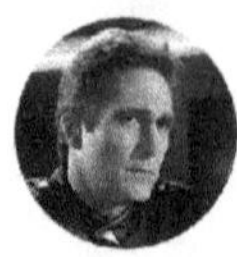

MICHAEL O'HARE
Yeah, yeah, yeah. It changes your life.

In what way?

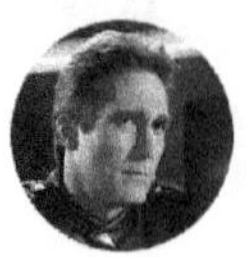

O'HARE
Well, you go to a certain place in order to play the part, and I think every part changes your life.

You mean a certain place in your head?

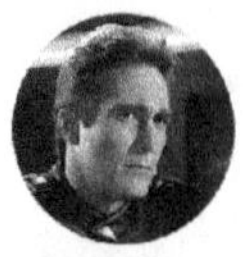

O'HARE
Yeah, and then it's difficult to let go of it, you know? I agree with Bruce that you have an obligation that just comes with the territory.

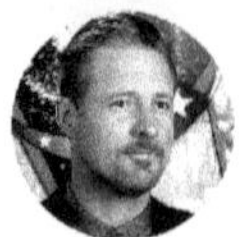

BOXLEITNER
Yeah, but, you're a person. We're people. We have our own personal whatever, and sometimes you want to go, "Listen! I'm allowed to fuck up. I'm allowed to do things. I'm allowed, you know what? Yeah, I'm a person." But, unfortunately, you still have to kind of live under it. You have to, and if you wanna continue, if you wanna blow it completely, that can happen.

We play very, very strong men. Difficult, I mean complicated, ones, but, nevertheless, what do they want in the end? They want a leader. It's a heroic type. Archetype. Yeah. Is that a good word? Archetype?

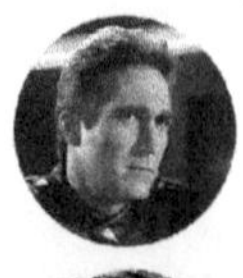

O'HARE
Yeah, it is an archetype.

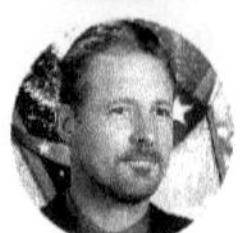

BOXLEITNER
And, they can forgive you. They will forgive you a lot, but I think today we have so many people who are screen idols—especially screen idols, I wanna say, who really go out of their way to live a notorious existence—like a Madonna or, so on and so forth, who really thrive on the tabloids and basically it's really their career. You know what I'm saying?

Yeah.

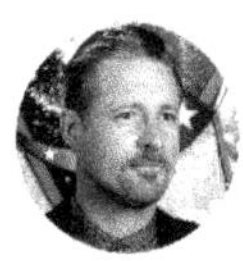

BOXLEITNER
I think that, I—myself—I think we're probably the same in that we'd rather have our work speak for us and not have to play the image out there. To some degree you have to do it, but yeah, it does change your life. You're right, Michael. It alters everything.

When you walk out here [at a convention], there's your perfect example. How do people look at you in these autograph lines? I mean, people literally afraid of you or don't know what to say. They walk up and they're just totally tongue-tied. You go, "Hey, we're all just people here."

Does that still happen to you, Michael? Because you've probably done more conventions now than Bruce, and so you've probably faced it more, I would think. Do people still get tongue-tied, or, because you've done a few conventions now, do they realize you're a regular guy?

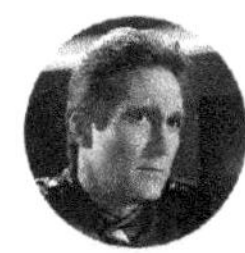

O'HARE
It depends. Both things happen, but you do still get the people who are tongue-tied, can't believe they're standing there in front of you waiting for your autograph.

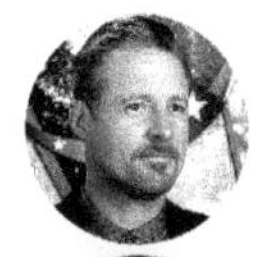

BOXLEITNER
It's so weird. It is.

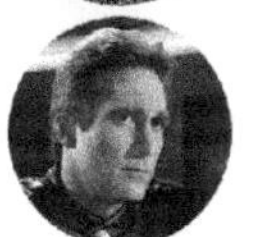

O'HARE
You just try to set 'em at ease. Like Bruce says, we're all just people.

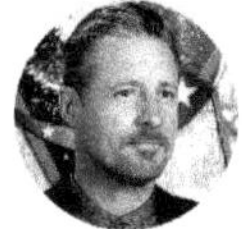

BOXLEITNER
Yeah, just a guy like you. It's just hard to still fathom that. I mean, I guess—I know—when I walked up to Buzz Aldrin, I stood in line. [Laughs.]

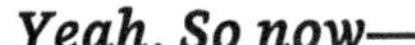

Yeah. So now—

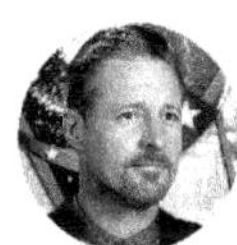

BOXLEITNER
He did a book signing. Here's an example: He did a book signing of the science fiction novel he wrote last year, and I missed him in London when we came to do this convention. I heard he was gonna be at Forbidden Planet and just missed it.

> Straczynski, Boxleitner, Mumy, Furst, and Katsulas traveled to the U.K. for a previous incarnation of this convention, Wolf 359 "The Gathering," held 7–10 June 1996.
>
> *Encounter with Tiber* was a 1996 science fiction novel written by Buzz Aldrin and John Barnes. Forbidden Planet, named for the 1956 movie, is a U.K. comic book and science fiction specialty shop, founded in 1978.

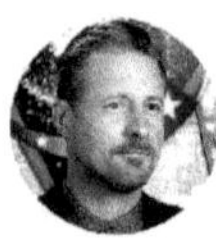

BOXLEITNER
So, when in Los Angeles, he's at this Barnes & Noble or Borders bookstore. I took my sons because I wanted them to meet somebody. I said, "Now, *this* is a hero." This is a real one, and this is also a man who wrote two books telling about how hard it is to be a hero, and how his life after walking on the moon went right down hill—the severe alcoholism problems, divorce, it just scarred—you know, after that peak he just spiraled down. "Show me a hero, I'll write you a tragedy," Fitzgerald says.

I stood in line to meet him, and I met him once before on a ski-trip thing, and that was even worse. I thought, he won't remember me. Well, all these people in line are going, "You're on *Babylon 5*," and they all want to talk, and I'm going, "No, no, no, no, you're losing— There's the man. That's the man." Dr. Aldrin was wonderful about it, and he took pictures with my son and his friend. I was trying to tell them, "If there is celebrity, to me, that's a celebrity." Dr. Aldrin. Because he achieved something none of us can ever hope to achieve.

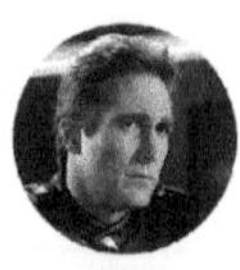

O'HARE
He really did go into space.

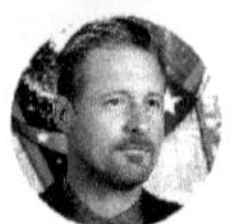

BOXLEITNER
Yes. Yes. I mean, he walked on another planet and no one's done that since. So he's one of 12 people that did this in the entire human history.

WELLS
Yeah, but it does come down to the "who do you feel is famous?" Who is *your* hero?

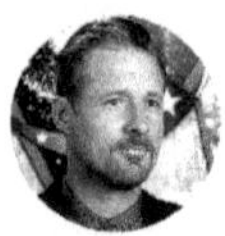

BOXLEITNER
And I want to get *his* autograph.

WELLS
We will all be heroes, a heroine, for other people. That's bound to be wrapped up in what you do. As you say, it comes with the territory. It's a cliché, but a cliché is only something, it's said by a lot of people because it's true.

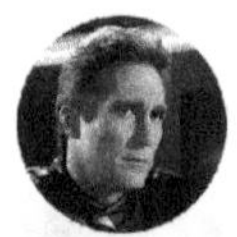

O'HARE
Yeah. And it is something that you take on board when you start.

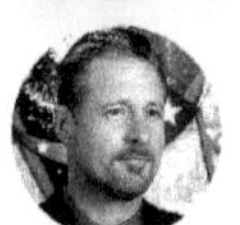

BOXLEITNER
Yes. I think sports heroes, some have kind of forgotten because the responsibility was felt much more in the past. In baseball, in the days of Mickey Mantle, Babe Ruth, he would stay and sign baseballs for children for hours and hours and hours. Whereas now, today they go, "I'm sorry, it's not the company ball that I'm supposed to sign," you know?

Yeah, "I have a contract with Adidas, or something."

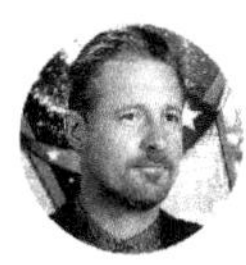

BOXLEITNER
Yes, I have a contract, and I cannot sign other than that.

I saw Reggie Jackson. I did a celebrity baseball game with the old timers, and I actually saw a young boy run up to him as we were all heading out to this field to play, and Reggie Jackson pushed the boy away. I think Babe Ruth would've come out of his grave with a baseball bat and hit him right in the head with it.

WELLS
That's terrible.

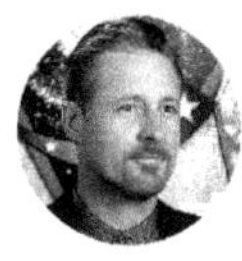

BOXLEITNER
This boy stood there, and that image is with me still—a child—he would turn on a child who had to work up all the courage that little kid could get, run up and—just doggonit! He had a program, "Would you please sign?"

Not unlike kids would do at a convention like this. They're working up to "I want to see Michael O'Hare or Bruce Boxleitner."

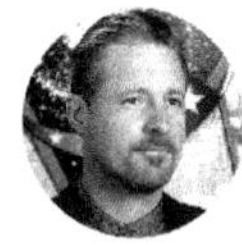

BOXLEITNER
There may be some adults here that you just go, please, please, but I would never—It's a policy with me. I don't care. A child, I would never turn that down. I will stop in the middle of the road, whatever.

Doesn't this go back to being a role model again, that you could be talking to a little kid at this convention who could be the next astronaut and the next physicist? In a way, they're using you as a hero in the abstract concept, but you can use your power as an actor to inspire them.

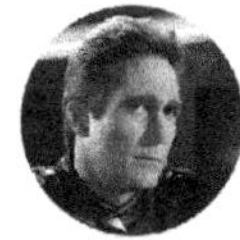

O'HARE
Yes.

Which sort of makes it worthwhile what you're doing, doesn't it?

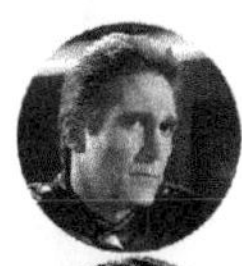

O'HARE
Yeah.

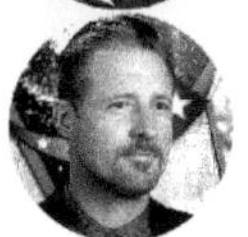

BOXLEITNER
I certainly think so. I think Leonard Nimoy and William Shatner [of *Star Trek*] don't realize how much they altered the modern space program. How many people are in that?

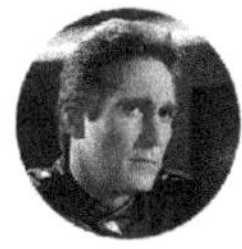

O'HARE
Because of *Star Trek*?

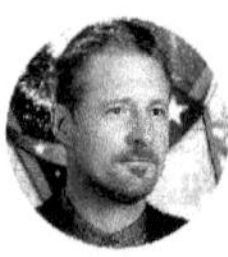

BOXLEITNER
Yes. Yeah. Gene Roddenberry. I mean, it truly is. The current generation, having talked to them, I think I told you, I was at NASA and talking to all these bright, dedicated people, which was so inspiring. I said, "I'm just a hack actor on a plywood space station."

I felt so intimidated by these minds and they said, "No, no, no. You don't understand. You don't understand what you all are doing." So it creates all this. You work in the area of the imagination and the imagination becomes inspired and then someone says, "You know what? I have an idea. I think we can do that." They need the imagery, the ideas to inspire them, and Joe [Straczynski] has certainly done that. They're tremendous fans.

Did you, Michael, have heroes when you were growing up?

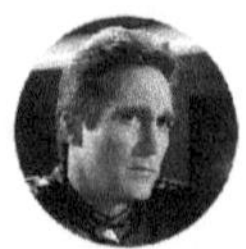

O'HARE
Mainly movie actors, like Spencer Tracy, or someone like that.

Stars?

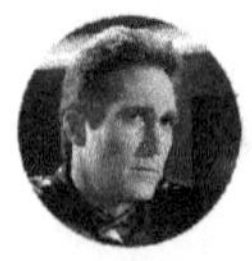

O'HARE
Yeah, stars. I could remember being deeply depressed when I heard that Lucy and Desi Arnaz were getting divorced. [Laughs.] I couldn't believe it.

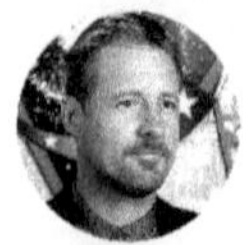

BOXLEITNER
Oh, I agree with that.

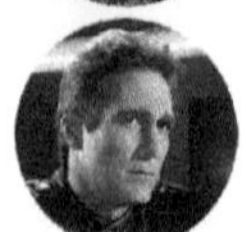

O'HARE
I couldn't believe they were.

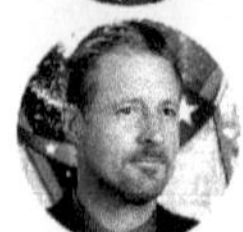

BOXLEITNER
They were icons.

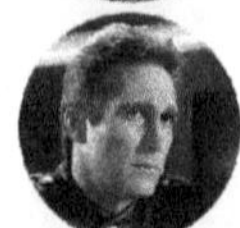

O'HARE
They were icons. [Laughs.]

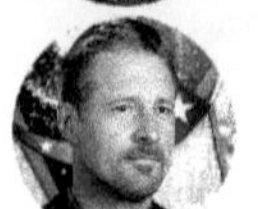

BOXLEITNER
Yeah. Me too. I loved the old movies moreso.

I'll tell you, I have a hero right now. Sean Connery is my favorite movie star. I would still probably spit up if I saw him. We were talking about this, here's an actor that started out as an icon and James Bond, but film-wise, anything he's in, he elevates it. Even if it's not such good material. His presence. That to me is what a huge star is. You know what I'm saying?

I thought one of the nice things about this convention was the moment that the two of you guys were actually up on stage, because it was one thing to accept these two actors on television together and say, "Right. They're on, on television together." It's another thing to actually see you together in real life.

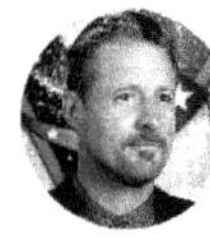

BOXLEITNER
Coming out of the jumpgate. [Laughs.]

> Guests at the Wolf 359 convention appeared on the stage via a "jumpgate" rigged with light effects.

But I was wondering, though, when, you came back to do this two-part Babylon 5 episode ["War Without End"], were you thinking about what it was gonna be like to be working with this guy? And you had said you thought that this guy was ten feet tall by then, from what you had heard.

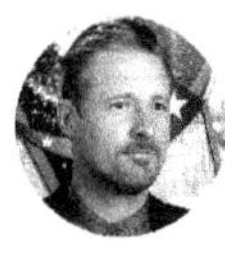

BOXLEITNER
Yeah.

Does that make the acting part of it more difficult? You know, all this stuff piled on?

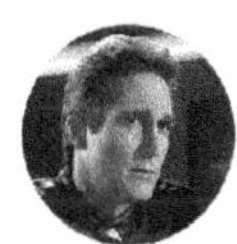

O'HARE
Bruce was very nice to me when we came in. No, really. Seriously.

WELLS
I'm sure he was.

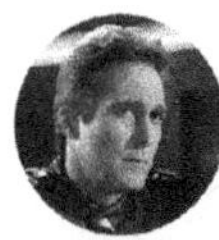

O'HARE
We didn't have any problem at all. If anything, we had a kind of good chemistry.

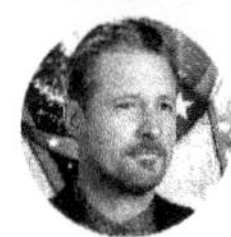

BOXLEITNER
I thought so. I mean, I think if you look at the episode, it works out fine. It works terrific. I mean, and Michael, I think more people made more out of it—

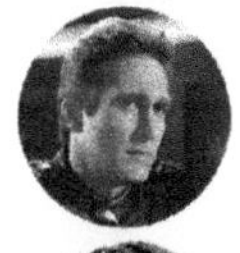

O'HARE
Yeah.

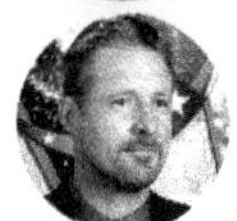

BOXLEITNER
—than you or I.

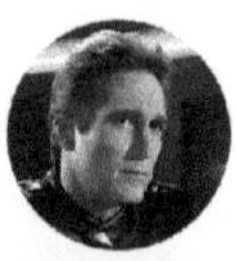

O'HARE
I agree. I agree.

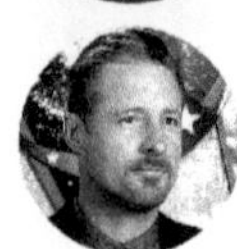

BOXLEITNER
It's how everyone [goes], "Oh my god. They're going to see each other. Oh, what?" And I'm going, "What?"

Where does this come from?

WELLS
Yes, exactly. Yeah.

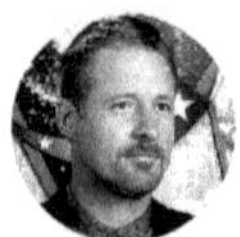

BOXLEITNER
We're actors, and we have a piece to do together here. And we did, and I thought it was a wonderful two-parter. Well, I'm just saying that I think people who have trumped things up moreso I would hear out of the corner of my ear. I never got involved in their conversations, you know? But I remember when Joe [Straczynski] told me [about O'Hare returning], and I said, "Yes! Yes! It's a great idea." I think we both are the same way. We both get to the job, get to the pace.

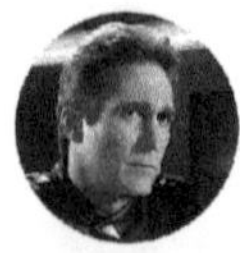

O'HARE
Right.

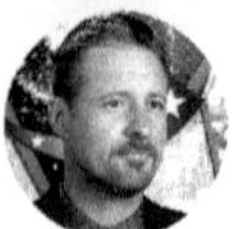

BOXLEITNER
You know, do the work. Yeah. It's not about this other stuff that seems to float around it, but it's generally people outside.

WELLS
Yes.

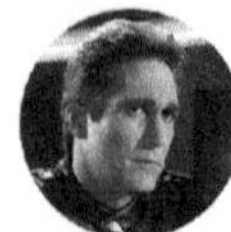

O'HARE
People making things up.

WELLS
Of course. Yeah. Yeah.

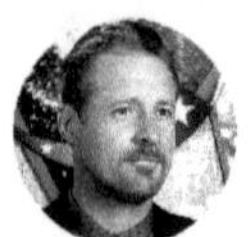

BOXLEITNER
It's their own sense of a drama they want to put together I think.

WELLS
That's exactly what it is.

It's the old thing. If there isn't a story, you make the story, and in this case, we take these two guys and we stuff them into our story. And it doesn't matter whether it's happening or not. It just sounds better that way.

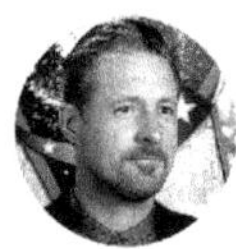
BOXLEITNER
But I think we're professional actors that've been around a long time and we've worked with all kinds of different actors, actresses—they're all mixtures of personalities and egos and experience and lack of experience.

WELLS
Well, certainly listening to the people over the last couple days, the excitement when the two of you are on that stage, side by side—

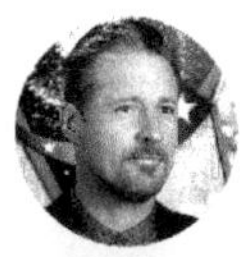
BOXLEITNER
No, I was excited. But what did they see?

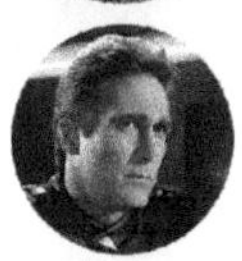
O'HARE
Yeah, what did they see?

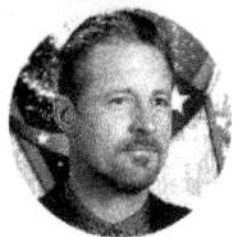
BOXLEITNER
What they project.

WELLS
I think for them, it was just as Joe [Nazzaro] says, you see the two of you on the screen. You have a script, you're playing parts, but when you two walked out and they saw you side by side, it's like the biggest present you could ever give them, because they've been there when it's happened.

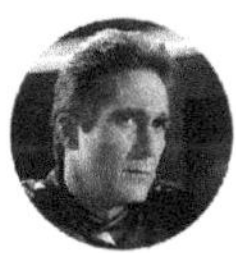
O'HARE
Right.

WELLS
It's not on that screen anymore. It's not divorced. It's not in the box in your living room or your family room.

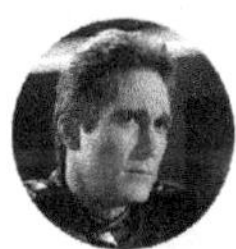
O'HARE
It's live.

WELLS
It's there, and they can go home and say, "I was there."

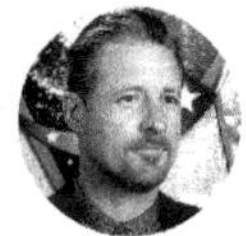
BOXLEITNER
Yeah.

WELLS
Yeah, and so they share that moment with you.

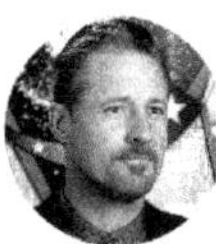
BOXLEITNER
Well, I was excited when [organizer] Brian [Cooney] said that Michael was coming.

WELLS
It's just wonderful to listen to people.

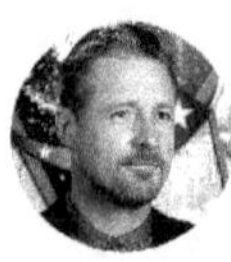

BOXLEITNER
I thought, we are putting on a show here, and how theatrical of him. [Laughs.] 'Cause I knew the two of us would have impact out there, and you put on such a sensational multimedia show there for all of us to come walking out there. I like that. I thought it was very classy.

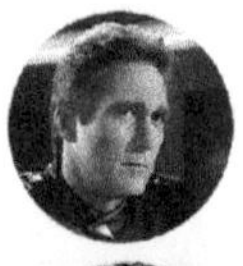

O'HARE
Yeah. I liked it too.

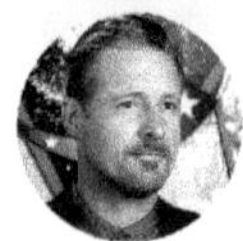

BOXLEITNER
It was very theatrical, and as we are, we're theatrical artists.

When you play the lead in a television series—and I know this is something you said before, Michael—you have to sort of take charge, because people will sometimes take the cue from the guy who's running the show. I don't wanna use the word "star" because it's deceptive, but the lead actor, the—

WELLS
The guy with the pointed end.

Okay, that sounds even scarier—

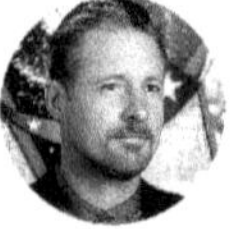

BOXLEITNER
—of the spear.

When you came back to do this two-parter, is that strange where there's somebody else who's on the pointed end? I'm not sure how that works as an equation: there's another guy in charge, or are you playing a different kind of a character?

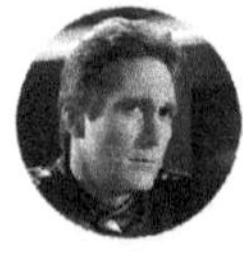

O'HARE
Well, in my opinion, it's up to the guy who happens to be in charge—on the pointed end—to make the other people come on the show at ease, and all that stuff—

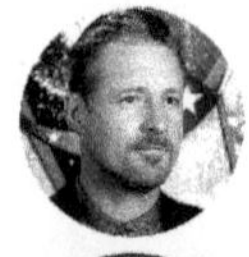

BOXLEITNER
Exactly.

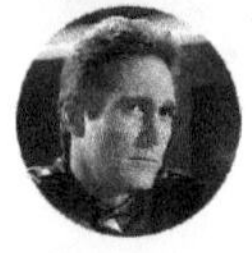

O'HARE
—and Bruce did that very much. He made me feel very much at ease. 'Cause I had a good time talking about [*Gunsmoke* star] Jim Arness.

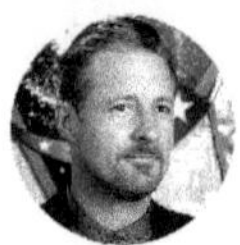

BOXLEITNER
Yeah, I did. I was talking about that. I learned from experience how to be that guy,

and that's to every guest star. You know, you're gonna be there. You're there all the time. They're coming on fresh into it. Michael, you know, he'd been there. It wasn't as awkward. It wasn't awkward.

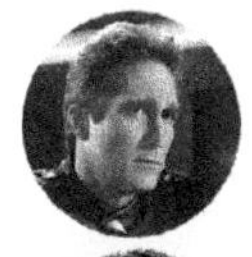

O'HARE
No, it wasn't awkward at all.

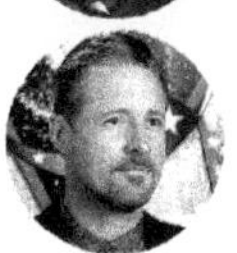

BOXLEITNER
Because this man was there and he is this huge, integral part of this saga, and we were really now going to show that.

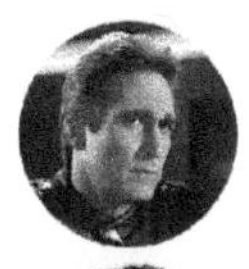

O'HARE
Yeah.

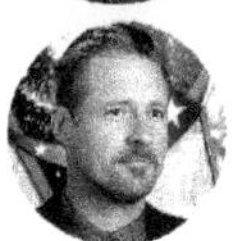

BOXLEITNER
You know what I'm saying? It's not like he was coming in, not having been. I was the come-lately, I was the guy.

WELLS
You're the new boy.

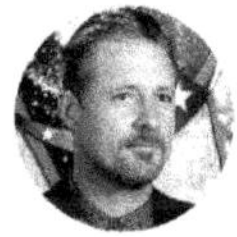

BOXLEITNER
I was the new boy, yeah. I was, I was. He was the beginning. You just put those thoughts away and just get to it. But I think you can come in the morning, on a TV show, and you can start the day or you can ruin it, you know?

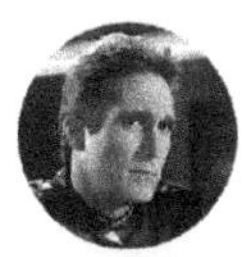

O'HARE
Yeah, right.

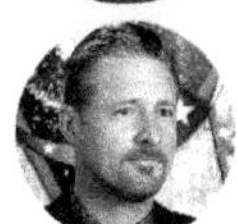

BOXLEITNER
A lot of the people do look to you, whether you like it or not. God knows, in some of the early hours, you're not feeling well or something like that. You don't do it all the time, but you really do have to pick up the reigns. You have to start it, and everybody kind of goes off of your cue. It's not always fun. You feel like shit and you've got other problems going on in your life or what have you.

But in a way, you had a marginal advantage in the fact that, as you say, you came in during the second season. So some of that groundwork was already laid by Michael. Michael had to go through those situations in the first season.

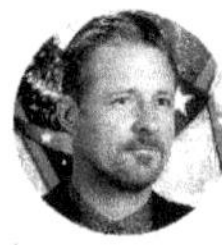

BOXLEITNER
He had to go through the first battles of it, the opening salvos. This show has been a struggle. It has been a struggle, and it has never ended. It's still a struggle. Still a struggle of acceptance. You wouldn't know that from here, but the powers that be, it is still; it's been dancing on the edge of dying, and I guess you guys ran into that.

There was a lot of naysayers at first, from the studio level, everyone going, "You'll never get this working." That's what I've gathered from Joe [Straczynski] and John [Copeland], but no, he did; he paved the trail. He did that.

But this is the other thing that comes with this role, doesn't it? We're talking about leading by example, as far as the set was concerned, but also in terms of publicity for the show. This has always been sort of the best kept secret of science fiction, or even of good quality television. Because of the parts that you both played, in a way, it sort of forced you to have to be the front man to sell the show too, didn't it?

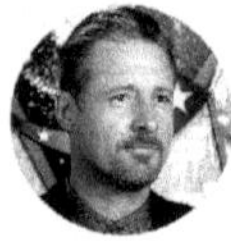
BOXLEITNER
Sure.

And Michael, you would've had an even more difficult job because nobody had seen it at that point.

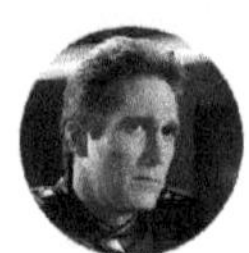
O'HARE
Right.

So you were introducing it as well.

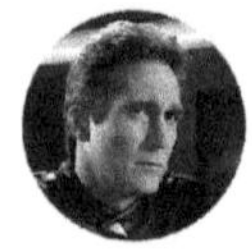
O'HARE
Yeah, I mean, we were trying to get people to write in so that the pilot would be picked up.

I remember talking to you when you were doing a play—I think it was in Florida—and at that point you were still waiting for this thing to go—

O'Hare played the role of Jim in *Lips Together, Teeth Apart* by Terrence McNally at the Coconut Grove Playhouse in Miami, Florida in January and February 1993.

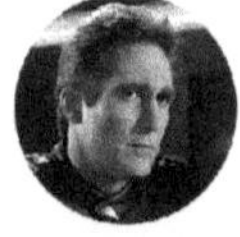
O'HARE
Yeah, sure.

—and working and saying, "Well, we don't know. We'll see what happens." And so now?

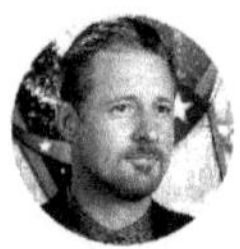
BOXLEITNER
Ironically, we say that every year—still. Well, we don't know. We know at the last minute, which is very frustrating.

Babylon 5's renewal for the fifth season came as the producers and actors flew to the U.K. for this convention. Contract negotiations were carried out during the convention.

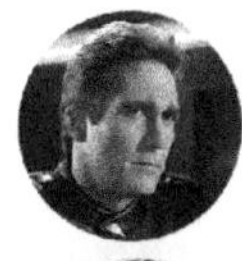

O'HARE
Yeah, and the show has moved up in popularity through the years, too.

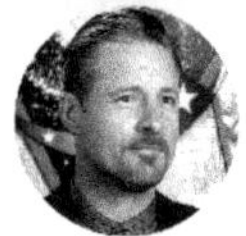

BOXLEITNER
Gigantic. That's why you wanna go, "Are they not looking?" I mean, they being the suits, but they are, but it has nothing to do with that. It has to do with markets, prices and blah, blah, blah. Computer—

Market shares.

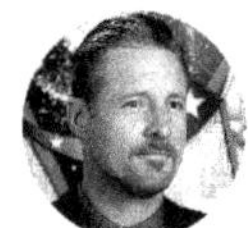

BOXLEITNER
—market shares, and who owns the rights. That's why this merger of Time Warner and TNT, this little show just started falling right through the cracks. Who owes what to where? Do we really wanna invest any more if something's on already, and, as it is, they're asking now for a six-day shoot. Yes, we're gonna try to do episodes in six days—good luck!—and a lot of other financial things, which has been my experience in television. The more successful the show is, the further you go on, they start taking money out of it.

WELLS
That's right.

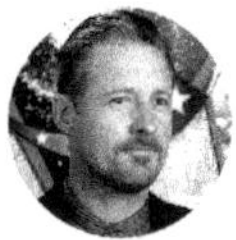

BOXLEITNER
They don't add money to it. They start doing it for less. Well, you're on already and you're running. Yet they don't realize that they're still asking for the same production quality.

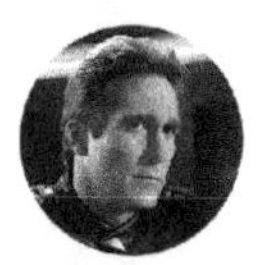

O'HARE
Right.

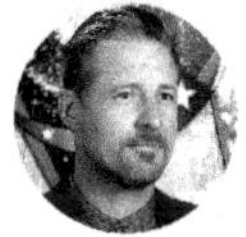

BOXLEITNER
Which costs. They want production quality but they don't wanna pay for it anymore. We're really in that state right now. Fifth season, they don't wanna pay anything for this. None of it. Neither. TNT is very enthusiastic, but, and unfortunately being the head point man here, you have to hear all this crap. Actually, there's a lot of people in the cast are blissfully unaware of a lot of the things. But unfortunately I hear about this stuff because, and I guess I want to, because I care about this thing. I want it to continue.

But it becomes your baby, in a sense. And you wanna take care of your baby. And somebody is talking about your baby out there you want to hear about it and come to its defense.

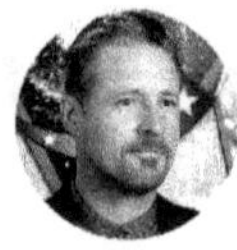

BOXLEITNER
I wanna know what they're—I'll stick my nose maybe where I shouldn't be.

WELLS
[Laughs.]

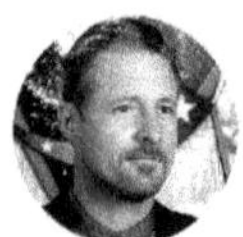

BOXLEITNER
By this time, I think—Michael, you agree—if your name is on it, I think you'd have a damn right to know to some degree of what is going on, because it's your name, your life, what have you out there. Reputation or whatever.

When it comes up to the starring and your name is the first one—

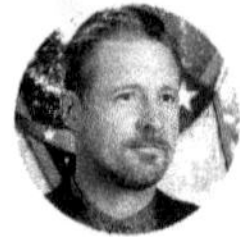

BOXLEITNER
Well, because if they hate it, it's that guy's show. They forget. Yes, you do get the praise. I mean, the actors are out there when it's brilliant and it's wonderful. Everyone's going, "Kudos, kudos, that's wonderful, too." But always remember the reverse side when it goes down. No one said it was a lousy producer. You know, no one ever claimed, "Jesus, the unit accountant was terrible."

How are you doing on time?

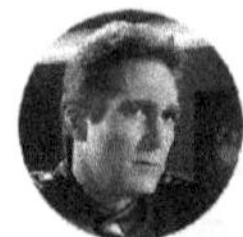

O'HARE
I don't have much time left. Five minutes—

I don't want to hold you up, because otherwise Brian [Cooney] will come and beat me senseless, or something.

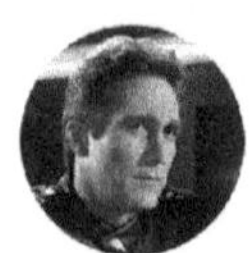

O'HARE
There is an actor who's gonna be coming here tonight who had to go through a very similar process and playing a role model on another science fiction series.

Who is this?

WELLS
Gareth [Thomas] is gonna be here. We've gotta keep it quiet, which is why Linda is here. Linda and I are going to create Blake from *Blake's 7*, and he's going to give Joe [Straczynski] his award as Blake, but we've gotta keep it quiet. We don't want Joe to know. It's gonna be a big surprise for him.

> Gareth Thomas played Roj Blake in *Blake's 7* (1978–81), departing the series after the second season. The series was frequently mentioned by J. Michael Straczynski as a personal favorite, hence Thomas making a special appearance to present the writer with an award. Wells was the makeup designer on *Blake's 7*, and co-wrote a history of the show with Nazzaro.

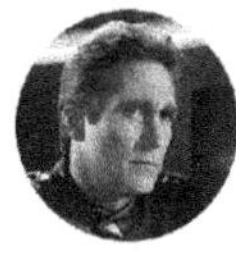

O'HARE
Oh, great. Sure, I won't tell him.

WELLS
But as this Joe was starting to say, he went through a very similar situation.

He went through the situation and a journalist came up to him from a newspaper and said, "Has this show been a milestone in your career?" and it's interesting because as I've talked to him a number of times over what the last ten or eleven years. His answer to this question has changed several times, depending on where his work situation is, what the continuing popularity of the series is, how it's made him maybe pigeonholed into a certain genre.

I was curious how the two of you felt as far as Babylon 5 is concerned? Which end do you feel that you've landed on as a result of this show, or is it still too difficult to tell at this point where it's going?

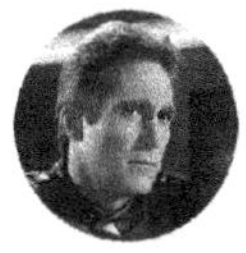

O'HARE
Well, it's a little difficult to tell, but from my own practical experience, I've ended up on the good side of it. It was good to have done it. It was a good job I've had.

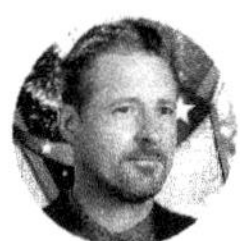

BOXLEITNER
I have to say milestone. I think it's you're saying. Yeah. I don't feel this is a millstone. This has been nothing but a great experience. I will never say otherwise. Never.

I'm anxious to meet him because he is sort of a brother in that, an older brother. If that happens to you and you've got sort of pigeonholed—I mean, maybe a lot of people would disagree with me—but I don't think that's such a bad thing in the long run of an actor's career. I think pigeonholed is a weird word. I think if you are known for a role and one's career, I think that's not such a bad thing. I mean, you may have played several great roles, but if there's one that people do know you by, I mean, I think we remember all our favorite movie stars from one or two movies—

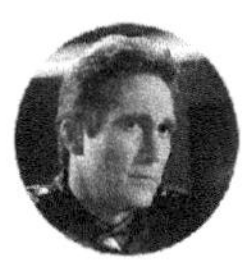

O'HARE
Right, right, right.

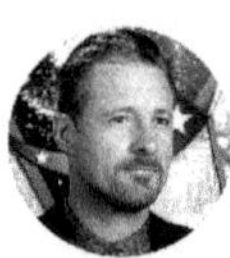

BOXLEITNER
—of the many, many, many, many. We remember them for something specific. I don't think it's such a bad thing. I think, even Dustin Hoffman, the guys like that—who I've often read is stereotyped—well, I see him in a certain type of thing.

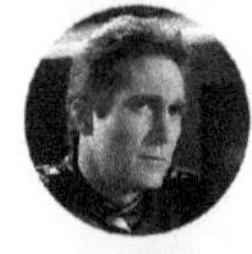

O'HARE
Yeah, right.

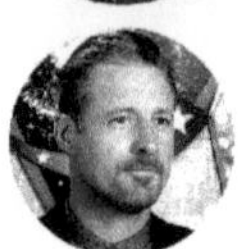

BOXLEITNER
You know, I'm sorry, Dusty, but that's the way it is, and it's been wonderful.

So if 20 years from now they look at Bruce Boxleitner and Michael O'Hare and say, "I remember him. He played this heroic character on TV." Maybe that's not such a bad thing?

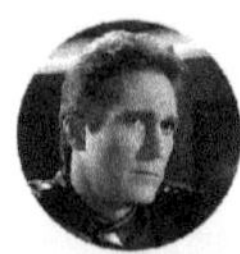

O'HARE
Not such a bad thing at all.

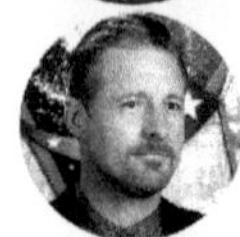

BOXLEITNER
Oh my god.

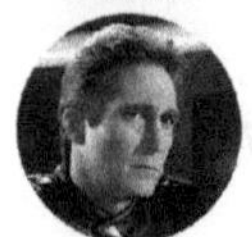

O'HARE
It's good to be remembered.

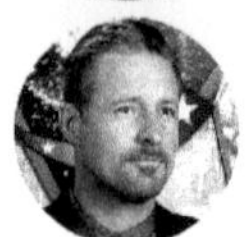

BOXLEITNER
I think that's essentially what I'm saying. You narrowed it right down there.

It's good to be remembered. In an occupation where so many are not, and are wonderful actors and actresses, they never get the recognition, but apply their trade throughout every theater and TV and movie set in the world, and will never be known. There are more who are known that really don't deserve it, I think, than the many that are out there.

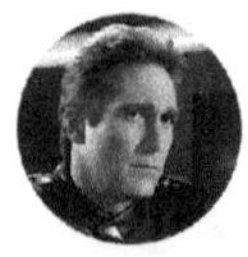

O'HARE
Yeah.

So for better or worse, it's an immortality of sorts.

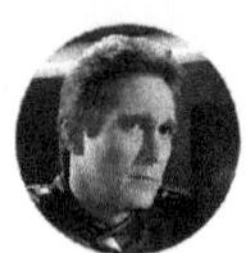

O'HARE
Yeah. I think it's for better. Oh, and Bruce agrees.

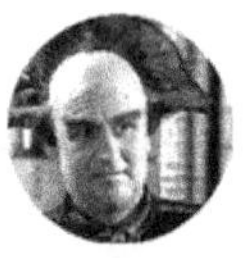

PETER JURASIK
Londo Mollari

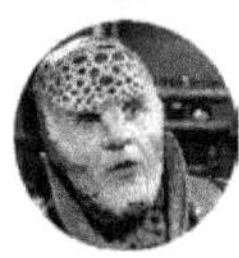

ANDREAS KATSULAS
G'Kar

13 July 1997, Norbreck Castle Hotel in Blackpool, U.K.

Babylon 5 Timeline
Last In Production
In the Beginning (MOW2)
Last on the Air
"Intersections in Real Time" (418)

> This interview was conducted by journalist Joe Nazzaro, with occasional input from his wife, British makeup designer Sheelagh Wells.

You've just finished the prequel [In the Beginning], which is the beginning of this whole thing, and now sort of at another crossroads where you're getting ready to start the fifth season, which is sort of neat.

Andreas, I was saying to you the other day—when I first asked you about the possibility of doing this prequel [in December 1996]—it was a little bit of a scary thought to be peeling back five years' worth of layers you've been adding to G'Kar. Now that you guys have actually done it, what was it like to play the original guys—from before day one, really, isn't it—because this actually takes place before the pilot. What sort of an experience was it when you finally started to do it?

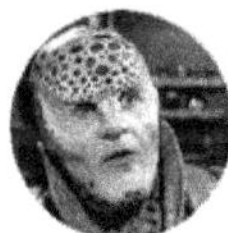

ANDREAS KATSULAS
I don't think I nailed it. I don't think I got back whatever it was, because the makeup was different. The costume was even different. A little different feeling, the G'Kar of the pilot.

> Both the costume created by Catherine Adair and the prosthetic makeup designed by Criswell Productions were replaced by the work of Ann Bruice and Optic Nerve, respectively, when *Babylon 5* transitioned from pilot to series in 1993. When *In the Beginning* was produced, the decision was made to stick with the aesthetics established in the series rather than to revert to those seen in the pilot.

But what I tried to recapture, as best as I could, was sort of a external energy. He was very out there in the pilot. I think, in time, he's become more internalized. Something vibrates a little bit deeper in him. But he was very sort of superfluous [in the pilot]. Not superfluous, but just external. I don't know any other way to put it. So I went that way with it, and I didn't have as much material to do that with, as I had in the pilot.

Pilot G'Kar was the size of Londo now. He's talking all the time and had all these big speeches so I could do more. So that's the way I went. I don't know. I'm almost afraid to see what the result is, because I'm about 20, 30 pounds heavier than I was in the pilot, you know? So who knows?

I think people will take into account that there are changes. The people who have been following the show are going to realize that there are things that have changed in the period of five years. Just like they're going to know—with the final episode, ["Sleeping in Light"]—some of these people who are playing 20 years older [aren't] 20 years older. That's the suspension of disbelief, isn't it? But you had the gamut, from beginning to end.

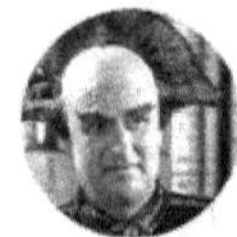

PETER JURASIK
Well, I had done the old guy already before [in "The Coming of Shadows" and "War Without End"], but I echo that, what Andreas said about playing the external energy. That's the first place I went, because you don't know what the soul, the insides the guys—Londo, it was just pulling inside-out and cleaning him up. He wasn't the drinker, but he was clean in a different way than we saw him when he stopped drinking, [in] season three or whatever it was.

He also had more hair, and I needed a girdle, too. I actually said that after I got dressed. I said, "Why didn't we have a girdle or something, make it fit?" I mean, I wish I was 20 pounds lighter. That would've been cool. But, he had hair of course, so—

The old Londo was the character you played as well. So you've already got that persona in your head, haven't you?

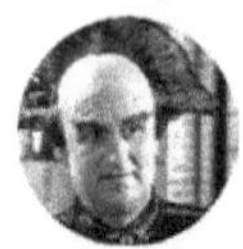

JURASIK
That was great to flesh out and play for a couple of scenes, and also I had these wonderful kids [Jacob Chase as Lucco Deradi and Erica Merr as Lyssa] to do the work with. So he's telling the story, it's all about memory and that was great to do. He was purging himself with a lot of stuff and confessing, getting a lot off his chest.

It's interesting now, when we look at this fifth season coming up, looking at the way your characters have ended up as we last see them in this [fourth] season; it almost seems like there's gonna be a completely different relationship for these guys coming

up, isn't it? Because the last time we see them [in "Rising Star"] is that scene with G'Kar picking the rice off of his uniform, or whatever, and they're actually speaking to each other civilly. The implication being that this is gonna be a new beginning, which will hopefully be seen.

> When "Rising Star" was filmed at the end of season four, it was believed to be the final appearances for G'Kar and Londo Mollari, Straczynski having been told there would be no year five. The rice scene was intended to shorthand the strange relationship the two characters would develop across season five, but became a prelude rather than precis, when the final season was given a last-minute green light days before this interview.

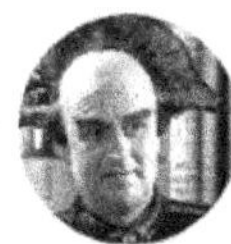

JURASIK
We have our worries about it, don't we, Andreas?

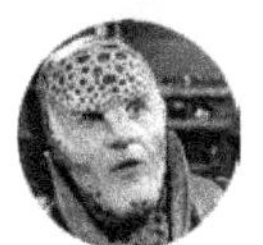

KATSULAS
Yes. [Laughs.] Where are we going to go?

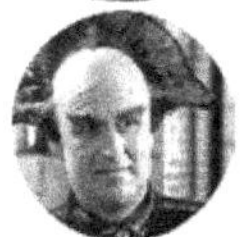

JURASIK
We don't know whether it's gonna be *The Odd Couple*, you know, Tweedle Dum, Tweedle Dee.

Which one is which?

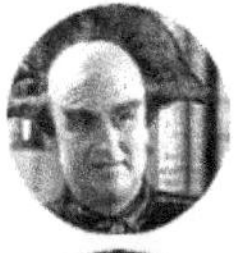

JURASIK
Does it matter?

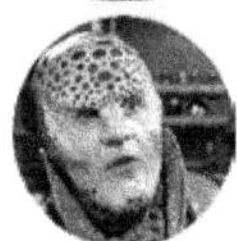

KATSULAS
Actually, I think we got the best idea for where to go last night at the fancy dress competition.

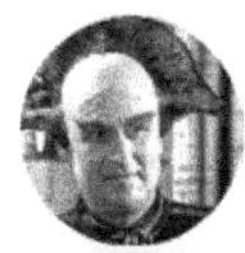

JURASIK
What was that?

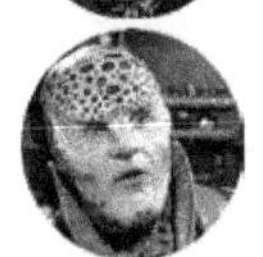

KATSULAS
The mice? Squeaky and—

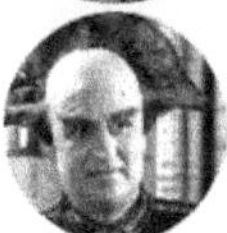

JURASIK
Squeaky and Mouse Man. Yes. [Laughs.] We're afraid—seriously—that the stories have been played, that both storylines have been played out a little bit by the end of the fourth series, that maybe there's not much left.

What were some of the ideas we came up with? They always end with "and then the hijinks ensue."

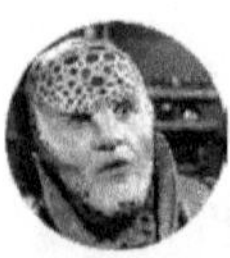

KATSULAS
And then the hijinks ensue. You're the one who was thinking them all up. I'm bone dry.

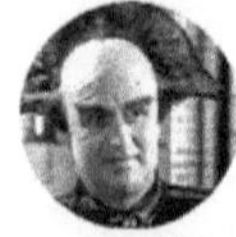

JURASIK
[Laughs.] Well, were they Kate? What were some of them?

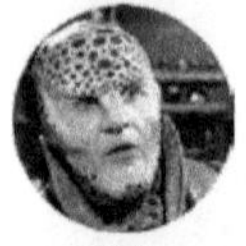

KATSULAS
Oh god, I don't remember.

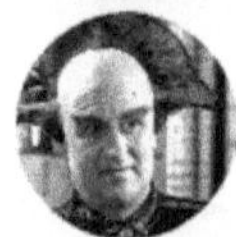

JURASIK
Londo goes to the—

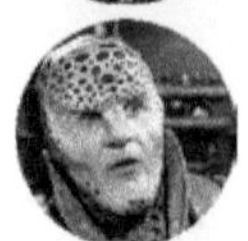

KATSULAS
What about the laundromat?

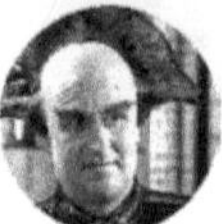

JURASIK
That's right. Londo has a big event to go to, and goes to the laundromat and picks up the Narn laundry instead—and the hijinks ensue.

G'Kar makes a pizza and Londo sneaks on hot peppers—and the hijinks ensure. [Laughs.] And so, what else are we gonna do?

So we've got 22 episodes of pure wackiness.

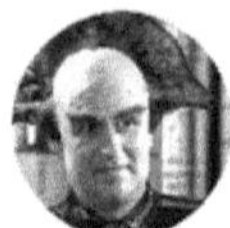

JURASIK
Exactly. It's a little like *I Love Lucy*. "I love G'Kar."

That's something I wanted to ask you about, because this final scene that we see these two characters together [in "Rising Star"]—I don't know how you felt about this—but this idea of G'Kar taking this false eye of his and putting it up on the dresser so he could be a voyeur to whatever's going on— It seemed to me that after four seasons of the raw conflict of these two guys, now G'Kar has sort of become episode one G'Kar, the voyeur again.

I actually asked Tony Dow about this, and he wouldn't venture an opinion, but I think his silence sort of indicated how he felt about it as the director, that he wasn't entirely comfortable with it. I was curious how you guys felt about that as the closing scene of the season for your two characters.

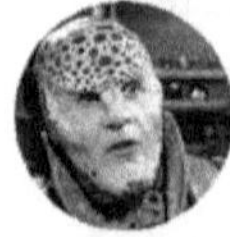

KATSULAS
Well, I wish he had saved it. I thought it was still too early to give away what's gonna happen with the eye. I wish he'd have thought a little more about it, Joe, because I don't know, it seems a little cheap.

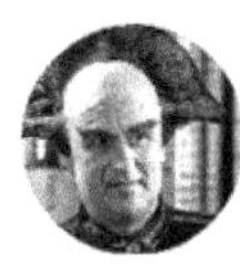

JURASIK
I don't think he's gonna play it out though. I think he's probably gonna use it as one joke.

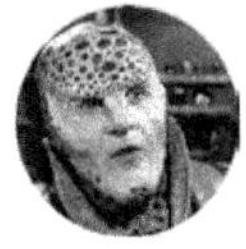

KATSULAS
Yeah. He'll never refer to that again. He may use the eye for other purposes later on, but there'll be no secret little film—I wanna show you what I know. I don't think so.

But that was exactly the adjective that came to mind for me, that it was a cheap gag. For these two guys, it almost seemed to be a disservice after what they had been through together.

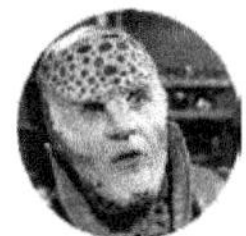

KATSULAS
Well, I don't know. You never know [with] G'Kar. It may look like a cheap shot and yet that might be, from a political point of view, such ripe material to have the goods on in some way. Well, they're officially married and everything, but that's not stuff that you can peddle, you know; you can't supply the next war with the money you get for that.

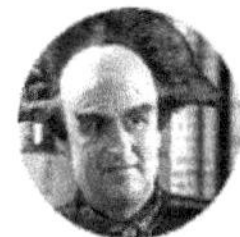

JURASIK
I have to disagree. I didn't see it as kind of a cheap shot. I liked it, actually, because I don't know if specifically it was the right time to use it or it was the right thing to do, but Joe [Straczynski], what he does is diffuses and disarms the melodrama of all the characters every couple of episodes by putting something kind of offbeat and farcical into the script.

Last night, we went to the fancy dress competition for these fans. We were both saying what a good spirit they have about science fiction, that they laughed at themselves and they're not afraid to laugh at themselves. I think Joe does that naturally in our scripts. Just when it starts to approach real pretense and B.S., he undercuts it by some silly little scene. I kinda like that. I think it brings it all back.

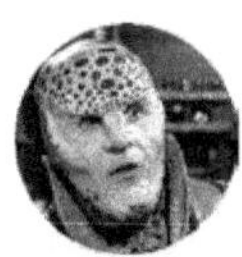

KATSULAS
Yeah, I think you're seeing the bigger picture there because G'Kar—it's almost like he's had a hell of a rough year—he just loosens up one night.

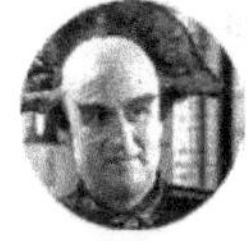

JURASIK
That's right.

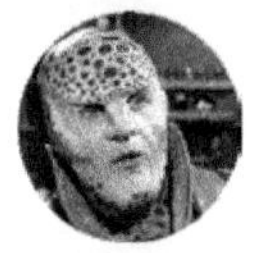

KATSULAS
The tension's over and he just, you know—

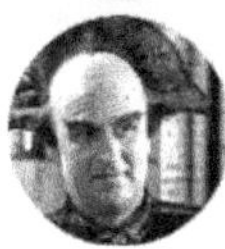

JURASIK
I just like what it does; it kind of resets.

It seems to me, though, the big scene as far as your two characters in this last season—once you've gone through the initial sort of hump of that first half dozen episodes [on Centauri Prime]—is really the scene where Londo comes in and offers him this drink and G'Kar sort of looks at him and reacts and then pours the drink back. That scene [in "No Surrender, No Retreat"]—which only lasts for whatever 30, 45 seconds—actually seems to go on for about 18 years, doesn't it? I don't know how you felt about that scene, but I thought that that was one of the high points as far as the remainder of the season for the two of you.

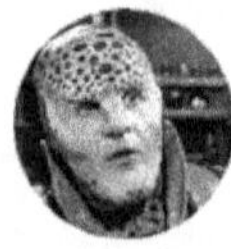

KATSULAS
Mmm. That's about all we have in the remainder of this season. That visit of yours to my quarters.

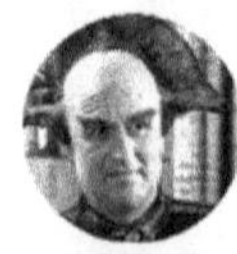

JURASIK
That's right.

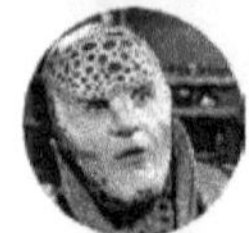

KATSULAS
And once again, you do all the talking in it.

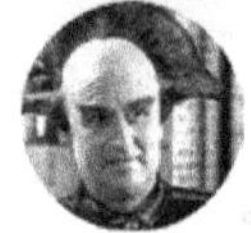

JURASIK
[Laughs.] He always downplays himself by saying I always do the talking, but it's funny because in this little gag scene that we've been doing in 416—the lost Babylon scenes—I'm doing all the reactions. I'm doing the classic G'Kar stuff, and you've been so appreciative of the fact that I don't have to stand and you do all the talking.

> At a November 1996 Creation Entertainment convention in Pasadena, Andreas Katsulas and Peter Jurasik encouraged the audience not to respond when J. Michael Straczynski took to the stage for his presentation. Straczynski, known to dislike public speaking at the best of times, was flummoxed by the gag and vowed revenge.
>
> Said revenge resulted in a fake script for "The Exercise of Vital Powers," in which G'Kar underwent a metamorphosis and became female. He then had an affair with Londo Mollari. The two actors performed the gag script live at the Wolf 359 convention shortly before this interview.

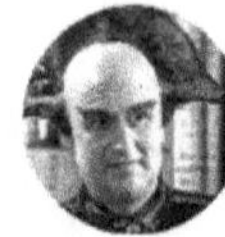

JURASIK
Actually all these scenes, the fact that you have to sit there and listen to me talk for a long time, you get a small medal, right? [Laughs.] I don't know. My remembrance of that scene is how rushed we were, when you said it felt like it went on for 18 minutes.

I'm not being critical when I say that, I'm talking about the dramatic tension of it.

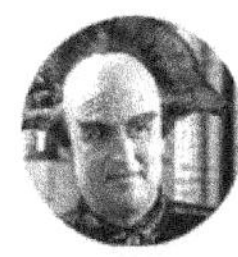
JURASIK
Well, I remember it was the end of the day and [producer John] Copeland and people on the set tapping their shoe. Do you remember that?

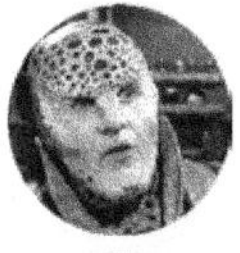
KATSULAS
Were they? No, I don't recall that.

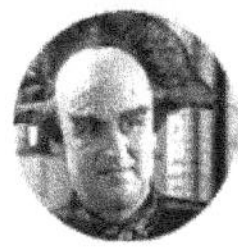
JURASIK
They were very aware it was going on for 18 minutes. They were like, "When's this ending?" [Laughs.]

So you're trying to be suitably dramatic and they're going, "Gotta go, guys!"

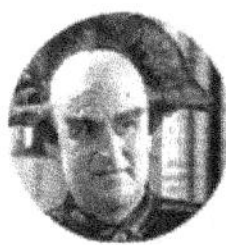
JURASIK
You got it.

> The scene in G'Kar's quarters was filmed during one of the show's rare excursions into overtime, wrapping at 8:42pm.

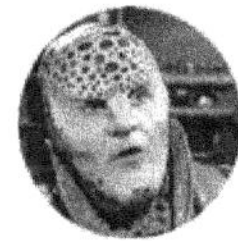
KATSULAS
What I remember playing during that scene was recalling all that you had done to me. Because here you are with a peace offering, but should I now forget the day when I met you in the Zócalo and said, "My friend, come, I'm going to buy you a drink," and poured my heart out to you and then found out that you had just killed 200,000 Narns [in "The Coming of Shadows"]. That's when I broke the stone table. You know?

So, am I to forget this now that he's here with this little flask? [Laughs.] That's what I had to play, and you gave me plenty of time to think about it.

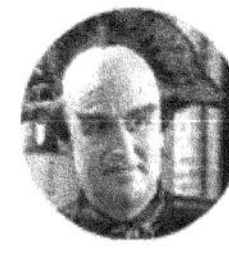
JURASIK
For me, it was all about kind of macho stumbling. Poor Londo really doesn't know how to—I mean, he's just not practiced at saying "I'm sorry." For me, it was a fits-and-starts and stumbling through, and I love that little macho idea of two men—let's have a drink and that'll make it okay, right? Then click glasses, then we're brothers together, eh?

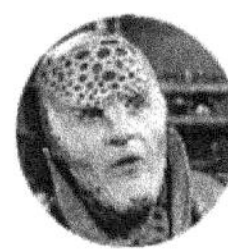
KATSULAS
But his reaction in the bar was so great, when I do come in and I chug one back and I turn to him and I said, "But not on the same page." You have the papers

signed. His reaction when I leave is just priceless.

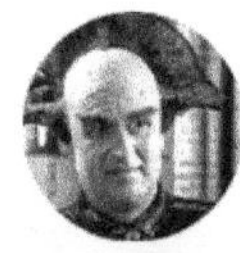
JURASIK
I don't remember what I did.

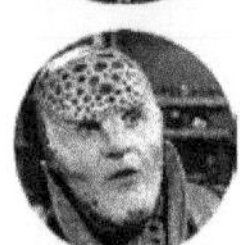
KATSULAS
Oh, you were like the fallen angel swept up again.

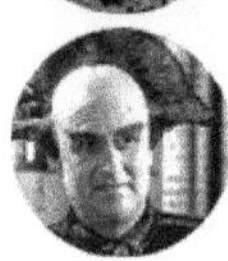
JURASIK
Sure I wasn't playing, "That's a wrap?" [Laughs.]

"I am outta here."

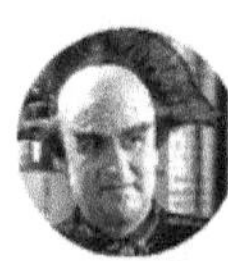
JURASIK
"Pete, the season's over." [Laughs.] Boy Joy.

Was that all disappointing to the two of you, that the two characters retreated so much into the background for a lot of the season? I know as a dad, you have another itinerary, right, because you get paid to be home playing.

Peter Jurasik and his wife, Barbara Guedel, became parents early in season 4.

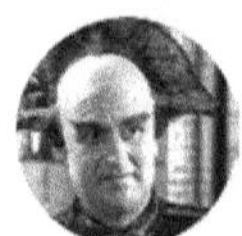
JURASIK
That's right.

Which is nice.

But on the other hand, as actors, you want to act. It's not like you can go out and get another job in the meantime, to sort of flex those muscles. How did you feel about that for that second half of the season? Was it disappointing in that sense?

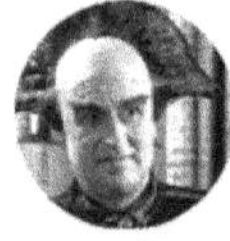
JURASIK
You know what? From my point of view, it comes as part and parcel of the ensemble. That's all. You have to be willing to, at some point, just step back. As you said, I had special circumstances, so I dunno how you felt. I felt I had something fill in my life.

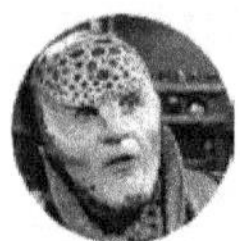
KATSULAS
For me, work is everything, so I would like to be called to the set every day from the first one to the last one to leave. If I really could lead my life the way I wanted to, that's what I'd like to do— work every day and have a good chunk of scenes to do every day—but that's just not the case. So, I try and fill in, you know, with gardening [or] whatever in between-time.

I think he needs a babysitter from time to time as well. Actually, no, I don't think he wants to be more than two feet away from this kid

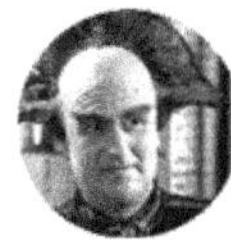

JURASIK
No. Really, it's true.

You guys have had a lot of fun now with, with this 416 script, now that it's been established as a joke and so forth. Obviously this is now, it seems, to be a fixture at conventions where I think people are going to ask everybody involved with it, what's this all about?

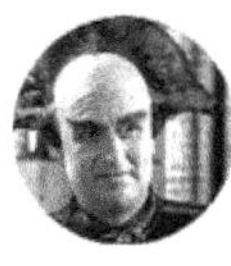

JURASIK
No!

SHEELAGH WELLS
It's inevitable.

You've dug your own grave very well on that.

WELLS
You've done this to yourselves.

And Pete, you told me about this thing originally, when it happened, but I'm sort of curious what your initial reactions were when this script hit your doorstep and you read it for the first time. We're talking out about it now and we could laugh about it, but what was it like when you turned those pages?

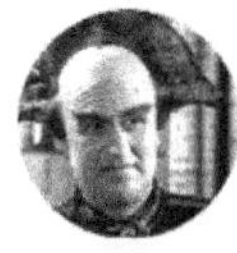

JURASIK
Well, tell yours, Andreas. Did you know it was a goof right away?

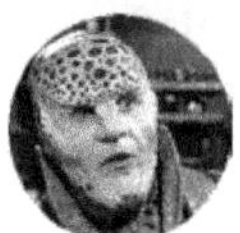

KATSULAS
I knew he was a goof right away. I hate to spoil Joe [Straczynski's] thing 'cause he loves to [think]—like he did in his [panel]—that he really had us going, but I never—

It was two in the morning when I picked up that script from my front door. I went in right away and sat down, two o'clock in the morning. I was tired. I started laughing out loud in my house, all alone in the middle of the night reading this. I never expressed second thought we were gonna do it, because I knew it was Joe getting back at us. It was so funny, just so funny. I just couldn't, you know—

But no, I never thought for a second. I'm disappointed that we're not. I still would love to do it. I'd love this.

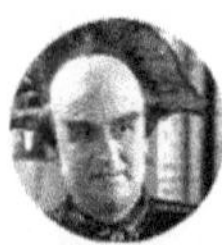

JURASIK
Andreas has really expressed that, too, that he really did want to shoot it. He kept saying, "Oh yeah, let's put it in front of a camera."

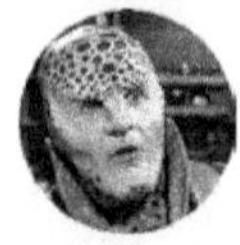

KATSULAS
Oh yeah. It would be the gag reel or the thing you'd take to conventions once a year.

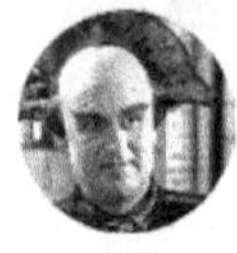

JURASIK
As you know, he's a very internal actor, so for days before we went in, he wore very tight brassiere. He's mincing around the set in low heels, not very high heels—

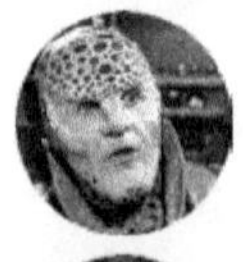

KATSULAS
He calls that internal acting?

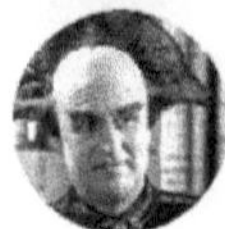

JURASIK
You know, getting in on it.

I don't think that's what they actually refer to as the Method, though, is it?

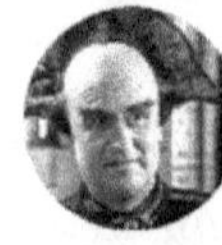

JURASIK
That's right. That's like, "Oh, sorry. You caught me in a brassiere. I was just acting."

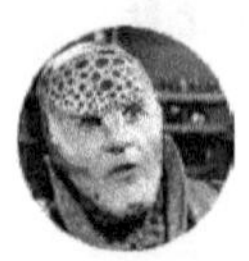

KATSULAS
It's not real.

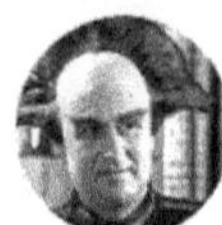

JURASIK
Well, despite what Andreas said about not being fooled, I was fooled, and along with Boxleitner and Bill Mumy and a lot of the people I was. Actually, I read it when my wife was in the other room having an important business meeting, and I was like gasping in the kitchen. I think she lost a job with the business partner because they thought her husband was—I didn't know what was going on, "No!No!" [Gasp.]

I did get calls from Bruce Boxleitner, and my favorite, of course, was Mira [Furlan]. She said, "Horrible. Horrible. Don't do it, Peter. It's horrible."

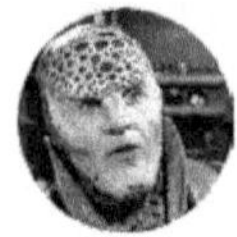

KATSULAS
But that was the clue: it's horrible. That's how you knew that it wasn't going to happen. Suddenly the man who's written brilliant things before, he—

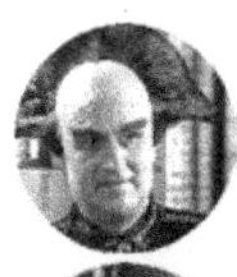

JURASIK
It was soap opera-y.

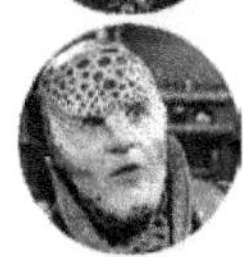

KATSULAS
You couldn't for a second think it was—

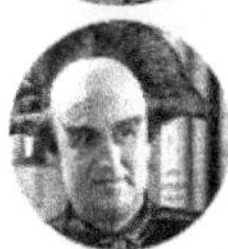

JURASIK
That's right.

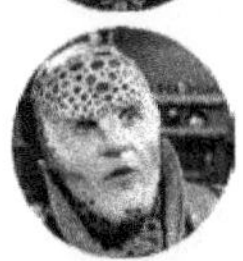

KATSULAS
—unless he'd had a major emotional breakdown.

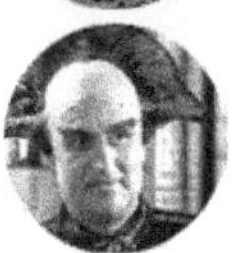

JURASIK
That's what everybody was saying. That's what Bruce said. Bruce said "He's gone mad! He's mad! Like he's gonna kill someone!" [Laughs.]

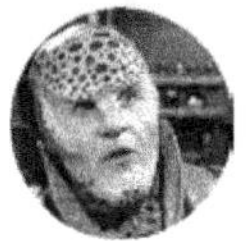

KATSULAS
If it hadn't been for the convention, we didn't have the onus of his retaliation, which I was looking over my shoulder every day. I hadn't forgotten it for a second. If there hadn't been that history, then I might have taken it seriously. If he was just initiating the first insult or whatever.

So, having spent three months looking over your shoulder, in a way was sort of a relief to know that it was finally—

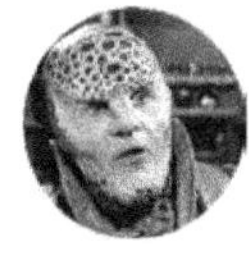

KATSULAS
I was relieved that that's all it was going to be. I thought it would be something maybe—

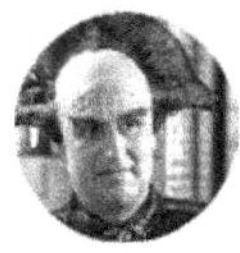

JURASIK
It should be said for the record, too, that it was—and this is true—was all Andreas's idea, the stunt. [Laughs.] So, this time, you know, 'cause I know fans think Londo's the bad guy and G'Kar is this kind of good—

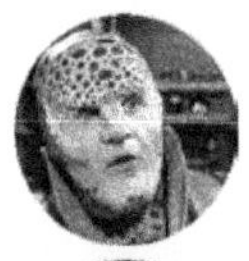

KATSULAS
You're getting the tongue today.

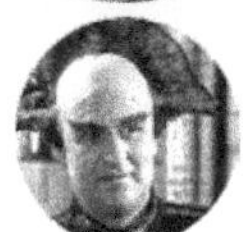

JURASIK
[Laughs.] Promise?

But the funny thing is, you guys still haven't learned, have you? You've got the executive producer who's writing these scripts, and you're still messing with him.

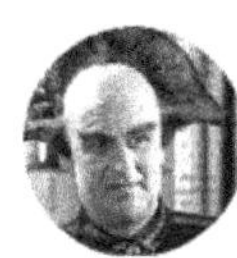

JURASIK
So I've heard.

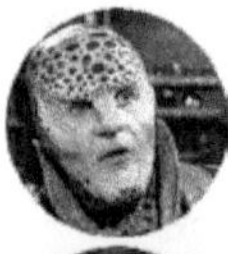
KATSULAS
You are.

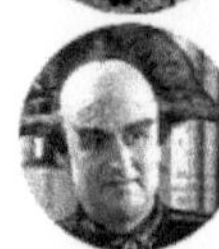
JURASIK
What did you do?

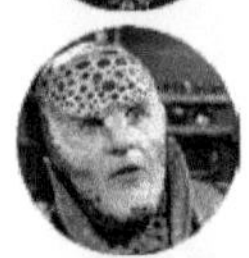
KATSULAS
He has to learn that that's our way of expressing affection, you know?

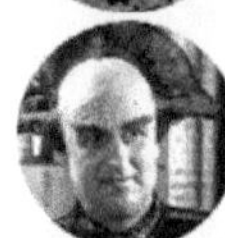
JURASIK
That's right.

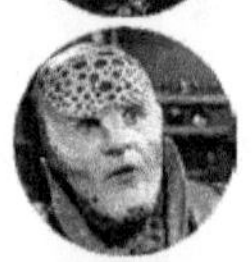
KATSULAS
It's part of male bonding.

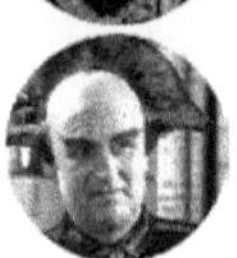
JURASIK
We love him so.

I think there's going to be two scripts for every episode for season five, and you're just gonna get it so that you won't know until you actually step in front of the camera.

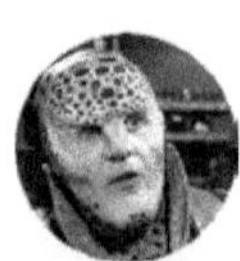
KATSULAS
Which one we're shooting.

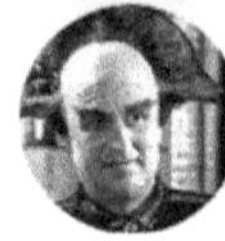
JURASIK
I'm gonna be drug into Andreas's muck.

[Laughs.] Do you guys work instinctively as a pair, now that you can almost second guess each other? When people work together, especially in theater, you get to know the rhythms of the other actor when you work very close. On this show, you two work very close together in that sense. Does that help that you can almost sense the way the other guy works at this point?

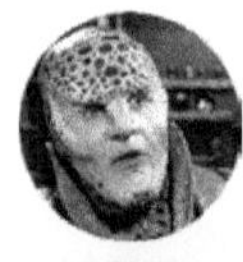
KATSULAS
Tell the truth, Pete.

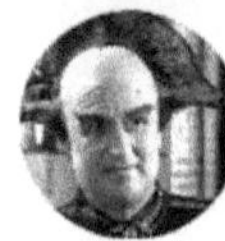
JURASIK
[Laughs.] No, you know what? The real answer to that is I feel like we work very easily together and the heart—where the sport comes in—is when we're both screwing up. When you're not good in a part of a scene, or I'm not good, we're very supportive, help each other through. I mean, that we know with each other. Right? That's a serious answer. The other stuff is just, I feel like it's pretty much actors who are just working together. Right?

What are you giggling about?

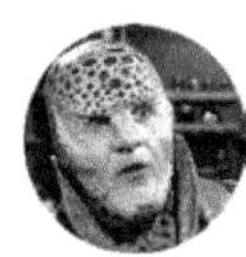

KATSULAS
I'm giggling, because when was it—towards the last part of this year—we were doing a scene and we realized that neither one of us had a clue about what the other one was doing. [Laughs.]

We were doing the scene. Each was in his own world doing his own shtick, and I said, "Do you realize I'm doing that at that time?" He says, "No, I have no idea." [Laughs.] And I had no idea what he was doing.

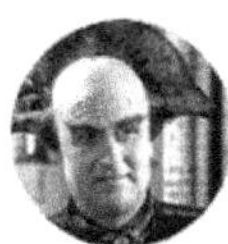

JURASIK
It's true. I remember that.

So far they have come.

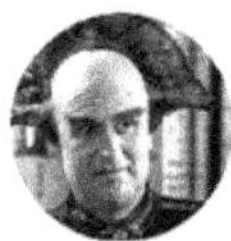

JURASIK
Right. So you're in this scene? Oh, I'm sorry.

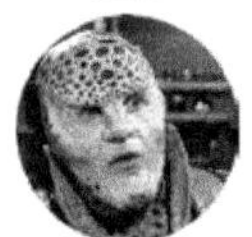

KATSULAS
It's like our chemistry is beyond us. We don't even have consider each other in the scene.

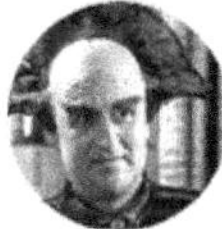

JURASIK
Yeah, we goof with each other and play with each other. So, we have a good time when we do it. But I think the working relationship is just like any other work. I think the best thing I get from you is that you sense when I'm in trouble and stay with me.

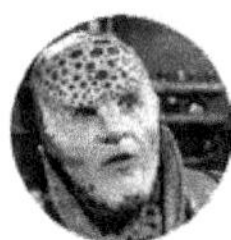

KATSULAS
I've never sensed that. That's why it feels secure. I'm the one who always feels insecure and thank god Peter's doing this scene with me because he'll be brilliant. [Laughs.] That gets me the confidence to get through the scene because I know he'll do it right. [Laughs.] That's how I feel about this [convention appearance] today. I'm scared to death. I don't want to do this. If I could find any way out of this thing today, I would, but I know Peter's gonna carry it.

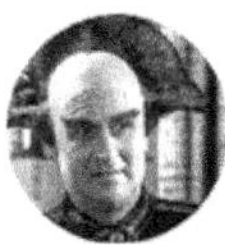

JURASIK
Typical Andreas response. Then he goes out there and wows them and turns into Milton Berle.

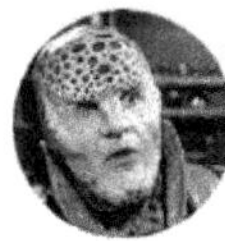

KATSULAS
It's because I believe I have nothing to lose. Because you're going to steady the ship and get us through the storm.

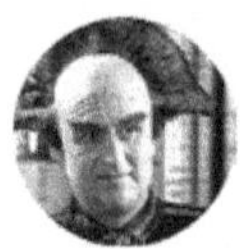

JURASIK
See how this works? See how this is now, right?

I know that Andreas doesn't like to look at a favorite episode of his and we've gone through this. You know how subjective it is for one person who will say that's the best scene with G'Kar, or whatever, but I'd be curious what each of you thought the other's best scene really was, where you looked at something that Peter did and said, "Shit, that was good. That really worked." Not necessarily looking at yourself and being self-critical, but looking at the other person.

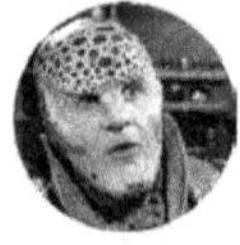

KATSULAS
I told you this year you've done some of the finest work in the whole four years in this last season. He just amazed me. It was because he was sweating this season. He was sweating the fourth season, saying, "God, I don't know where to go," and yet, boy, you found places to go, though, that were really stunning. I thought his whole thing with the emperor—all that stuff—the way you treated the emperor and that whole thing. It's just—

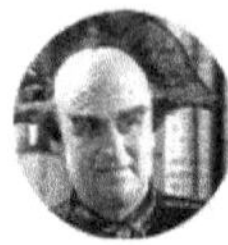

JURASIK
I speak so much easier about my own good work than his good work. You sure you want me to do this?

Force yourself. Be a pal to this guy. Throw a bone.

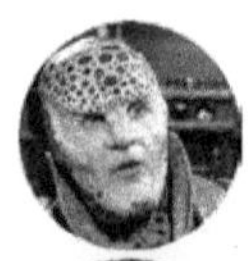

KATSULAS
I wasn't in the fourth season. I carried a cross and groaned.

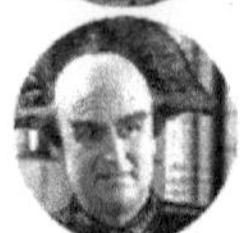

JURASIK
I think it's difficult to pinpoint one scene. It then becomes about mutual admiration and patting you on the back for good stuff. I feel almost like I don't need to blow his horn much. Everybody pretty much concedes that Andreas's work is the best work. We know how lucky we were to have him and his work is the best in the show, and all that. So that'll be another five dollars.

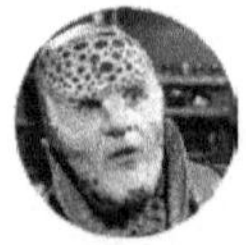

KATSULAS
I'm grateful.

That was only worth about two pounds.

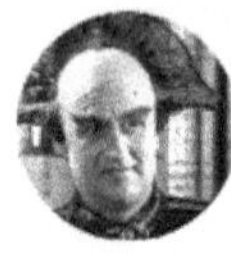

JURASIK
Again, the stuff in the fourth season, Andreas is in some ways, may have been making jokes about the fact that he doesn't have these long speeches to say. All actors really know that they're reacting and hanging and scene in a quiet way, the quiet stillness that he plays in G'Kar, the sense of the change that he has made the character, is really the most difficult.

But it is easier to hang a moment on a word than it is on silence, isn't it? You could play a word—you've got a script to depend on—but if you're playing the silence, it's that old cliché, silence is golden isn't it?

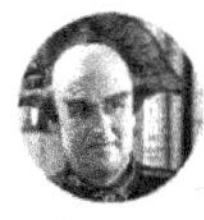

JURASIK
Absolutely. Yeah. It's much more difficult to stand there with no lines.

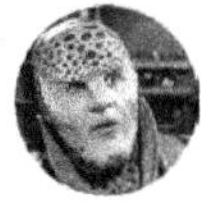

KATSULAS
As you found out in that scene, with the presidents. [Laughs.]

> The press conference with Presidents Luchenko and Sheridan in "Rising Star" was a day-long shoot with Furlan, Jurasik and Katsulas sitting quietly in the audience for most of the day.

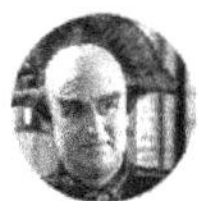

JURASIK
It's true.

WELLS
I think this is something that the British people particularly appreciate about the show, because our British television is a big industry. It is far bigger than our film industry, which is nonexistent. We get some very good dramatic moments on TV, and I think we appreciate and love the silence that can exist between two actors doing their jobs superlatively well.

This is something that I've heard many actors in Britain say about *Babylon 5*. It's most beautifully dramatic piece in a very strong, quality atmosphere. That yes, the words are there, there's a lot of action, there's a lot of movement, there's a lot of talking, but there are those moments of silence, which are the pure gold moments between people. I'm sure that's something that the British fans appreciate. Maybe they don't actually talk about it, but there are some wonderful dramatic moments where nothing is said at all, and that's quite unusual for an American production in our eyes. I've heard a lot of actors say, "I watch that show because it's so superbly done."

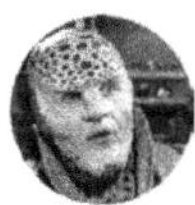

KATSULAS
You know, where what you're saying is evident, is the videos we've been watching, especially Friday on the opening night, there were a few during the fancy dress. These silences were captured by people, I guess, who instinctively know. It was actually those takes of reaction to something someone had done. It was all built on that—

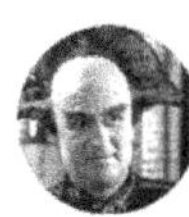

JURASIK
Definitely.

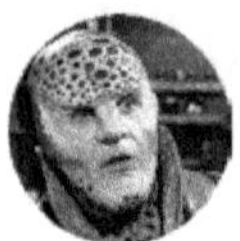

KATSULAS
—and was the right music. I was actually moved on Friday by some of the quality of the emotion and the how emotional the piece really is.

Katsulas is referring to fan-made music videos in which images from *Babylon 5* are edited together to music, often pop songs or instrumental pieces.

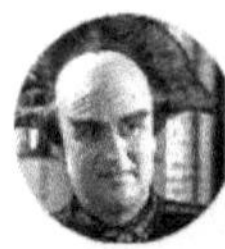

JURASIK
It is definitely true. Last night, after that one video, I said it's better than the series.

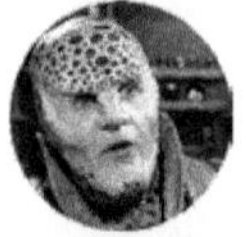

KATSULAS
Yeah.

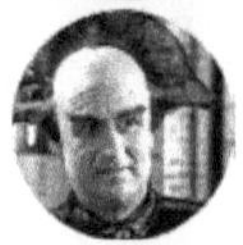

JURASIK
But it's true in a sense.

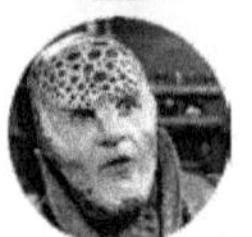

KATSULAS
You don't really [appreciate it], until you see it all put together like that. Because it's all here and there in the episodes, but it's really there, it counts for a lot, I think.

WELLS
And the moments of silence are yours. The words may be Joe's filtered through you, but the moments of silence are the actor's. They don't exist without them. I think it's a combination of the two that makes this such an outstanding production.

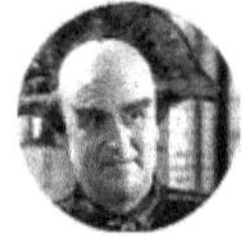

JURASIK
In a sense, though, Joe has, forced—for instance—your character to be quiet and taken your voice away. That's one of the things, by putting you Centauri Prime, he did by locking him up where he took his ambassadorial stuff away in the third. Yeah. He has forced you into that, and forced that drama that works so well.

WELLS
I think it works superlatively well.

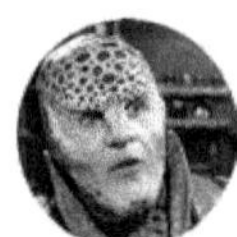

KATSULAS
That's why that picture is so eloquent, that one of us that I showed you sitting on opposite ends of the stage.

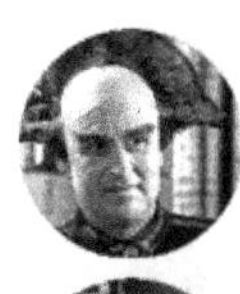

JURASIK
A fabulous picture.

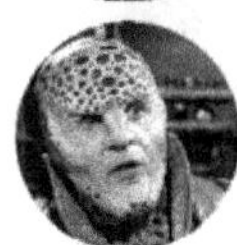

KATSULAS
A dozen chairs in between us. It's really that distance between two human beings, and we just take what there is in life and we put it on the stage.

WELLS
I'm a makeup designer, so I work a lot with actors, and I know there are a tremendous number of British actors watching the show, not because it's science fiction, but because of the pure drama between the working people. It really is appreciated.

Sheelagh Wells, Joe Nazzaro's wife, was a makeup designer for *Blake's 7*, *Doctor Who,* and Neil Gaiman's first series, *Neverwhere*, to name a few.

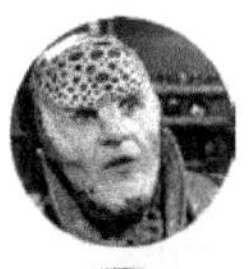

KATSULAS
I'm delighted.

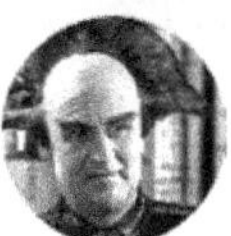

JURASIK
That's quite a compliment.

I think now that they're taking it out of that horrible six o'clock time slot and bringing it into a time where people can actually see it—

Babylon 5 initially ran on the UK's Channel 4 at 6pm, necessitating edits to the more violent installments of the series.

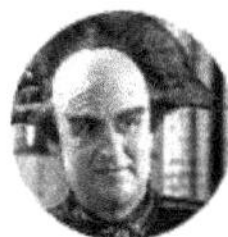

JURASIK
That's a great move.

—will possibly open it up to a whole new audience over here.

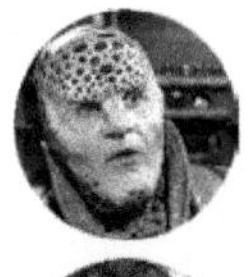

KATSULAS
Or maybe, when we're out of work, we'll come over here for a job.

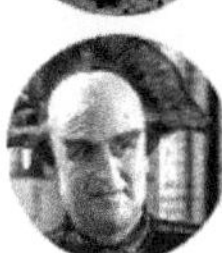

JURASIK
I've thought of that, man. I'm on that already.

WELLS
I think the door is open any time you'd like to. [Laughs.] I don't think you'll have

any trouble at all.

[Laughs.] It's interesting that this seems to be such a crossroads for the series right now. As we're speaking, TNT is going to pick this up for a fifth season and people will all be able to tune in at the same night on the same time all over the United States, and actually be able to see it. So, in a sense, maybe in America the show is gonna be getting an additional lease on life, isn't it? That people will be able to discover it for the first time.

> Prior to the TNT cable channel's acquisition of *Babylon 5* between the fourth and fifth seasons, the show's timeslot was determined on a market-by-market level, with programming directors at the local PTEN affiliates—many of which had dual allegiances to Fox, UPN or the WB—determining when the show would be broadcast. Someone moving, mid-week, from a market where the show aired on Friday night to one which screened the series on Mondays would miss that episode.

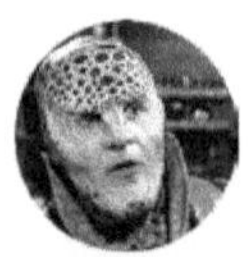

KATSULAS
I believe the best thing that's happened in the history of *Babylon 5* so far is TNT's involvement right now.

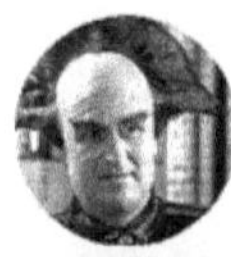

JURASIK
From a business point of view, that's true.

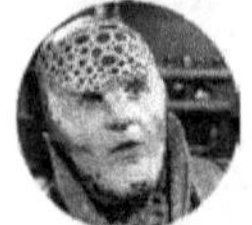

KATSULAS
It's going to extend its life enormously. I really think if they hadn't entered the picture at this point, it would've taken a nose dive and been buried in the depths. I think TNT is just that energy now that's needed, because the little train that could, that could, that could was just one thing to get in push gonna push it over.

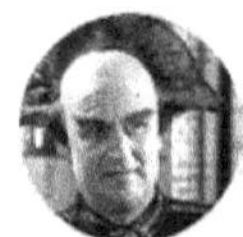

JURASIK
I have heard, when I'm here on conventions, so often people say about the British fans that the reason *Babylon*'s more successful here is that they have a better understanding of the long story and literature, all that. A couple of the fans have said to me that that is true. But a couple of fans have said to me, it's because they can really follow the story and sequence here and they don't get the way that Warners was airing it, where they show six and then stop and rerun and then show six. It broke it up for the American fans.

TNT is now gonna show it every single night [for] continuity of story. It's gonna be wonderful. It's a great thing to do. I think you're really right Joe, it's gonna pull a lot more people on board because you're gonna be able to—in one year, they said—they'll show the whole storyline twice, or something like that.

WELLS
You can be able to follow it right the way through, which is wonderful.

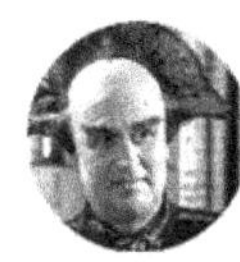

JURASIK
Night to night.

It's true what you're saying, because when they're doing the repeats, I know Sheelagh was over [in the United States] and she saw like episodes two, three and four—let's say—while she was over. Then we were both doing some work and she went back to England and then when you came back you said, "Oh good, I'll be able to see some new episodes, which ones?" I said, "Well, two, three and four." Terrible, because there isn't any continuity, which does disservice to the story structure, doesn't it? When you're doing an epic and you're just sort of showing bits and pieces of it.

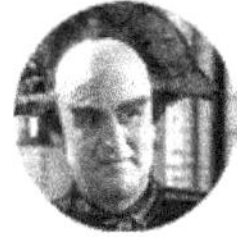

JURASIK
Not only does it frustrate the loyal viewers, but the people who are just tuning in are totally confused. I just saw an episode, now we're cutting back?

WELLS
Yes, we've been lucky. We've seen it.

> During PTEN's original presentation of *Babylon 5* in the U.S., the series was broadcast in six- or eight-episode bursts, with repeats screened for four to six weeks between each salvo of new shows, interrupting the weekly continuity. In the U.K., each season of *Babylon 5* was screened in a continuous run of 22 weeks. When TNT commenced repeats of the first four seasons, they ran episodes Monday through Friday, taking 17 weeks and three days to get through the extant 88 episodes. Once the fifth season had completed its debut run on Wednesday nights, the 110-episode package took 22 weeks to broadcast.

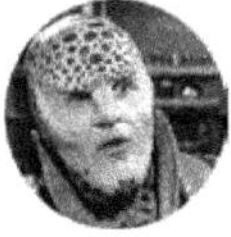

KATSULAS
But we didn't have a good table full of bottled elixir, you know? Warner Bros. just chose to leave it out on the street corner and said, "Help yourself. Please leave a dollar for each bottle sold." But TNT's up there saying, "Folks here it is! Come and get your elixir!" They're barking. You know? That's what it needs to sell that elixir.

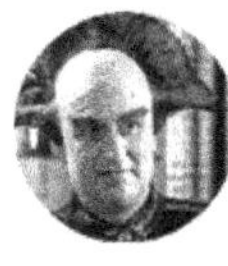

JURASIK
That's right. That's selling.

I wasn't able to go out when you were shooting the prequel because I was over here, but I was out when they were doing part of Thirdspace. The sense that I got—which I told Sheelagh—was that there was like even more of an electricity in the air than there normally is. It's a happy crew, but I was there, Jesús [Treviño] was directing, he had ordered an iced cappuccino machine that was put on one of the stages. There were TNT executives all over the place. I said, "This is amazing."

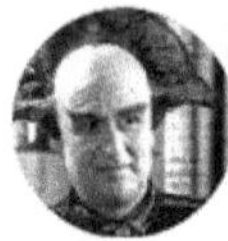

JURASIK
Yeah.

So did you find that to be true when you came in to do the prequel? That people were that excited?

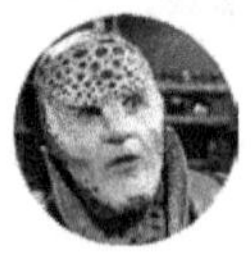

KATSULAS
Oh yeah. I mean the first thing was there was a sort of a gift basket for us in our trailer. For four years, we've never gotten a gift basket from Warners.

WELLS
Not even a donut?

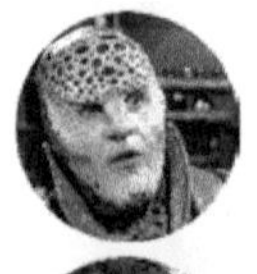

KATSULAS
No. Well, maybe a donut.

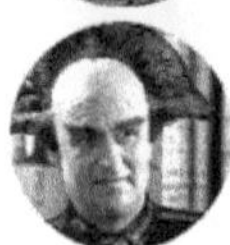

JURASIK
Think they were day-old. I don't wanna pick on them.

But you could put 'em in the microwave to soften it.

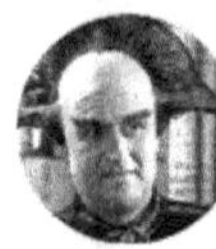

JURASIK
That's right.

What would you like to see in this final season? Not necessarily for your characters, but for the show as a whole?

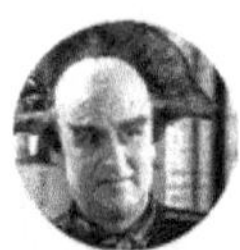

JURASIK
Well, it is wrapping up time. I know what I don't want to see is them necessarily throwing out the line, spending a lot of time throwing out lines to spinoffs in the next series, and maybe they're gonna do that. I would really like them to take the time to finish these storylines now and really complete them and fill them out and fill them in and fill in the holes and the spaces between the things that were left and done.

Joe got a lot of mileage out of the prequel in the sequel in doing that, but filling in lines. I just hope they don't spend time throwing lines out to new story ideas and spinoffs, that kind of stuff. I think there are plenty of loose ends that need to be wrapped up with all the characters. I wish they would do that.

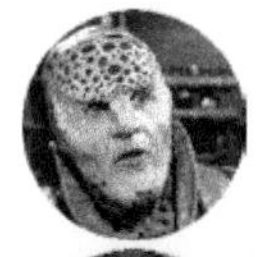
KATSULAS
Yeah. I would like to get some closure to the whole thing about the *Book of G'Kar.*

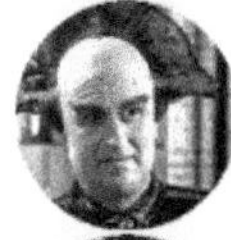
JURASIK
Definitely.

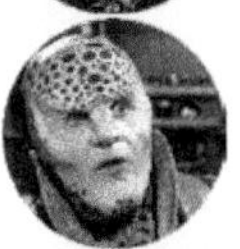
KATSULAS
He started, when he was in prison, writing his book. I'd love to see—

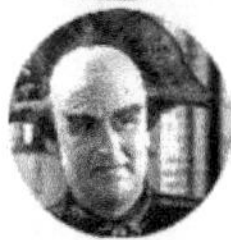
JURASIK
Where does it go?

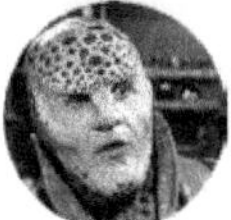
KATSULAS
—how he's balancing what's in his head with what his actions are now. I'd like him to have more speeches. I'd like more explanation from my character.

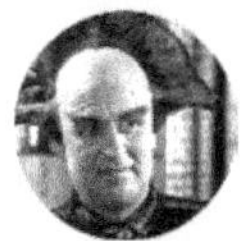
JURASIK
That's right.

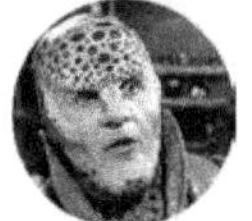
KATSULAS
So yeah, just on that level, I'd like to see. Maybe we have the chance now—because since Joe is telling more of the story in the fourth season in case there wasn't the fifth—we've got some breathing room in the fifth season to do a real Londo episode and a real G'Kar episode.

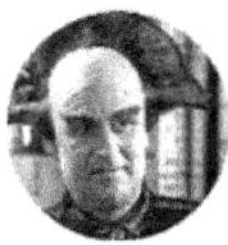
JURASIK
That's a great idea to spend time one episode at a time on characters. That would be fun to do. You know, just lay into it and really fill out one character, give it one character an episode. I think they would be great.

Pretty much nobody had the luxury of making big speeches, did they? Because there's too much story to cram in there.

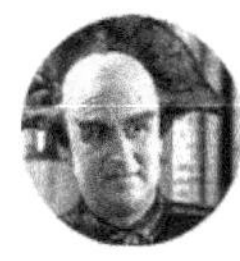
JURASIK
No matter what Joe says about that, he was able to truncate—push it all together—and make it happen. I know he had to edit stuff out, stuff out of his big story arc. So he needs to make sure those are filled in.

WELLS
Yes, that'd be interesting. Will he be writing all of the episodes?

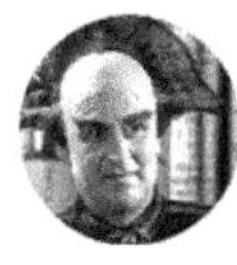
JURASIK
Let's hope not.

WELLS
Because I've heard that various people might have been asked.

> Wells is referring to Neil Gaiman, writer of "Day of the Dead" for season 5.

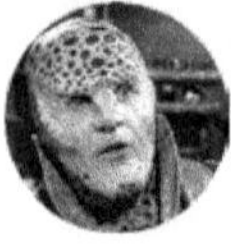

KATSULAS
I heard him say 15 of the 22.

> While there was an attempt to lighten Straczynski's writing duties for season five, only Gaiman's script and two Straczynski teleplays from ideas developed with Harlan Ellison, made it to production.

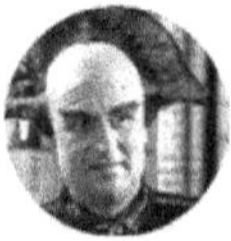

JURASIK
We heard on the way over this morning that he's got the first one done and the second and working on the story for the third, basically doing the first three.

> Because the series finale, "Sleeping in Light," had been produced at the end of the fourth season in expectation of the series concluding, Straczynski was under the gun to write a new fourth season finale that could be produced before PTEN reached the final week of the fourth season in its broadcast schedule. The preliminary draft of that replacement script, "The Deconstruction of Falling Stars," was dated 8 July 1997. The first drafts of the subsequent episodes, "No Compromises" and "The Very Long Night of Londo Mollari" were dated 29 July and 30 July, respectively, and were likely already on Straczynski's laptop in Blackpool.

Well, he had an hour before breakfast this morning.

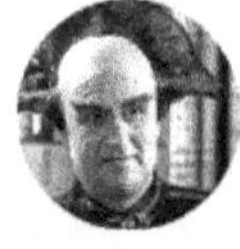

JURASIK
That's why I said I hope not, for his own brain and for his own work schedule. It's killing.

WELLS
It is, isn't it?

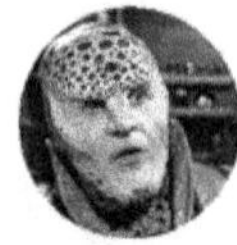

KATSULAS
I think these events give him energy, too. I think when he feels the feedback from the fans and everything, boy, he goes home and writes 20 pages.

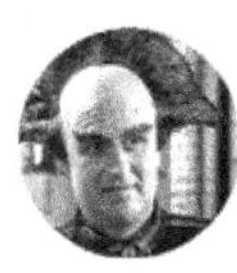

JURASIK
Definitely that's true. He needs the fan support.

WELLS
It's the equivalent to doing something on stage when you've that huge burst of adrenaline that comes from your audience, that unique moment that you have with the audience, that it will exist for that and that only. Of course, that's the first time he gets a chance to get that, is when he comes to his conventions.

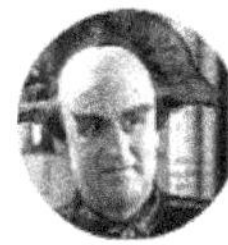

JURASIK
And Joe's not out in front, he's the writer.

But doesn't that happen for you as well? I mean, Andreas you said it's sort of scary to be up there, but you know, as a stage actor, this is the closest that you'll get to getting feedback from a television performance that you'll ever get.

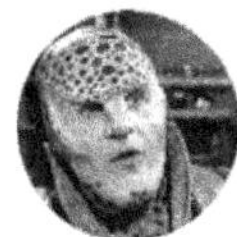

KATSULAS
Yeah. That's, that's how I feel about it. Even though I don't do it very often, this feeds me enough for a year. An event like this, it'll give me the impetus to really get into this next season, knowing that the people are over here waiting for what we're going to do.

WELLS
Well, the camera's a cold creature and that's what it comes down to really, isn't it?

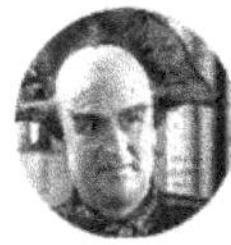

JURASIK
I try to give Andreas feedback, Joe, but he doesn't accept it. I've tried for a long time, but he's not the kind of actor who listens.

WELLS
[Laughs.]

So, hopefully we'll see that in season five—as the hijinks begin to ensue.

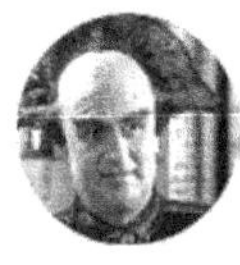

JURASIK
That's a good idea!

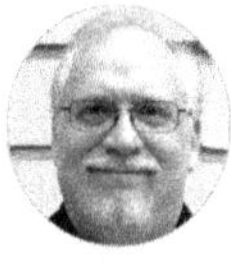
J. MICHAEL STRACZYNSKI
Creator/Executive Producer

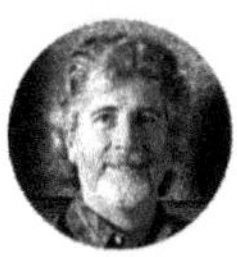
JOHN COPELAND
Producer

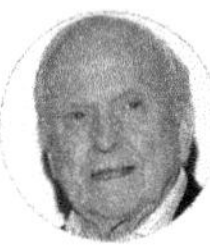
DOUGLAS NETTER
Executive Producer

21 January 1998, Babylonian Productions Office

Babylon 5 Timeline
In Production: "Darkness Ascending" (517)
On the Air: "No Compromises" (502)

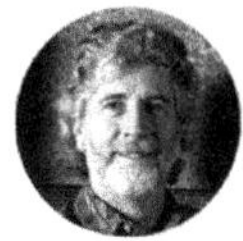
COPELAND
You've got us all here. Let's take advantage of it.

All right. What [Babylon 5 Magazine editor] John Freeman basically wanted to do was to—this is a sort of a companion piece to what we did in the first couple of issues by speaking to the cast. I thought that it would be nice to get the three of you [producers] together, rather than do another cast interview, to get a different slant on the show.

But what John [Freeman] thought would be quite nice, is to look at the current season as a crossroads of Babylon 5, as far as what's going to be happening in the future with the show. You know, if there's going to be a spinoff, the movies—there's lots of debate right now on what's going to be happening with the show in whatever incarnations—and it seems best to go right to the sources and talk about what's going to be happening now.

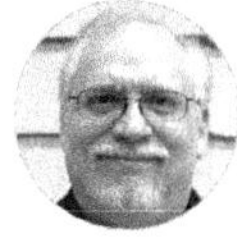
STRACZYNSKI
Of course, the difference in getting us, and the cast, together is the cast all like each other.

Well, we can work around that. Let's start by looking at it this way
We're sitting here now as the first regular episode of Babylon 5's fifth season is about to air—

"No Compromises" launched the fifth season of *Babylon 5* at 10pm EST on Wednesday, 21 January 1998 on TNT. For the first time, the series would be seen nationwide on the same night, the timeslot an hour earlier moving west across the time zones, due to TNT's lack of a West Coast feed.

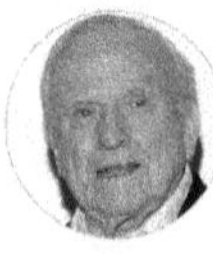

NETTER
Which I want everybody to know! I've been called several times. I guess it got a very good review in *Hollywood Reporter*.

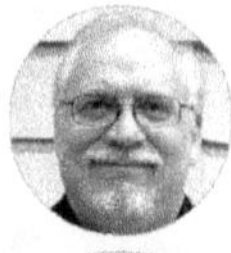

STRACZYNSKI
Oh, really? Cool.

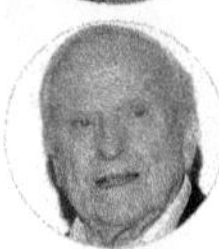

NETTER
Kate [Forte, Netter's daughter and a television producer] called me—

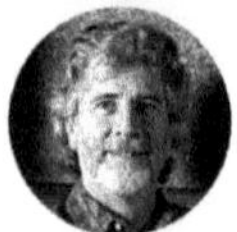

COPELAND
Well, I heard on my way down from the stage, an absolutely incredible radio spot from TNT on KLOS. On 95.5 [FM].

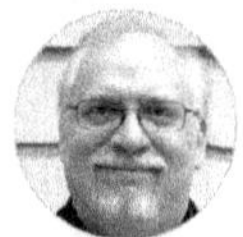

STRACZYNSKI
Oh, really? I never hear these things. I'm in an alternate universe, I guess.

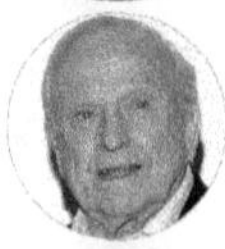

NETTER
Yeah.

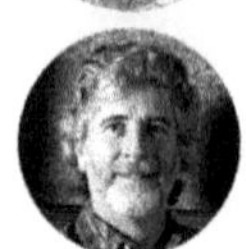

COPELAND
I mean, if you have to be somewhere, it's probably just as good as any, but it was really good, and it's the first time. This is not the first time that we've ever had radio spots, but this is the first time that I think we have—

Let's talk about being at a crossroads. The crossroads is the crossroads of TNT and Warner Bros., and I think that the TNT road that we're on, we're all really happy about. And going back to this radio spot that I heard on the way down from the stage, it is the first time that anyone has hit on the buttons of it's the show that everybody's talking about. It's won two Hugos. It's this, it's that—make sure you don't miss out on [it], and talking about the fifth season and on TNT, and they really did a wonderful little 30-minute package that are all of the things worth saying about *Babylon 5*—

Babylon 5 won the 1996 Hugo Award for Best Dramatic Presentation for "The Coming of Shadows" at L.A.con III in Anaheim, California and the 1997 award for "Severed Dreams" at the LoneStarCon 2 in San Antonio, Texas. It was the fourth series to win the award twice, after *The Twilight.*

Zone (1960, 1961, and 1962), *Star Trek* (1967 and 1968), and *Star Trek The Next Generation* (1993 and 1995). From 2003 onward, the award was split between long- and short-form categories.

Thirty seconds.

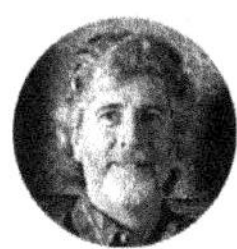

COPELAND
—30-second spot that had an audio montage from episodes mixed in with some of Andreas [Katsulas's] voiceover from one of the television spots that TNT shot. But it really hit all the things that are good about the show, and what works about the show that we've never had anybody focus on before.

TNT filmed special scripted commercial spots with Claudia Christian as Commander Susan Ivanova and Andreas Kastulas as G'Kar during the production of *Thirdspace* and *In the Beginning* that were broadcast, in long and short edits, during TNT's commercial breaks.

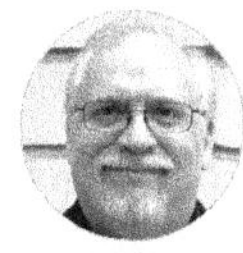

STRACZYNSKI
It's a comprehensive approach rather than highlight one aspect per episode.

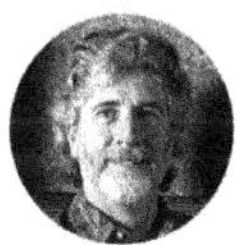

COPELAND
All new episodes tonight on PTEN!

PTEN's promotion of *Babylon 5*—and its other series—was typically limited to 15- and 30-second previews for the upcoming episode.

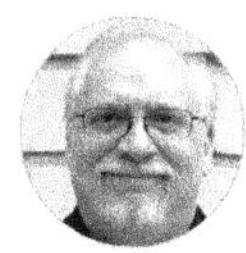

STRACZYNSKI
What about them? What makes special? Why should you wanna watch it?

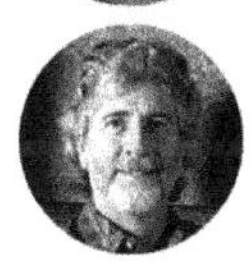

COPELAND
And what is it about *Babylon 5*—the last best hope? It was very good. I mean, we've got some great people working on our show.

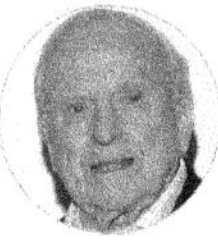

NETTER
Wonderful. When I went to Atlanta [to TNT's headquarters], at their marketing meeting that Friday—they had every department go through radio spots, TV spots, different departments, what they were doing, their contacts with the cable operators, what they're doing to promote [the show] with the cable operators, their trailers, and how they were doing the trailers. Their approach to the

advertising on their own outlets—CNN, [the TBS] Superstation, et cetera.

Then, what they would do with the others, spots that they took around *Star Trek* and around *X-Files*. And then what they were doing with the magazines, with the interviews, what they were gonna do on the hundredth episode, how they were gonna regenerate the activity again after they got the first episode on, which goes on tonight.

> "Phoenix Rising" was the 100th produced hour-long episode of *Babylon 5*, to be broadcast on Wednesday, 1 April 1998.

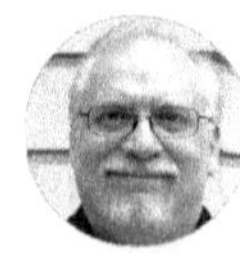

STRACZYNSKI
What it is, really, is that they took the approach the network would take to any decent show—

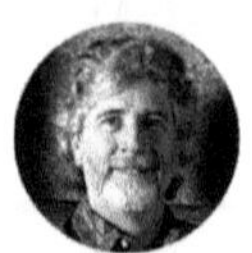

COPELAND
Absolutely.

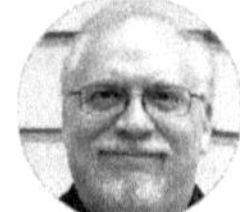

STRACZYNSKI
—and having that for the first time, we sort of merited that approach. Someone said, quite appropriately I think, that after the [*In the Beginning*] prequel [movie] aired [on 4 January 1998], that *B5* had come of age.

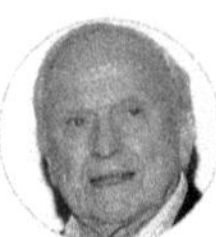

NETTER
Yeah.

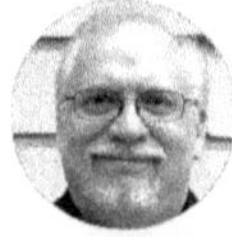

STRACZYNSKI
For the first time.

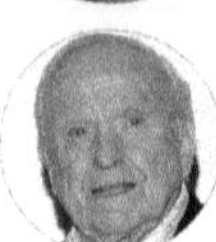

NETTER
Yeah, it did.

But that's a strange thing to have somebody say, that it's come of age in its last season. I mean, I don't know that you would agree with that, would you?

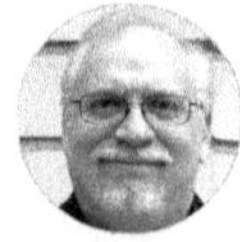

STRACZYNSKI
Well, it's come of age in terms of the mainstream consciousness. The show itself has been mature since about midway through the second season.

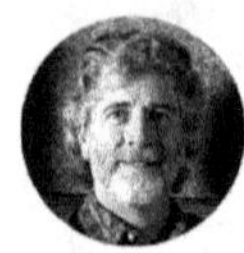

COPELAND
Well, it's continued to season and mature. I like to feel like we've improved ourselves every step of the way. I think the second season, though, we started hitting on all cylinders.

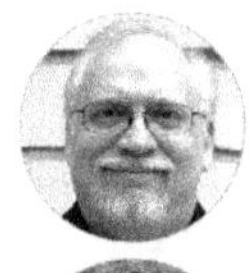

STRACZYNSKI
Yeah.

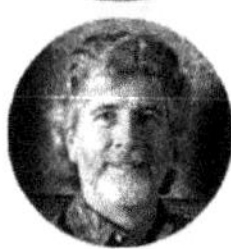

COPELAND
But, you're right. In terms of popular awareness, of just the buzz out there. That's another thing that TNT did in the buildup to January 4th with the airing of *In the Beginning*, and the re-edit of *The Gathering*. They did a really concerted push across the country so that people knew about *Babylon 5*. They may not have ever watched it before, but they heard about it, and that's part of getting an audience.

> *Babylon 5* debuted on TNT with a four-hour block on Sunday, 4 January 1998 after an advertising campaign progressively strengthened throughout December 1997. The all-new *In the Beginning* led off the block, followed by an all-new "special edition" edit of the 1993 pilot movie, *The Gathering*, which reincorporated much of the footage deleted by director Richard Compton five years earlier. From Monday, 5 January, the first four seasons were stripped, an episode screening every evening, Monday through Friday. Several late first-season episodes had never been repeated by PTEN and received their first reruns.

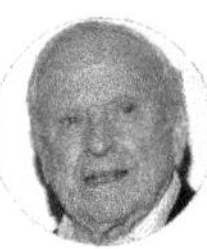

NETTER
There's other things you pick up, like on Sunday, we moved *Thirdspace* up. They moved *Thirdspace* up, but how are they gonna use it? They're gonna use it at the beginning to [re-]launch [the] *Babylon 5* series as they continue, because we learned there's a hiatus coming up, which we didn't know. But [TNT] just don't go into hiatus and then run other episodes and nobody knows the difference like they did at Warner Bros. So now they're gonna put [up a] big *Thirdspace* campaign.

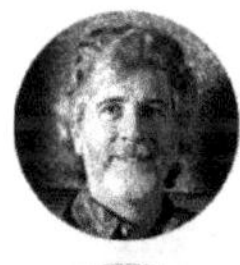

COPELAND
Another big campaign.

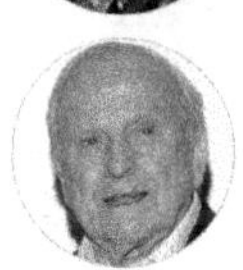

NETTER
Yeah. Another big campaign.

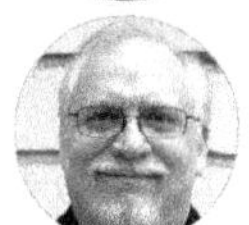

STRACZYNSKI
What's really kind of interesting about all this whole thing—what I think often gets missed, something I mentioned the other day—was at the critics' thing—the [Television Critics Association] meeting in Pasadena—what the ongoing lament in television is studios and networks that interfere with the creative process. They get in there and give notes and they take over and they'll have their own particular voice.

We're in a unique position. It's almost like [Pope Clement XIV] sponsoring Mozart, and writers and artists, where they would say, "Look, I don't entirely understand what it is that you're doing, but you're doing something significant and I won't get in your way." Warners, and now TNT, have given us an extraordinary patronage for the last five years, where they would say "We don't necessarily understand science fiction. We don't quite know what it is that you're doing, but you're doing it well enough. We're gonna leave you alone."

The fact that we have not gotten a note on stories since episode two of year two ["Revelations"] is a profound statement on any show, and that TNT has continued that process, and given us carte blanche, to say, "Look, we believe in this show, we believe in this story. We're commissioning a fifth season to see the end of the story, and you tell us." I mean, way back when [Warner Bros.] wanted to know what the end of the story was, I said, "I'm not gonna tell ya." They said, "Okay, just go ahead and do it," and that's truly extraordinary.

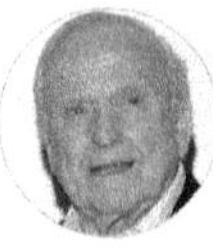

NETTER
That's carried another step. The internal drive to make *Babylon 5* never stops. Nothing ever gets in the way of making that show better. No compromises on the show, and we believe that.

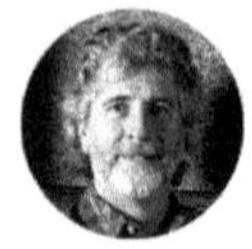

COPELAND
Well, I think it has been recognized by both Warners and the folks that we deal with there, and now the folks at TNT, that we are [more] severe critics of our own efforts than they could ever be, and I think that our self-judging process is something that never stops. This is not a group that's afraid to say, "That didn't work very good, and we've gotta do better." And, unfortunately, in the production of a television series, everything's not gonna be a home run. You have a schedule that really makes you march to a certain drum beat, and every so often, you have to turn over a finished episode, so you can only do so much.

Whereas a motion picture can stay in post for additional months, and they can go back, three months later and do some re-shoots or something like that. I mean, we just don't have those options. So, we try to nail it as good as we could and can at the time.

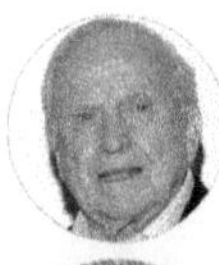

NETTER
Little mistakes should always be corrected.

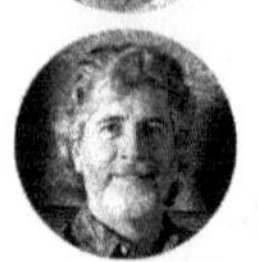

COPELAND
We do try to recognize where we have had our failings and shortcomings so that we don't go there again. I like to think that we don't make the same mistakes twice.

What sort of adjustments did you make going into season five, knowing that this was

going to be a very visible season in terms of the show's history?

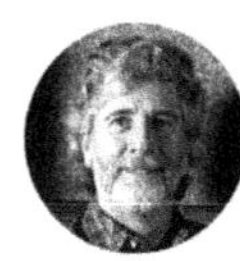

COPELAND
Well, on the production side, there were several, because of the change of venue to TNT. Cable television has its own unique set of economic realities, and we were tasked with doing a show, which—thank god—we had several seasons under our belt. We also had a crew that had been with us for a number of years. We still have 75% of the folks that started with us, still there on a day-by-day basis.

In making the transition from seven days [to film an episode] to six days, we were able to do that. Now, there were certain things that we did out there at the stages to help accommodate that. One of the things that we did was we decked the stages. We decked over the concrete floors of the old hot tub warehouse, which gave us a couple of things. It made the putting up of walls and sets very easy. It also made it much easier to unscrew them and take them out. It also meant that we had—for the most part—a level floor that we were dealing with, so we did not have to lay dolly track.

So, every thing that we could do at the front end would save us time when we're shooting on the stage, because losing the day, you've gotta pack it all into six days, and you've gotta have everything that saves you effort and labor there and workable. So, I mean, those were some of the things that—

> Due to the difference in broadcast and basic cable union agreements, the move from PTEN to TNT necessitated the reduction of *Babylon 5*'s shooting schedule from seven days per episode to six. In an effort to prove that the transition could be made without a loss of quality in the finished product, Straczynski volunteered to direct the final production of season four, "Sleeping in Light" over six days rather than seven. If Straczynski, a first-time director, could meet or exceed the show's usual standards with one day less, a more seasoned director should have no difficulty.

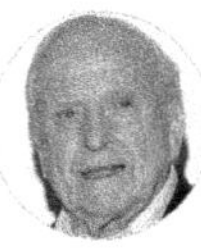

NETTER
Well also—unrelated—graphics. No curtailment of schedule. So therefore you have to continue to improve and do better, and get more graphics to complement the shows all the time. That had nothing to do with the live-action schedule. So that's going on all the time.

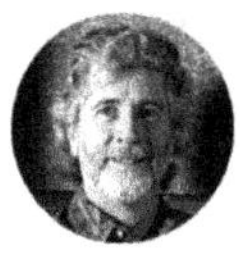

COPELAND
Even though we're on six-day schedule shooting, our turnaround, in terms of the time that it takes to complete an episode, really didn't contract. It's still a seven-to eight-week completion cycle that we have always been on.

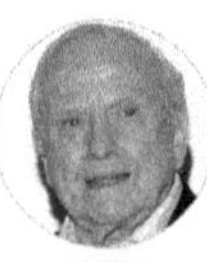

NETTER
Right. Yeah. That's very important.

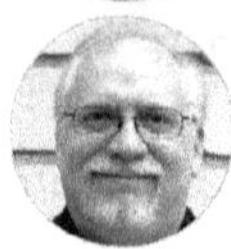

STRACZYNSKI
On the creative side, my task was a way to sort of continue the process of each season. The tone of the show changes to one extent or another, and there's a certain maturity I wanted to get across in the season where you see a story you've been building up for so long coming into fruition, and now to stop, letting things spin off.

My problem with the characters is, the characters in my head know that their time is almost done. So they keep saying, "Look over there! There something happened over there, this to that." I said, "No, you can't go over that. We have to stop this now." And, and it's hard to make them stop doing that. Even in [episode] 20, there a little more going on, than I probably had anticipated, but the character said, I want go up and do this. So it's just, it's hard to make 'em shut up.

> Straczynski delivered the final draft of episode 520, then titled "The Alien Inside" but renamed "The Wheel of Fire," the day before this interview. The lives of the characters were far from settled, with only two episodes left in the series, not counting "Sleeping in Light," which served more as an epilogue.

But this is one of the questions I was sort of leading up to before. The show may now be at its most successful, in terms of being recognized by the general public, just in time for it to finish. You have thousands, if not hundreds of thousands, if not millions of fans that want to see more Babylon 5—and you're gonna have a lot more new fans that are gonna be discovering the show in the coming months that will undoubtedly want more Babylon 5—but you've always gone on record as saying it's five years; that's all you get.

Will that decision change because of all this stuff that has now happened, as far as the show is concerned?

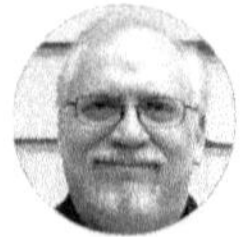

STRACZYNSKI
No. My feeling is you want to go out on a high note, as far as the series is concerned.

That outpouring of enthusiasm is this great in part because they sense we have kept our word and created a novel, which will have a definite finishing point. If we were to violate that promise, it'd become any other show that goes on and on, indefinitely. Then we wouldn't be the thing that has gotten their enthusiasm, and we have betrayal to the fans and to the intention and purpose of the show.

Certainly, we're looking at the possible follow up series, *Crusade*. We're doing one or two more movies for TNT. There are discussions for a feature film, and, in one fashion or another, that universe will keep going. I created this universe, and found it kind of a fun place to play in, and I look forward to going back there through different venues, but this particular venue is closed-end. The universe goes on; this particular telling of it stops.

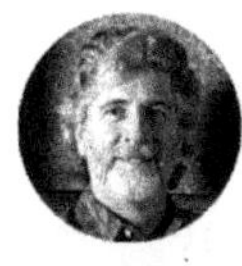

COPELAND
The form changes.

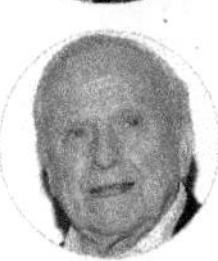

NETTER
The form changes. You see what they said is, the five-year arc is over.

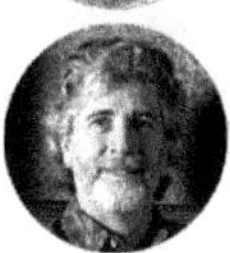

COPELAND
The story. And likewise, as you know, Joe [Straczynski] described this as a novel; you have to get to the end of it. Now, in the continuation of this—as this has moved off—because Babylon 5 is the name of a space station. If it is not set on a space station, how can you call it *Babylon 5* to begin with?

Yeah, yeah.

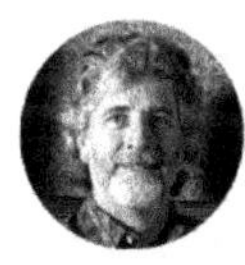

COPELAND
You know, it's like we left Babylon 5.

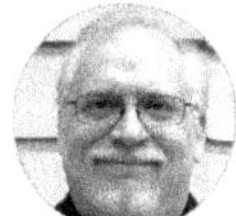

STRACZYNSKI
Yeah. See, what no one has really understood—I think, on some level—is that this [has], for me, always been an artistic venture, not a financial venture. Right? If I wanted to be in the finance, I would say that on *Murder, She Wrote* I was getting twice what I got to come here and be executive producer. I came here because this form appealed to me, and if I were to walk away from that now, it would be to sort of abandon everything that I've fought so hard to get.

The only concern, way in the back of my head, is if someone said, "We're doing it with or without you," in which case, the last bullet in my gun would be a *Tales from Babylon 5* anthology series. But that would be sort of the last resort, emergency parachute thing, to keep it from getting handed to someone who wouldn't understand what we're trying to do.

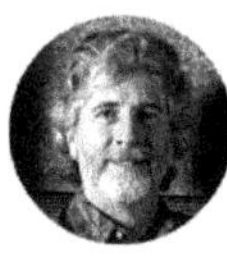

COPELAND
But even that is not *Babylon 5*. It really isn't, because this novel is done, and even if this comes back, these are more stories set in familiar places that we have discovered during the past five years, and with characters that people have met or spent a lot of time with over the last five years.

With the spinoff, it's in the universe of *Babylon 5*. There's gonna be a lot of familiarity there. There's going to be places that are familiar to viewers, and then there's going to be all sorts of new and exotic places that we've never seen before. So there will be the real wonderment again—just like the start of *Babylon 5*—of starting to discover these new characters and new worlds. There'll be a sense of wonder and exploration.

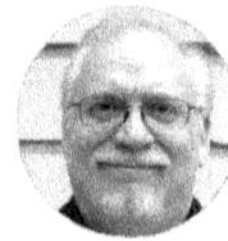

STRACZYNSKI
It's kind of funny that the critics first were saying that you won't go up for five seasons because the money is against you. Now they're saying, well, of course you will go past five seasons 'cause money's in your favor now. Money ain't the issue with me. Never has been.

I think that's the thing that I was alluding to. You have the creative concerns versus the business concerns, and from the business concerns, you have people that would not be able to comprehend, sometimes, why would you want to stop a series on your own volition when it's at its peak?

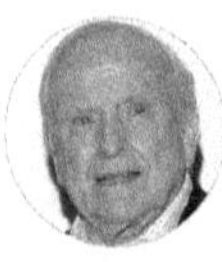

NETTER
That story arc is stopping, you see.

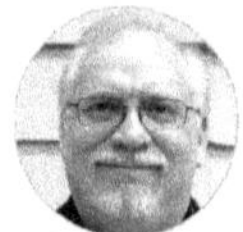

STRACZYNSKI
Michelangelo painted the Sistine Chapel. He sort of got to the edge of the ceiling and stopped, didn't keep going it down to the walls—

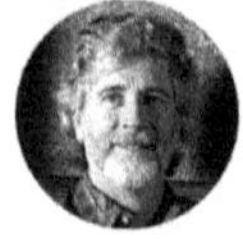

COPELAND
No, but he went somewhere else, and he did other statuary, and he did other paintings. Maybe it didn't take him the 11 years or the 18 years that it took him to paint the Sistine Chapel ceiling, but it went on. You look at all Michelangelo's work, and it's all a related body of work. Because it is back then, the biggest patrons of the art were either the families like the Medicis, or the Church.

Would you say that, if there is a future of Babylon 5 as an entity, it would more likely be in longer forms, as you say, maybe doing the occasional TV movie or a feature film, where you have the creative people behind you to do it. For your participation, it's like, "Well, if I can come up with a really cool, really good idea, we just do that every once in a while."

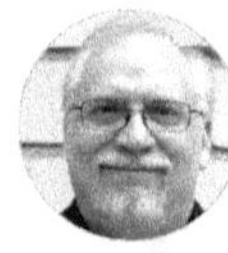

STRACZYNSKI
Yeah, absolutely. That's the key to it. The fact that the fan population is there now, and we know that there are 11 million core viewers of this show means that if we were to do a feature film, of say $25, $30 million, you're gonna make a profit. Now our job becomes to do those as we come up with nifty stories. If I haven't got a nifty story, we ain't doing it, but, if you do it, the audience will come and find you.

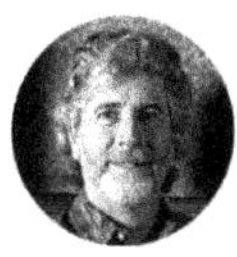

COPELAND
However, I think that you're also missing an element of the world of *Babylon 5*, where it will continue to be there in other forms. It's gonna continue in different forms. The novels are gonna keep coming out. I mean, there are three arcs—

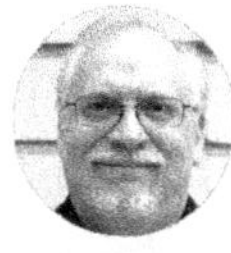

STRACZYNSKI
Yeah. I've finished that outline for the first two of the first arc.

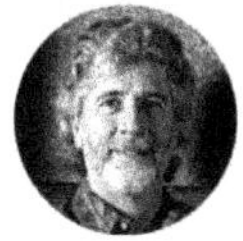

COPELAND
But there's essentially three arc stories that will be covered in three novels each that will deal also with portions of *Babylon 5*. One of the things that we just simply cannot deal with, in making of a series or film entertainment, is you can't go into all of the detail that you can in the written word, and for some of the fans that really want to immerse themselves and get lots of detail and everything. Those novels are there to further enhance their understanding and also give them alternate points of view of things that were covered in the series.

From 1998 to 2001, Del Rey published three trilogies exploring aspects of the *Babylon 5* universe introduced in the television series, but only explored to the extent that they affected the five-year arc. Straczynski provided outlines for a history of human telepaths and Alfred Bester by J. Gregory Keyes (referenced as two-thirds outlines above), the reign of Emperor Mollari II by Peter David and passing of the techno-mages by Jeanne Cavelos.

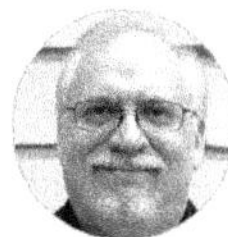

STRACZYNSKI
I showed Walter [Koenig] the outlines for the first two Psi Corps novels—the Bester storyline. He was knocked out by them.

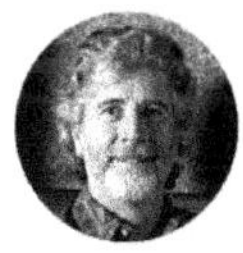

COPELAND
Yeah. He called me at home on Monday night. I'll tell you about that later. It's kind of interesting conversation.

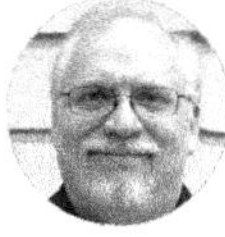

STRACZYNSKI
But that's why it was important for me. *Babylon 5*, what is at [its] core root, is future history, which is why I took the pains of establishing it from a thousand years before the story begins, a thousand years after, in rough strokes. So, like an onion, you can slice it up and take any piece of that and tell the story about that, whether it's the Dilgar War [referenced in "DeathWalker"] or Valen and Zathras, the [original] Shadow War [set up in "War Without End"], whatever—the great burn [referenced in "The Deconstruction of Falling Stars"]; it's all there.

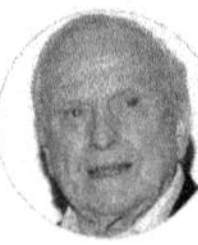

NETTER
It can be extrapolated; the novels are doing it now.

Well, you have a bigger special effects budget when you're doing a novel.

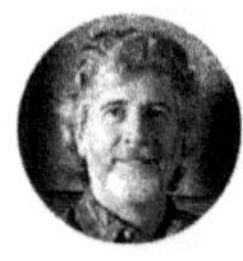

COPELAND
Well, yeah. Then you're only limited by the reader's imagination.

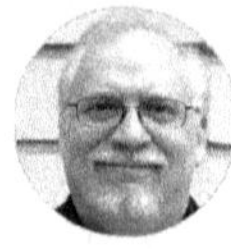

STRACZYNSKI
The writer's skill.

So, are the novels actually in place? I mean, is this something that, you know—

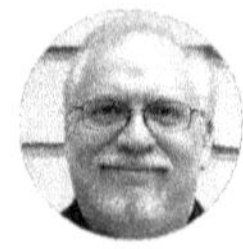

STRACZYNSKI
Oh yeah, It's a done deal. I wouldn't have done the first two outlines on them, given the schedule.

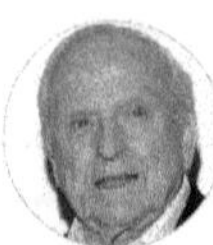

NETTER
Tells me it's just the beginning.

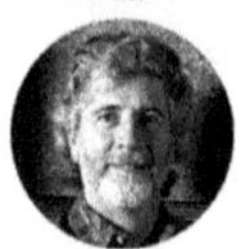

COPELAND
How many of the other novels are out right now? Ten?

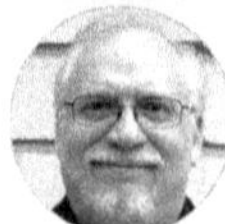

STRACZYNSKI
Nine from Dell, and there's nine more that are coming out from Del Rey. Plus, they will do individual standalones, plus they will do the nonfiction books as well.

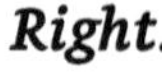

Right.

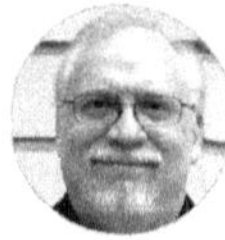

STRACZYNSKI
So, on one level, we're turning into a cottage industry, and there are times when John and I have talked about this, when we feel it's almost getting a little too big, and my concern now is to make sure that we don't grow so fast that we lose control of it. We guarantee the fans a certain level of quality, and I will not let this thing expand too fast and we lose that.

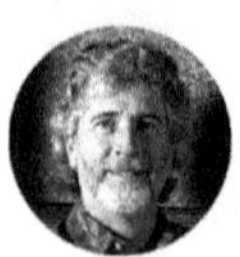

COPELAND
Well, it's the big concern that we've been struggling with for the last several months making sure that there is a consistent through line in terms of the facts of this universe. What's been a little alarming is the discrepancies that we're discovering, coming out in different—

What sort of things?

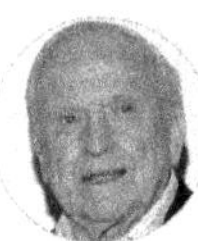

NETTER
I'll give you an example. You don't want to get it outta control, you know, on the electronic game. It's getting bigger, so all of a sudden they're going into another medium. Okay. It's a different medium. But how do you protect with a group like that?

> A *Babylon 5* game from Sierra Online was in development at the time of this interview. Live-action footage for the project would eventually be shot with series actors on the Babylonian Productions soundstages in April and May of 1998 under the direction on Janet Greek before corporate developments at Sierra led to the project being shelved.

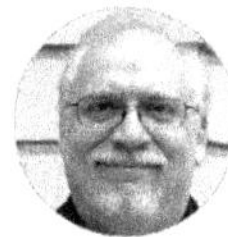

STRACZYNSKI
Well, basically that, for instance, the role playing game [from Chameleon Eclectic] has one series of facts about the background of Earthforce. The [*Official Guide to Babylon 5*] CD-ROM [from Sierra] has another set of facts.

The problem is these come in to me, and often they're hundreds of pages long, and after a while I go into a severe case of M.E.G.O.—my eyes glaze over—and I've been writing all day and I'm at night dozing over a role-playing strategy book which I barely understand to begin with. So, [what] we have to do now is pull back and say, "Okay, let's take these various stories that are out there and begin to consolidate them and say this is canon, this is not canon," and have a series of established facts to build on in the future so the fans don't have to worry about conflicting information.

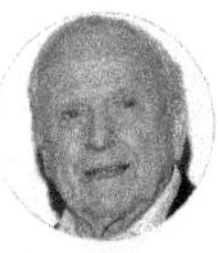

NETTER
So there's a continuity of story, a continuity of quality. That's hard, very hard.

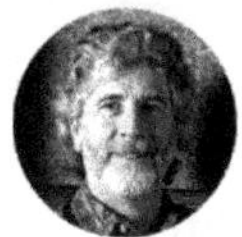

COPELAND
The fans get concerned about these things. We get these inconsistencies brought to our attention with no uncertain fervor on the fan's part. Because they want to know. They'll get into some argument and somebody's pointing to, you know, "In the Earth Force Sourcebook [from Chameleon Eclectic], it says this and, gosh, in [the non-fiction book] *Creating Babylon 5* [by David Bassom, from Boxtree/Del Rey], it says this, so who's right?"

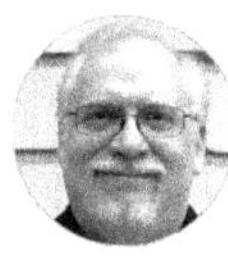

STRACZYNSKI
Yeah. So it's become more and more onerous on me. Every day, I come home with a larger and larger stack of things to approve and read through because I have to have my hands on what everybody's licensed to make sure what they expect, and

it's got to the point now where I'm just getting overwhelmed and I have to pull back and find somebody to stop that.

> During the latter part of the fifth season, reference editor Fiona Avery was brought on staff to maintain continuity among the various licensed properties.

It seems with the groundswell going, it's very hard to stop that wave.

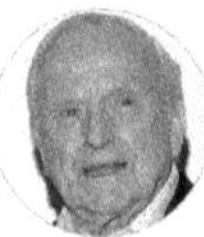

NETTER
Particularly when you spread out. Well, if they have their ideas of what they want do and they do it well, but that sometimes may not be consistent with the way *Babylon 5* should be done, or as, you said, the CD-ROM or the electronic game or the publishing.

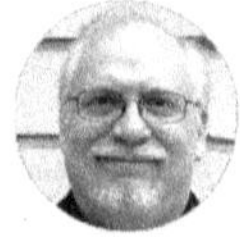

STRACZYNSKI
There was a time I could hold all of *B5* in one hand. And it became two hands. Then it became kind of like this [Straczynski mimes juggling many things]. Now my fingers are extended to the maximum level and that makes me look crazy sometimes.

Just because it's gotten so big.

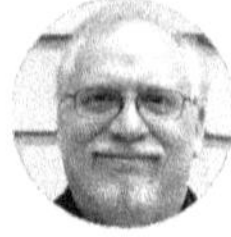

STRACZYNSKI
Yeah. It's one thing you never really count on, man. I went into this figuring [I'd] tell a story, we'll sell a few products here and there—as an ancillary thing, not at the point of it—and we'll get out. I never stopped to really consider how big this thing was gonna get. I'm a writer, I'm a storyteller, I'm not necessarily a guy looking at products, so it's got kind of difficult at times. But we learn. We adjust. We correct.

Well, you bring to mind an interesting point because I remember you telling me back in 1992—I think we'd just been talking about seeing Michael Piller on QVC hawking Star Trek memorabilia—"This is the executive producer of Deep Space Nine, selling his products." I have to paraphrase, but I think you have said something like, "If you ever see me on QVC hawking Babylon 5 products, you have my permission to hit me in the head with a baseball bat."

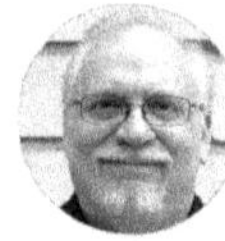

STRACZYNSKI
I don't think it's gotten to that point yet, but do you think that there is going to be a point where the proliferation of *Babylon 5* merchandise can just get to be too much? I mean, it's all new now.

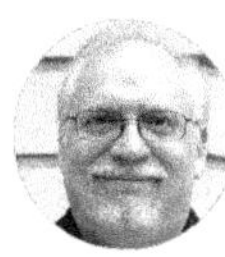

STRACZYNSKI
It's a yes-and-no scenario. I mean, the reality is *Babylon 5* is a very smart show. Consequently, I think it will never be as mainstream a show as *Star Trek* is, because you have to bring a lot to the table to follow it. So I think that the merchandising will never quite get that substantial.

The day I approve *B5* Underoos, someone shoot me in the head. At the same time, already we've had to make in-house decisions on how far we do and don't want to go. Doug and others mentioned a possibility of there being a Las Vegas thing and my reaction was to veto it completely out of hand. Because I think that if you go into Las Vegas, you're supporting a corrupt situation.

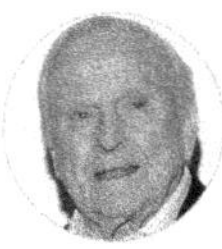

NETTER
We're talkin' only in Las Vegas, if we discuss anything like *Star Trek*—

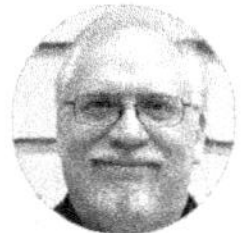

STRACZYNSKI
And the response is, well, Vegas isn't really that bad, to which I said that if Vegas really isn't that bad then god owes Sodom and Gomorrah an apology. So I think there is a certain level where you have to say, this far and no more. And we are doing that.

The thing I've noticed this last couple of days when I've been talking to people is there seems to be this sort of air of—wistful uncertainty, I think, is the only way I can describe it, because people are now counting the number of scripts that are left and they know what's gonna be coming up.

What can you say now as far as what is definite? What is probable, as far as what is going to be happening once the final episode of **Babylon 5** ***finishes up in the next, well, several weeks, really?***

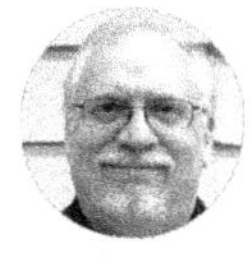

STRACZYNSKI
Well—

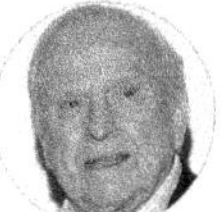

NETTER
See, the trouble is you are asking questions that are preceding certain announcements that will be made.

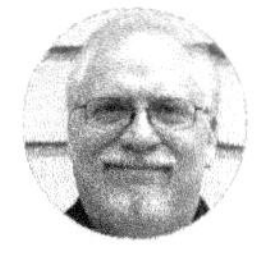

STRACZYNSKI
Of course, this will appear in a paper long after.

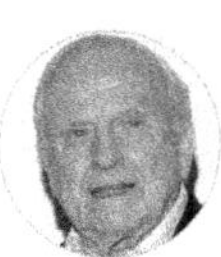

NETTER
Yeah, and the problem is those people who are involved with financing the life of *Babylon 5*, or whatever you want to call it in the future, do have a certain right to make those press announcements.

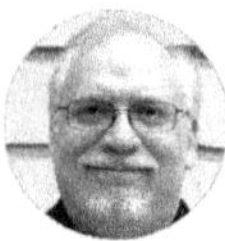

STRACZYNSKI
Well, on the assumption that anything that shouldn't be appearing here, we can pull out before it appears.

Well, generally it comes on your desk anyway.

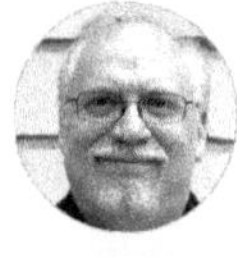

STRACZYNSKI
Exactly. So, you know—

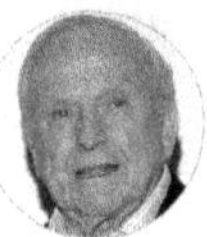

NETTER
I mean, that's odd for us, and with everybody, because of—

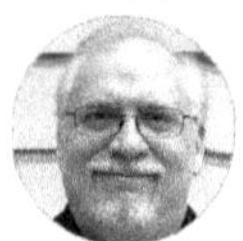

STRACZYNSKI
—but assuming that, everything that we are saying here will end up being able to be printed, that things have been announced and done by that point. In theory, there is a Showscan ride we'll be shooting toward the end of the season—

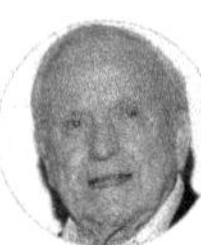

NETTER
Maybe, or shortly there thereafter.

> The Showscan ride never came to pass.

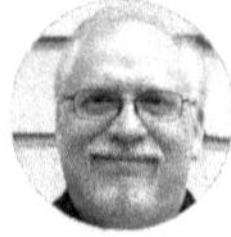

STRACZYNSKI
At least one film for TNT, the possibility of two, but at least one. Then we have a break of a couple of months, we began shooting, in theory, *Crusade*, in August?

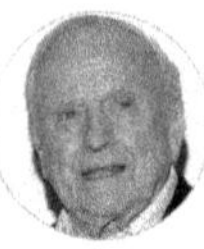

NETTER
Or July. We're trying to move it up to July.

> As the end of season five neared, the movie-of-the-week *A Call to Arms* was already green-lit by TNT to serve as a segue from *Babylon 5* to the already-in-preparation spinoff, *Crusade. The River of Souls* was in discussions at this point, though it would eventually be given the go-ahead, shooting ahead of *A Call to Arms*, prior to the station sets being dismantled for *Excalibur. Crusade* began production on 3 August 1998.

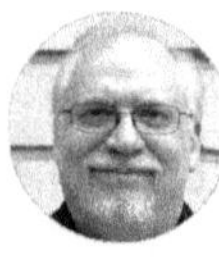

STRACZYNSKI
My suspicion is that sometime during this process, Warners will come to us, as they have already done so to a limited degree, and suggest a feature film. If that indeed comes to fruition, my suspicion would be I would write it sometime late in the year, we go into prep, maybe '99 sometime, shoot it

maybe fall '99 and come out with it in 2000.

Right.

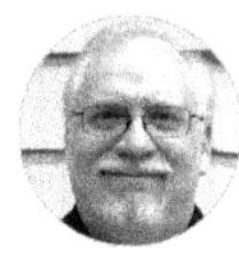

STRACZYNSKI
Which would be most appropriate for *Babylon 5*, usher in the 21st century with the *Babylon 5* feature film.

> Though Straczynski wrote up a treatment for a theatrical film and talks with Warner Bros. were had circa 1998, a *Babylon 5* film did not manage any serious traction until the 2004 attempt to produce a movie subtitled *The Memory of Shadows*, though the project had been shelved by 2005.

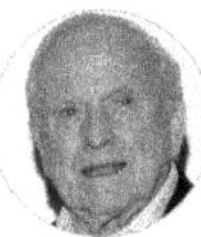

NETTER
There's more things. I mean, as long as you can edit, there's more and more things. Now they're talking about an animation film. So you talk about animation film, do they understand—

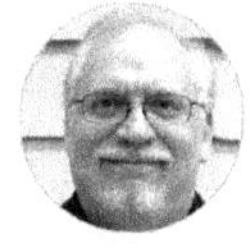

STRACZYNSKI
Series.

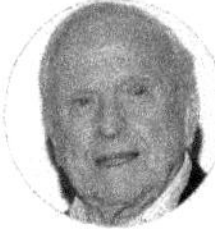

NETTER
—series, I mean. Do they understand this is not for children? This is not a show for children.

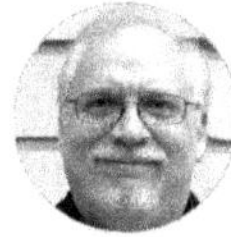

STRACZYNSKI
That didn't come from the animation division; that came from the publishing division.

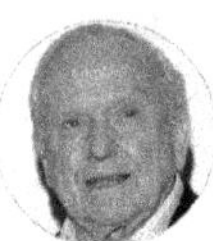

NETTER
Yeah. But I think it's—

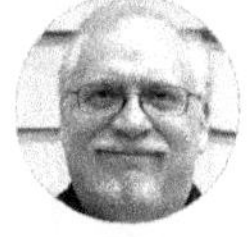

STRACZYNSKI
That isn't serious conversation yet.

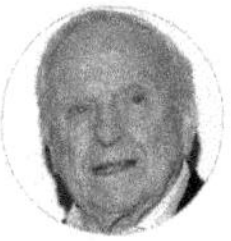

NETTER
Yet. But I mean, it's one thing after another that comes up.

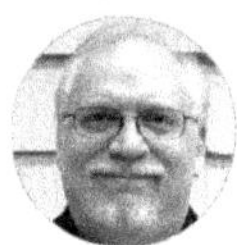

STRACZYNSKI
I think I'd go to hell for that.

As far as the spinoff, then, you're already making plans, obviously, to keep the crew that you have.

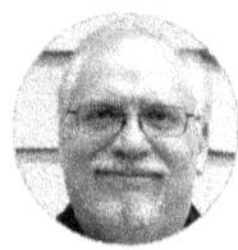

STRACZYNSKI
Absolutely.

You don't want them to be out of work long enough to go out and find other jobs.

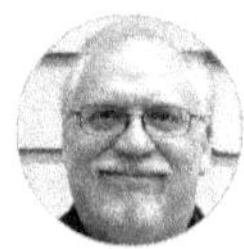

STRACZYNSKI
Yeah. Those crew we wanna keep along with the show. We definitely want to make sure they know they can return and have a warm place to come back to.

What about with the cast, though? I know you said at the beginning of this conversation, "This is a different story." Do you feel secure enough doing a spinoff on its own, as far as the story that you can cut it off, character-wise, from Babylon 5? You don't have to have, say, a Sheridan or Delenn or whatever?

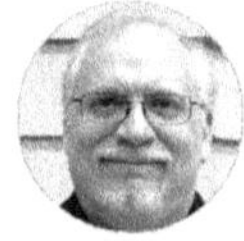

STRACZYNSKI
Well, that's currently the point of ongoing negotiation with Warner Bros. Some say let's have the cast from the old show. Some say let's not, and some are somewhere in-between or some are hearing voices saying "Go save France." I told 'em, "I've seen the movie don't do it. You wouldn't like the ending."

> The nature of the spinoff's connection to the parent series was an ongoing debate with the studio and network from the time Straczynski first proposed a *Ranger*-based series premise featuring many of the characters from *Babylon 5* in 1996. Early versions of *Crusade* featured Marcus Cole (Jason Carter) and one of the brothers Zathras (Tim Choate).

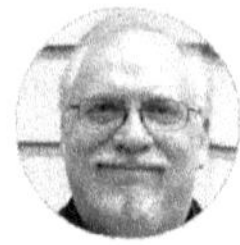

STRACZYNSKI
So that really has not been set at this time. Certainly—because this takes place in the same universe—from time to time, for instance, we would come to Babylon 5. There's a chance that you would see some of the same characters, from time to time, regardless whether it's three or four episodes, just where you run into and see Sheridan, Delenn or Lochley or somebody else. Because, if you look at the structure of last part of season five, it's being built so that A) we establish the *Babylon 5* universe goes on and, and B) that our people are in different places now, and available to us. Franklin's going to Earth to run the xenobiological research division. Garibaldi is gonna go off to Mars, with Lise. G'Kar and Lyta are going walkabout. Sheridan and Delenn are going to Minbar. And who am I losing? Londo, of course, gets emperor. Lennier goes off into the Rangers.

You have Vir, Lochley and Zack that you haven't—

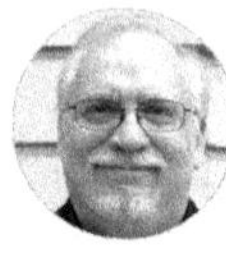

STRACZYNSKI
Yeah. Who are still there [on the station]. So, basically you've got all these characters in different parts of the *B5* universe now—scattered to the four

winds—who therefore become available to a road show.

Sure. So these people can become part of the new texture.

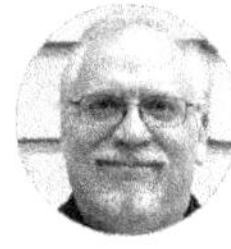

STRACZYNSKI
Yeah. The story the takes place about a year or two after the events of *Babylon 5* and Londo is still emperor. He'll be emperor for the next 17 years. Sheridan is still president of the Alliance, along with Delenn. Franklin's still working back on Earth. So there're those characters still there. I tried to create a realistic universe, and those characters go on for at least another 17 years.

> *Crusade*'s timeline was shifted further into the future before production, the series beginning in 2267 rather than 2263 or 2264. Only Captain Elizabeth Lochley (Tracy Scoggins) and Dr. Stephen Franklin (Richard Biggs) would appear during *Crusade*'s brief run, the former in three episodes as a series regular, and the latter for one episode as a special guest star. Return appearances for Lyta Alexander (Patricia Tallman) and Alfred Bester (Walter Koenig) were scripted but not filmed, and Michael Garibaldi (Jerry Doyle) was excised from a script at the outline stage.

From a pragmatic point of view, as producers, it's very difficult. Even if you wanted to bring back, say, character A and B, it wouldn't be an intelligent idea to be saying it because once people know that they're wanted for it, the agents realize that they're a hot commodity and that can—

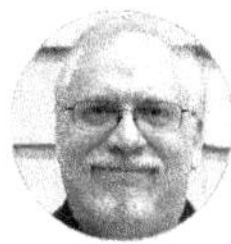

STRACZYNSKI
And then you bring characters C and D instead, and our cast know that about us.

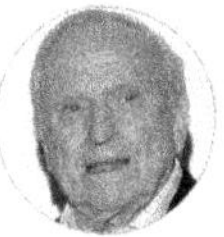

NETTER
That's a practical problem in the business. That's not unique to this.

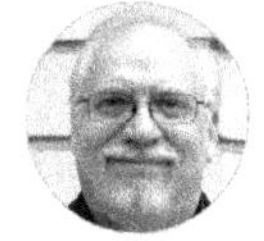

STRACZYNSKI
No.

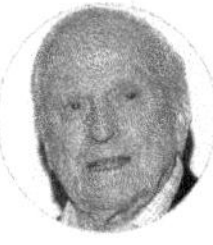

NETTER
If you've had them before, and you go back to 'em again, you have to have a new negotiation, and there's not much you can do to change that because that's happened before *Babylon 5* and will happen after.

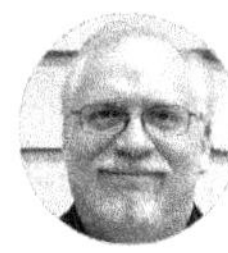

STRACZYNSKI
The cast know by now that this is a modular show; you can plug in various people.

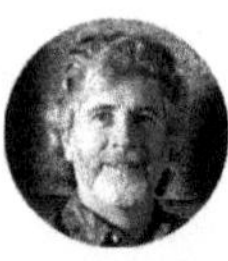
COPELAND
People can come and go, and they have.

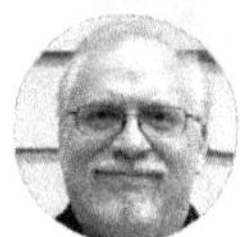
STRACZYNSKI
If I wanted to make the head of security a large, stuffed bunny, I could find a way to make that work, you know? [Laughs.]

What sort of regrets do you guys have, looking back at these five years? I want to end this on a positive note, as well, but I'm curious, if you had your druthers about certain things that could have been done or changed or altered or improved as you went along, looking back at this over the last five years now, what would they be?

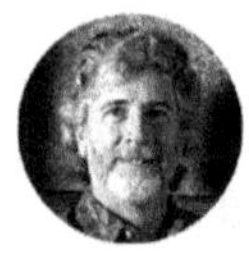
COPELAND
That we wouldn't have done pastels on Centauri Prime. Get them out of those purples! [Laughs.]

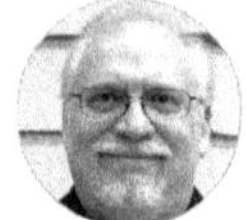
STRACZYNSKI
I don't have any real regrets. I mean, on one level there isn't a frame of film I wouldn't want to see and edit one more time. There isn't a line of dialogue I wouldn't wanna go back and tweak one more time. The exigencies of television production being what they are, you have to at a certain point, let it go and move on. And you think, well, "Shoot, I should have said 'the' instead of 'a' in that sentence," and sure, I could have had a sharper hook on the sentence.

In terms of the show overall, no, I have no regrets. It's what I wanted it to be, and I'm very happy with it. John, I don't know about you.

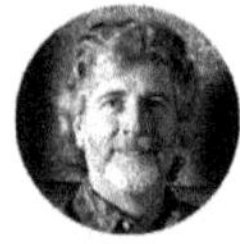
COPELAND
Well, you know, overall there really aren't any regrets. Certainly, hindsight is golden and it's much more 20/20 than trying to have a perspective towards tomorrow from any given point. But I think, all in all, with what we've had to do this show with, there's really not anything to be ashamed of or horribly disappointed with.

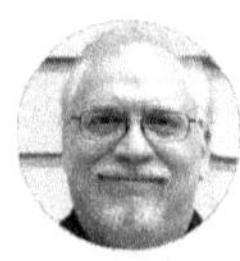
STRACZYNSKI
Well, the pilot, but we fixed that.

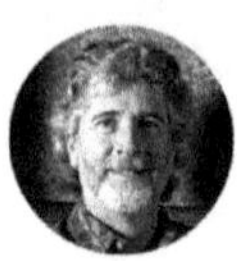
COPELAND
But, I mean, that was our first time around the block, and there are some things that I would have jumped up and down and been a lot louder about at the start of the first season, with had I known how the first season unfolded, that we were gonna go there. Because I kind of felt that that was gonna be where we went, but you grow so much stronger from the experiences that you have, and it makes you so much better. Even the bumpy roads are worth going over because of what it does to you.

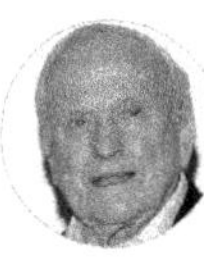

NETTER
Regret kind of means you look back, or it's negative. What about what's coming up, where you are going to?

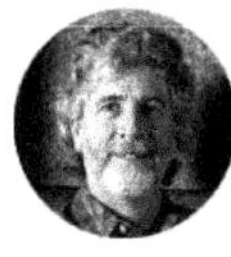

COPELAND
It would've been nice to always have had more money. It would've been nice to have had a more consistent play spot [in the U.S. television markets] in the scheme of things. Those are things that would've had an immediate and dynamic impact on the show, that would have sent it into something different and it would've been a different show because of that. But, for the cards that we've been dealt, I think that we've done pretty good at the poker table.

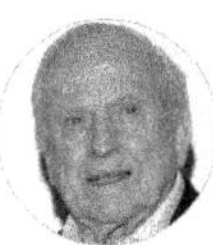

NETTER
I mean, if you wanna say, "Was it a network show? What could you do?" You get into conjecture.

That's a whole different ball of wax, really.

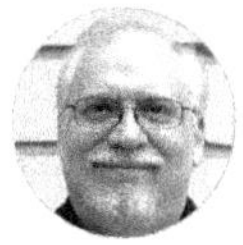

STRACZYNSKI
Basically working in television, it's like going to Vegas and trying not to lose your entire life savings in the process. We walked out with our pants on and our shirt in place, a couple dollars in our pocket, to use John's metaphor, and you can't regret that.

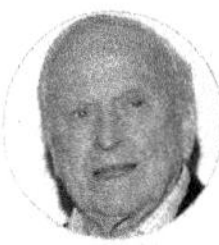

NETTER
I don't regret anything on *Babylon 5*, really, if you look at it objectively.

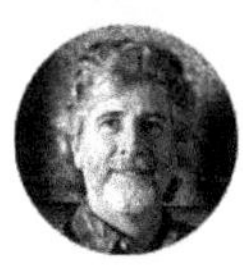

COPELAND
You look at the things that we have succeeded at, where nobody succeeded until we came along. I mean, my god, it's the first space-based series besides something that's branded with *Trek* that's lasted more than two seasons.

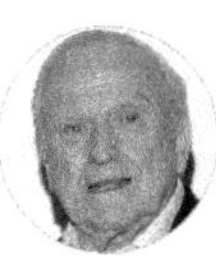

NETTER
They told us at the very beginning, Number one, you could not make another science fiction show other than [*Star Trek*]. They were wrong. Number two, you couldn't make science fiction with quality.

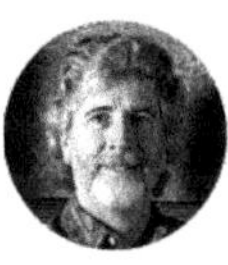

COPELAND
Everybody believed the big myth. There were a lot of naysayers about the way that we did our effects, about the way that we went about posting the show. No, you can't do this. Don't tell us we can't do it! That just makes us that much more determined to go out and succeed.

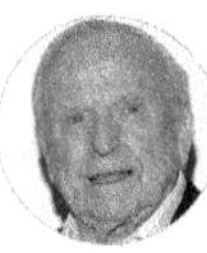

NETTER
Quality and science fiction were directly tied to extravagant budgets, which was strictly not true. We learned that lesson with the stupidity that went on on the show in Canada.

> Netter is referring to *Captain Power and the Soldiers of the Future*, the series on which Copeland and Netter met Straczynski.

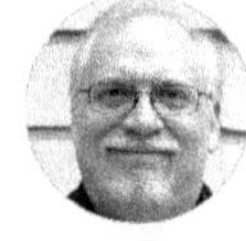

STRACZYNSKI
Everything we set out to do, we did; everything we sought to prove we proved.

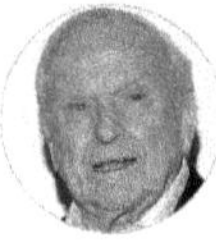

NETTER
Yeah. So that's not regretful.

No, I think what I was going to come around too was exactly what John said is what would you look at as the accomplishments.

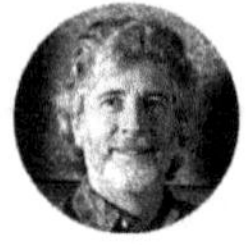

COPELAND
I also think one of the big pluses that we did was to, in a way-back in 1992 when we started on this with the pilot, and then in '93 when we went into the series—was we said, "We can make this for a price here in town," and that kind of thing has helped regenerate this community. It's also made it possible for other science-fiction-based storylines—in terms of series and television movies—to find their way onto television and in front of viewers, because people have said, "*Babylon 5* is kind of working."

> At the time *Babylon 5* began production, many television series had fled Los Angeles for less-expensive international locations like Vancouver or Melbourne.

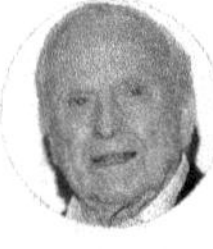

NETTER
Syndication, cable TV—all these things were helped by *Babylon 5* substantially.

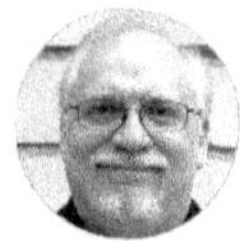

STRACZYNSKI
We introduced the term of the five-year arc, which, of course, *Dark Skies* began to use and then *Earth Final Conflict* began to use. Others are now in the process of saying we have a five-year arc, too. That was a term that wasn't in existence before we came up with it.

Creatively, I think that what you're always told—the okeydoke—is that television does not have auteurs, television does not have one creative force behind it. It's all done by committee. I took the position that you can have something that is one vision, one voice. Granted, you can go too far with that, but nonetheless we proved that you can do it, that you can present one sustained vision across a period of five years.

The amusing thing is that the process that I showed in "The Deconstruction of Falling Stars" is already happening. I know some folks who were at the conference in Europe—an academic conference—and the one overriding thing was that [Gene] Roddenberry and Straczynski are similar and they both had to pretend to create monster control on the show in order to make it seem as if it's their vision. They're assuming, from the git-go, that in fact, I don't have that much control with their vision of the show, that it's others, doing it for me. I take the credit for it, and that the scripts really aren't as detailed as everyone's been led to believe. It's not one person; it's the gestalt that comes together and creates a thing, which is what they said in "Deconstruction"—that one person doesn't change things. It's that the group sort of—when it's ready—to begins to change things.

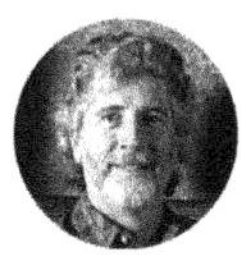

COPELAND
The group decides to buy into the change and then makes it.

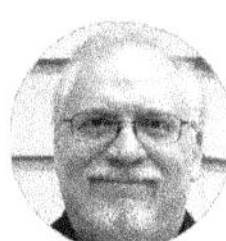

STRACZYNSKI
Yeah. Exactly. So that process has already begun. I think they were so disappointed to find out that Roddenberry wasn't as much in control as he would've liked to have believed, that they figured they won't go for that a second time. So I'm anticipating that process of folks saying, "Joe was actually very nice but it actually was all John's idea, which of course it was." [Laughs.]

The man behind the myth. [Laughs.]

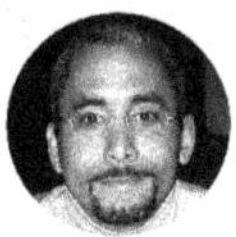

RICHARD BIGGS
Stephen Franklin

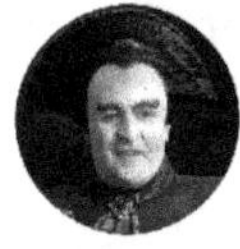

PETER JURASIK
Londo Mollari

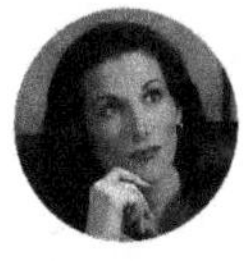

JULIE CAITLIN BROWN
Na'Toth & Guinevere Corey

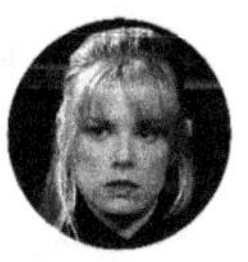

MARJORIE MONAGHAN
Tessa Halloran

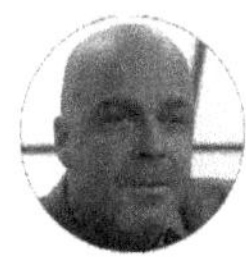

JERRY DOYLE
Michael Garibaldi

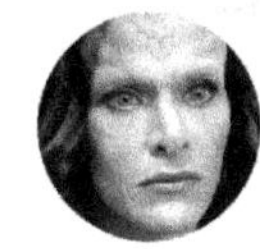

CARRIE DOBRO
Dureena Nafeel

27 April 2001, Sheraton Meadowlands in East Rutherford, New Jersey

Babylon 5 Timeline
Last in Production: *Crusade* "Appearances and Other Deceits" (113)
Last on the Air: *Crusade* "Each Night I Dream of Home" (105)

This interview took place at the Chiller Theater Convention on 27 April 2001, a few weeks before *The Legend of the Rangers* went into production in Vancouver. At the time of this interview, Julie Caitlin Brown served as the booking agent for most of the *Babylon 5* and *Crusade* cast when they attended conventions, hence her managerial comments throughout the interview.

Jerry Doyle, who joins the interview after a break in the recording, had run for a seat in the United States House of Representatives as the Republican nominee for California's 24th congressional district in 2000 and lost.

So everybody's on autopilot. The thing that I'm so curious about is now we've come to the end of Babylon 5, we've come to the end of Crusade—because I've got people from two different shows.

There's an actor [Gareth Thomas, of Blake's 7] that I interviewed—that was on a very major science fiction show in England—and he was interviewed one time and [was asked], "Was this show that you were in a milestone in your career? Or was it a millstone?" He said, "Every five years, my answer to this question changes because of what's happening with my job."

How have these shows actually affected your respective careers now? Have they done

anything for you? Or is it nothing really? What sort of things have you been finding over the last couple years?

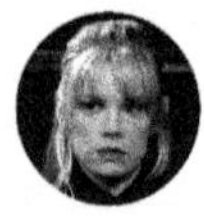

MARJORIE MONAGHAN
Well, what's been really positive about it, for me, is getting involved in doing these conventions and getting to meet so many fans. It's so much fun. They're just lovely people, and connecting with people and then seeing as they support the other work that you do—

But the truth is that, in the industry, they do not pay attention to science fiction.

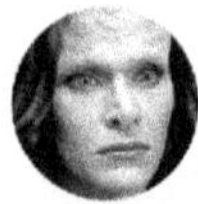

CARRIE DOBRO
None at all.

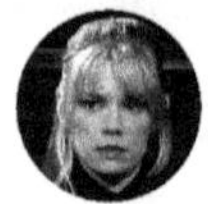

MONAGHAN
Unless you're on like a show that runs for years and years—and even with *Babylon 5*, because it was in syndication, honestly—nobody in Los Angeles watched it. Nobody in the industry watched it. Most of them never heard of it. So, as far as that, it doesn't really seem to do anything one way or the other, because just nobody watched it.

From what I understand on the rumor mill, you had actually gone in to audition for the new Trek series, didn't you?

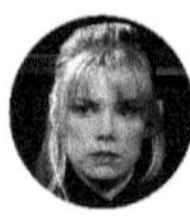

MONAGHAN
Yes, I have. I've gone in twice.

> *Enterprise*, the sixth television series in the *Star Trek* franchise, would begin production on 14 May 2001, just over two weeks after this convention. Monaghan was considered for the role of Sub-Commander T'Pau, a part subsequently reconceived as T'Pol, played by Jolene Blalock.

Was that just basically on your credentials as an actor or do they say, "This person might have a little bit of marketability in the science fiction arena from things that she's been in"?

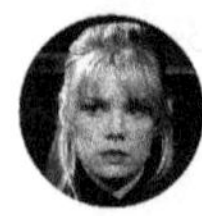

MONAGHAN
Well that's possible because I've noticed, there's a girl who does a website about me, and I found out through accessing that, there's a lot of talk that I've got it. I'm reading for it. I'm not reading for it. It's very funny. None of the rumors have been true, but it's been funny watching them and and flattering that anybody cares. [Laughs.] It discusses *Babylon 5* and *Space Rangers* and other things, so I don't know. You kinda have to ask [*Enterprise* executive producer] Rick Berman.

It's all hypothetical now.

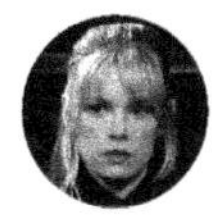

MONAGHAN
He would know because he deals in the science fiction genre. He would know other science fiction shows. As far as people casting features, people casting hour-long series, they don't really follow science fiction.

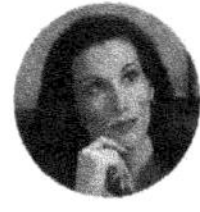

JULIE CAITLIN BROWN
Although we've had a few directors cross over, like Jim Johnston and Mike Vejar who have gone on to *JAG* or other things. I started [for Vejar] on *Renegade.*

I took back the name Julie. So I wasn't just Caitlin Brown anymore. I was Julie Caitlin Brown. It was Caitlin Brown and Joe [Nazzaro] knows this, 'cause when he first met me, I was Caitlin Brown. Not a good story for now, but anyway—[Laughs.]

I get called in to read for a role on *Babylon 5*, for Guinevere Corey, a lawyer in the second season. I walk in and—oh god, what's her name?— [casting director] Mary Jo Slater says, "What are you doing here? We're, we're reading Julie Caitlin Brown," and I go, "That's me." I got the part because Mike [Vejar] wanted me to do it, but I also got the part on *JAG* because Jim Johnston wanted me to do it.

I think if you're a good, solid actor, do they look at your science fiction and say, "Yeah, we want her, baby." Not necessarily, but if you're a good, strong actor, it doesn't hinder you.

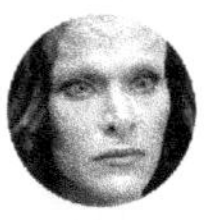

DOBRO
It doesn't hinder you, but I think it absolutely does not help you.

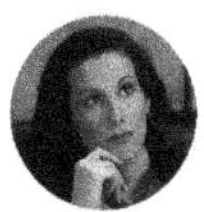

BROWN
Except in the genre.

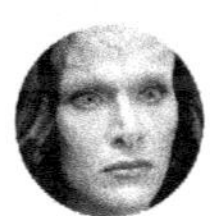

DOBRO
Right.

The other obstacle that the two of you had was if you were identified with roles that you were involved in makeup. It doesn't necessarily put you into certain roles, does it? Because they're not thinking of you in glamorous terms, are they?

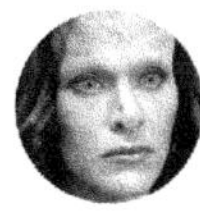

DOBRO
Well, I've done two sci-fi series [*Hypernauts* and *Crusade*] and I've been in major prosthetic makeup in both of them. Nobody ever knows who the hell you are. Do you know what I mean? For one thing, as an actor, it's good to know that they didn't hire you for your looks because god knows, you don't see them, which is kind of a nice thing as an actor.

I don't think it helps or hinders us either way, because the crossover between sci-fi and straight stuff in Hollywood—like Marjorie said, they don't look at sci-fi—they don't care unless you're like [Jean-Luc] Picard [played by Patrick Stewart in *Star Trek The Next Generation*]. Do you know what I mean? I don't think it helps or hurts us, one way or the other.

But don't you think, as women, you have a different situation than men? Being married to a makeup artist, I hear this all the time. A lot of women say, "My face is my fortune," and they're not being vain. They're just being pragmatic because that's the way it is. I should think that you always have to factor that into your decisions for roles that you're playing, don't you?

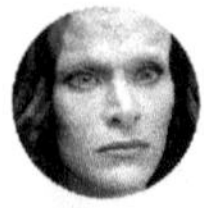

DOBRO
In terms of—

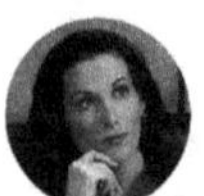

BROWN
—wear and tear.

In terms of what your appearance is going to be, too.

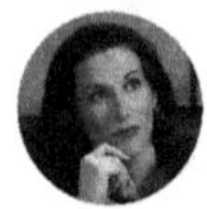

BROWN
That's why I turned down [continuing on] *Babylon 5*. I couldn't stay with it. That was the bottom line is that they weren't willing to protect my investment. I'm 32 years old, at the time, and I have just came out [to Los Angeles] from doing a lead in the Broadway musical and I'm with a good, strong agent. Yes, it's wonderful you wanna put me in a series, but you're gonna cover me with a ton of makeup that's not gonna help my career, that could potentially harm my face, and they can sue you. They can sue you for breach if you come come back and say, "I have to get out of this makeup."

Okay, they can force you to work. I asked for a medical out. I said, "If I bring, from a doctor, evidence that I'm having skin damage, I'd like you to let me out of my contract." Warner Bros. said, "No," and that was their prerogative. They had parameters about the role. I had parameters about the role, and I couldn't do it. Didn't stop me from going back and doing it occasionally.

> Brown took on the role of Na'Toth as a favor to casting director Mary Jo Slater when the original actor cast fled from makeup on her first day on the series. Brown was released at the conclusion of the first season, due to the concerns mentioned, and the role was recast. The third Na'Toth did not work out, and the character vanished from the series midway through year two. Brown returned to the role in the fifth season episode, "A Tragedy of Telepaths," to resolve the character's story.

But you weren't in a position of strength.

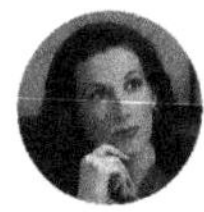

BROWN
No. Because who the hell was I? I mean, I wasn't like a big name.

Yeah. I remember with Carrie, I was there for part of the time when they were messing around with your makeup and this became the giant task for the makeup and hair people. It was like a daily ritual, wasn't it?

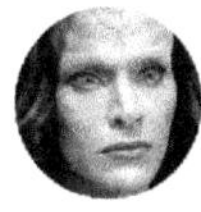

DOBRO
My makeup changed three times. I had three different prosthetic makeups and I had three different hairs.

> Dobro's three distinct Dureena Nafeel looks are seen in the movie-of-the-week, *A Call to Arms*; the first five produced episodes of *Crusade*; and the last eight produced episodes of *Crusade*, which were originally screened first, inverting Dureena makeups 2.0 and 3.0.

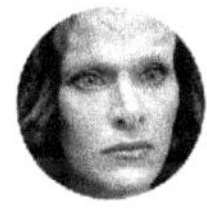

DOBRO
But the first series I did was worse, *Hypernauts*, because that covered from here all the way through to the back of my neck. That was major wear and tear on my skin, but they got me every skin product I asked for, and they were very gentle.

Crusade was only a little piece on my forehead. It wasn't a big deal for me.

The other thing was literally all over, and I got them to not put the glue all over the face, just on the edges. I worked every single day on that series and that was rough on the skin. But they work with you. If you really work with them, they'll do less amount of glue and less amount of scrubbing. I didn't let them do the scrubbing thing, very little, gentle brush. Although while doing *Hypernauts*, I got Detachol in my ear and had to be rushed to the emergency room. I woke up the next day and there was like blood on my pillows, I was bleeding out my ear.

> The makeup for *Hypernauts* was provided by Optic Nerve, which also handled the makeup on *Babylon 5* and *Crusade*. Dobro worked with them on all three series, having played a Brakiri in "Racing Mars."

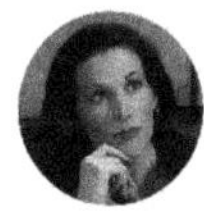

BROWN
See? This is the stuff they don't tell. You're gonna go and take this role. You're not gonna get paid a lot of money, and your gonna bleed. No.

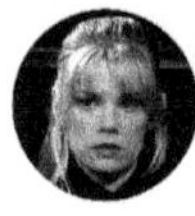

MONAGHAN
I was was offered a role in a kid's morning show thing that involved a lot of prosthetics. I knew [*Star Trek* makeup designer] Michael Westmore and I went to him. I said, "Look, I'm thinking about doing this thing. If I do it, what should I ask for?" Because I knew that he knew. He knew what the deal was with prosthetics.

[Richard Biggs enter, with much banter .]

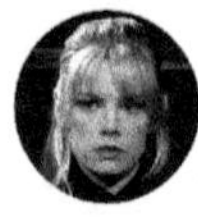

MONAGHAN
First of all, he said, "Why?" And then I asked him what would I expect and what should I require in my contract? I decided not to do it, for a lot of reasons. But, yeah, because there's a lot of stuff that you just don't know going into this. Now, I've never had to do prosthetics.

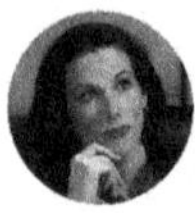

BROWN
Well, she's so beautiful, dammit, that she's always getting to be a real chick.

After doing *Deep Space Nine* and *Star Trek: The Next Generation*, I knew exactly what was coming, and I was terrified when I saw how much makeup it was [for Na'Toth] the full face mask and the head cowl and the skin's not breathing.

But here's the thing, science fiction roles for women are usually some of the best-written roles of television. There's the rub. Yeah.

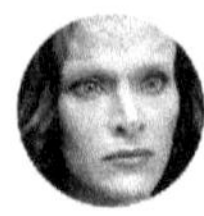

DOBRO
It's very hard to get a strong role for women in any genre, and sci-fi, they tend to be strong. I don't know why that is.

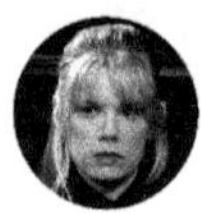

MONAGHAN
But especially, I found Joe [Straczynski's] women— They're strong. They're competent. They're intelligent. They're female, you know, they're feminine. They're not trying to be guys.

They're all very different. I mean, you look at Lyta and Delenn and Claudia's role and mine and Julie's and—they're all completely different. And yet they're all very strong together, cool, feminine women. So it's like, wow.

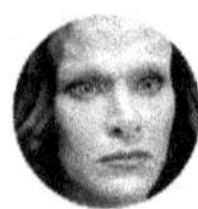

DOBRO
I remember for *Hypernauts*, after the producer session, before they went to network, they went, "We want you to see what this makeup looks like." And it was literally the whole—

> In casting a television series, the final stages are typically the producers who are making the show, the studio that is financing the show, and the network that will be broadcasting the show.

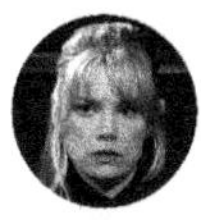
MONAGHAN
She's a fish.

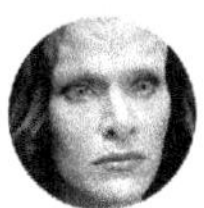
DOBRO
I had not a clue. I knew nothing about the sci-fi world, knew nothing about prosthetics. I was like, "Oh, okay. That looks like fun." You know? I had not a clue.

Famous last words, aren't they?

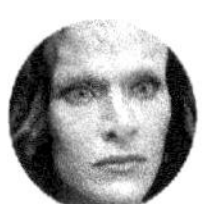
DOBRO
Well then they do that mold on you. Have you ever had that? It's like the freakiest thing in the world; you feel like you're dying, because they cover everything but too little—

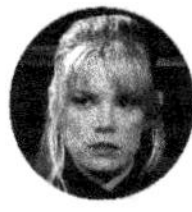
MONAGHAN
—snake holes [for the nostrils]. We did neutral mask in college. So we had the thing and that was like all I ever want to do. Yeah.

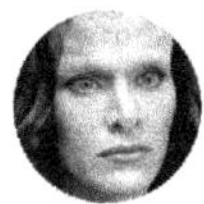
DOBRO
It was intense.

It's funny now that we have two people here who are actually involved in Crusade, one as a regular, one sort of peripherally.

> Nazzaro is referring to Carrie Dobro, a series regular on *Crusade*, and the newly entered Richard Biggs, who guest starred in the episode "Each Night I Dream of Home."

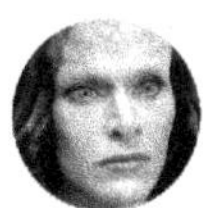
DOBRO
I was sort of curious about this, because I never got a chance to talk to you about this because of the show going [SPLAT! noise] out the window.

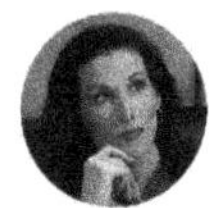
BROWN
So eleganté.

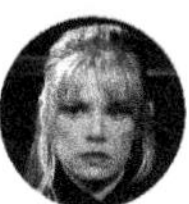
MONAGHAN
I wanna know how you're gonna transcribe that.

Yeah. Well, we use our creativity.

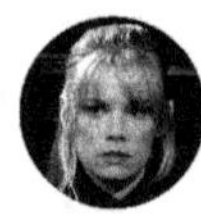

MONAGHAN
Having both of you been involved in the original show and then going into *Crusade*, did you find that there was actually a difference in the working atmosphere going on to the successor? Or was it business as usual? Rick, you only came in for one episode, so I don't know, you know, how you necessarily experienced it.

> Dobro appeared twice on *Babylon 5*, playing Dr. Harrison in "Exogenesis" and a Brakiri in "Racing Mars" before being cast as Dureena Nafeel for *A Call to Arms*.

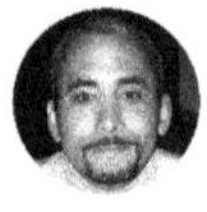

RICHARD BIGGS
Well that one episode was definitely different. As you say, the atmosphere, the energy was different. It was small ship. It was a small crew, and they were all by themselves, you know, going from place to place. It really felt like it was real tight-knit, you were enclosed kind of, it was a much smaller space, it felt like.

Babylon 5 was just huge everywhere you went. You could see different aliens and different rooms. It just felt bigger and the energy was much more frantic.

That was the thing I couldn't really put my finger on, and I think you've just said it. I sort of felt it as a different energy on set because I'd been on both sets a number of times and it just felt different, but you couldn't put your finger on it.

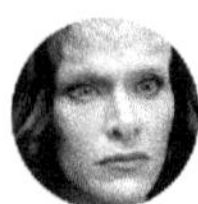

DOBRO
Well, I think there's a lot of reasons for that. I think you take a show that's been on for five years, that has its own success rate, and there's a relaxedness there and there's a camaraderie and there's all this wonderful stuff. Then you do the spin-off, which has its own problems as well, and pressures. We had 90% of the same crew; the crew was amazing.

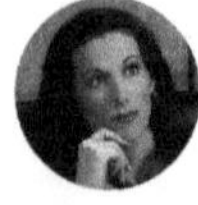

BROWN
But didn't you guys drop a day in your production too? Didn't you go from seven to six?

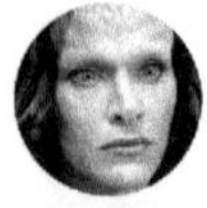

DOBRO
We were always seven.

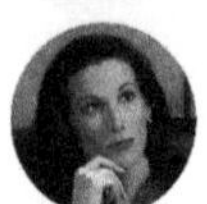

BROWN
Why did I think it was six? *They* did a six. It was the last year of *B5*. Then they went back to seven.

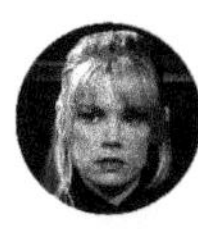
MONAGHAN
It completely baffled me.

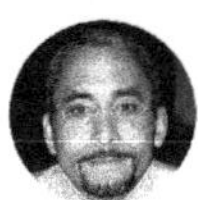
BIGGS
It was to save money.

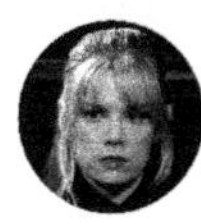
MONAGHAN
I've done episodic, I've done almost all like hour-long dramas. Every single show I've ever done shoots in eight days and barely gets by, and we did 14-hour days.

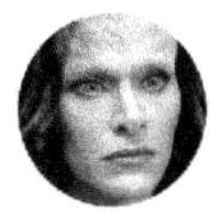
DOBRO
We did seven [days per episode], and they *never* let us go into overtime.

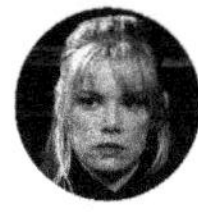
MONAGHAN
Babylon 5 shot eight hours a day for six days, and then we were done. It was amazing.

> For the first four seasons, *Babylon 5* shot seven days per episode. Due to the economic impact of moving from broadcast to cable between seasons four and five, it was necessary to shorten the shooting schedule to six days per episode. J. Michael Straczynski, a first-time director, volunteered to shoot the first show on the short schedule, to prove a novice could accomplish the task. For the most part, *Babylon 5* shot 12-hour days, beginning at 7am and wrapping as close to 7pm as possible.

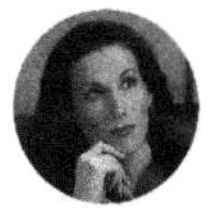
BROWN
Every time we got close, it was like, "Wrap it up! Wrap it up!"

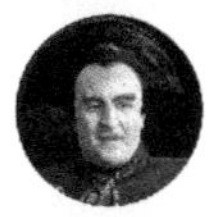
PETER JURASIK
Are you being interviewed here, what's going on?

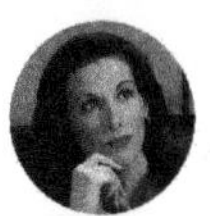
BROWN
Sit with us. Would you like some water?

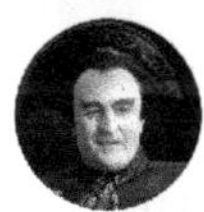
JURASIK
I want a drink!

Are you being interviewed right now?

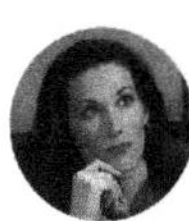
BROWN
We all are. It's a gang.

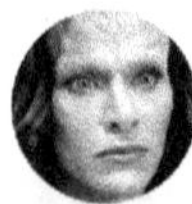
DOBRO
I don't think we've ever met, I'm Carrie.

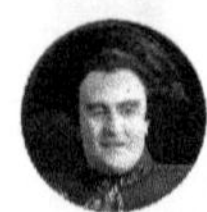
JURASIK
How are you, Carrie, I'm Peter.

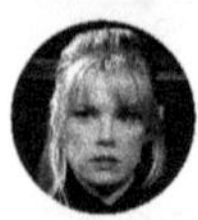
MONAGHAN
I'm Marjorie.

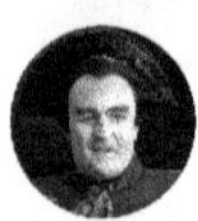
JURASIK
Hi Marjorie, we've met.

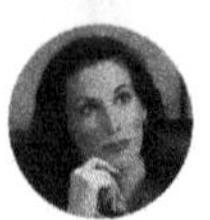
BROWN
Drinks, we can make happen.

[Richard and Peter look at baby photos.]

I think everybody with a baby should prop a photo of them up on their dealer's table.

[The discussion of children continues, with lots of incoherent talking over one another.]

Peter, just as you were coming in, we were talking about the difference in the energy and the chemistry going from Babylon 5 into Crusade. Funnily enough, you're one of the people who decided not to make a transition. I think there's one of the TV movies in the interim that you decided you'd had enough of it at that point, hadn't you?

> The role of brothel owner Jacob Mayhew in *The River of Souls* was originally offered to Peter Jurasik, but he passed on the part.

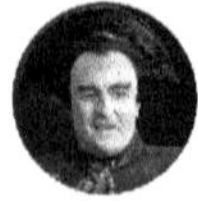
JURASIK
Well, at some point they pretty much had told all the stories, I mean, unless you wanna do Londo opens a dry cleaner, and he loses the Narn laundry. Boy, the chaos begins. They pretty much told the story, so I was happy to step away.

As the series ended, you have your absolute maximum amount of money you've earned. So you think, "Oh yeah, I'll step away." Then, three years later you're like, "Wait, don't step away!"

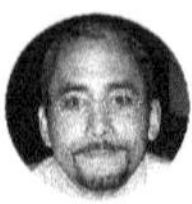
BIGGS
I mean, the shows go for seven, eight, ten years [in] science fiction. There had to be more stories out there.

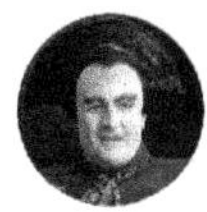

JURASIK
Oh no, of course. I felt like I had played it out pretty good, you know, to move on to something else.

Not too long after that, you'd got offered the role in Sliders and they wanted to bring you in there for a while as well. Having just come off of a science fiction series, that's a difficult decision to make, isn't it?

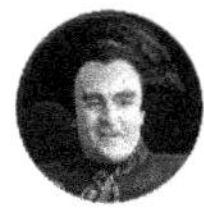

JURASIK
That really was a financial decision. They didn't have enough money to get me on. They wanted me on all season, but they didn't have enough money to pay me. So I signed up for however many I did.

My heart wasn't in it either because they were pursuing me, but another sci-fi was not really what I was anxious to do. I wanted hang out with my wife and my son, and fish and goof off. [Laughs.]

> Jurasik appeared in three episodes of *Sliders* as Dr. Oberon Geiger.

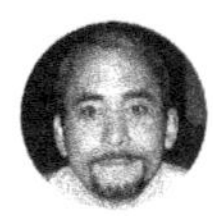

BIGGS
That's what you're doing now, huh? Is that what you're doing now? [Laughs.]

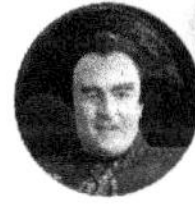

JURASIK
I am. Basically. I live in a town now that actually has a lot of movie and television work.

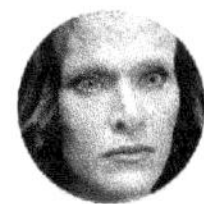

DOBRO
Where do you live?

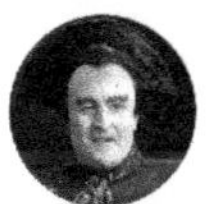

JURASIK
I live in a little town in North Carolina.

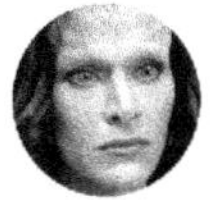

DOBRO
You're kidding.

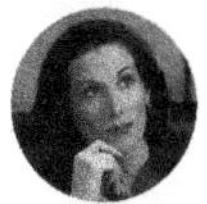

BROWN
A lot of work in North Carolina.

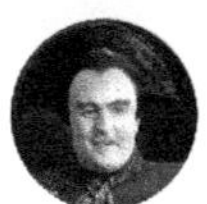

JURASIK
There's a town, Wilmington, right nearby that has studios.

This is where the De Laurentiis studios were put in, weren't they?

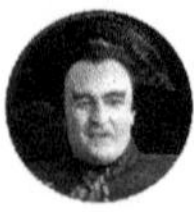

JURASIK
Exactly. So I've been working for *Dawson's* [*Creek*], that shoots there, and shooting a television movie. They found me there, but I disguise myself. You know, I wear moustache and a hat.

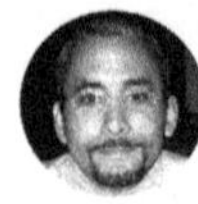

BIGGS
Good for you. That's great. Did you move to North Carolina specifically because there's a lot of work there?

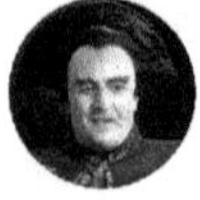

JURASIK
I have family south in Charleston. [My wife] Barbara's family is in Virginia. Because the studio was there, I worked a number of times. We wanted a beach. We wanted East Coast, and we wanted on the ocean. I tried to get my wife to move to Maine, but then she checked out the snowfall—

> Jurasik had been filming *Matlock* in Wilmington, NC, when he auditioned for the role of Londo Mollari in 1992.

If you want the winter that lasts for five months, then go to Maine.

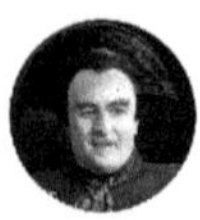

JURASIK
It's really, it's a great choice. We really love it. It's a great little town. I've got everything you'd would ever want.

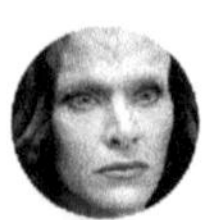

DOBRO
Was it shocking to kind of move from L.A. to North Carolina?

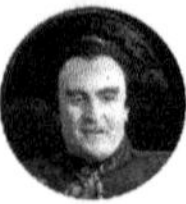

JURASIK
No, it really wasn't. The move was a giant pain in the ass, as you might imagine. But, yeah, once I got there, there was like nothing not to like. It's got a lot of culture. There's a university, so it's a hip town. There's music, there's theater, there's arts.

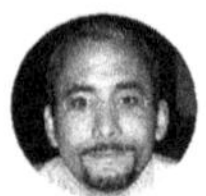

BIGGS
Yeah. But you've been living in L.A. how long?

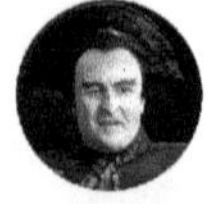

JURASIK
A long time.

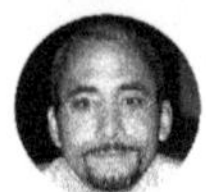

BIGGS
And you just up and left?

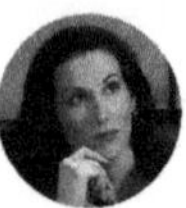

BROWN
Good for you!

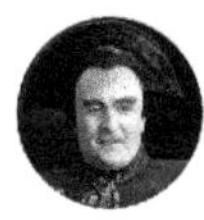

JURASIK
[Laughs.] Elvis has left the building. Know what I mean? You sell the house in Malibu.

I'm sure one of the subjects of discussion for a lot of people that are coming this weekend—and I'd be interested to hear how you answer it—is how do you all feel about this, this new B5 pilot/possible series that Joe [Straczynski] is coming up with? What was your reaction when you heard this thing was actually kicking around? Because one of your old friends, Andreas [Katsulas], is going to be in this from what I understand.

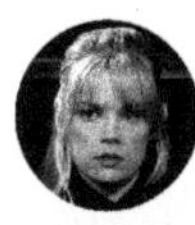

MONAGHAN
I kept hearing that somebody was gonna be recurring.

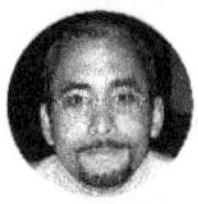

BIGGS
Andreas, probably.

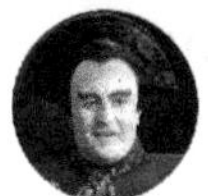

JURASIK
Not probably; he's in it.

So what was your reaction when you first heard that this thing—?

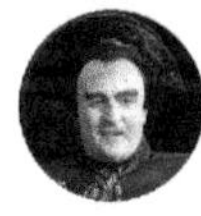

JURASIK
Chatted with Joe this week because I was doing a little charity con in town and he sent some stuff, and I said to him, "No wonder you [are] struggling with a script. You have no Centauris in it." [Laughs.] So that was my reaction to it. I'm sure it's gonna be great. People really want it.

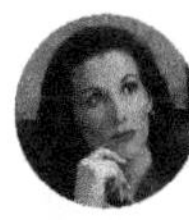

BROWN
It's funny when Jerry [Doyle] comes up, we had a conversation about it and it was interesting. He said, finally Joe's gonna give them what they've been screaming about *Crusade*, about *Babylon 5*—more action. *Rangers* is gonna be more action.

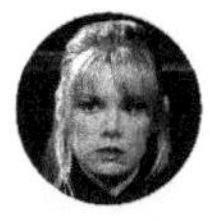

MONAGHAN
I wanna learn more about the *Rangers*.

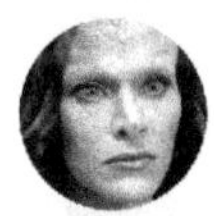

DOBRO
I don't know very much about it.

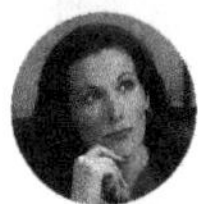

BROWN
The great thing about Joe is that everything comes from something. In other words, when he's making stuff up, he really makes it up organically, the way you would layer and build a character. He has these worlds in his brain and

they're deep. So when you're getting to do it, there's layers and layers for us as actors to play with and get into. Whereas what's unfortunately happened with some of the other franchises out there is that they go, "Okay, let's stick a forehead on you and stick a forehead on you and you're a new race!"

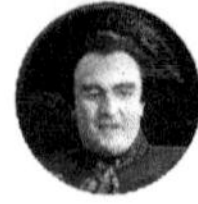

JURASIK

Another thing, Julie, they do is they pass it to different writers. You see Joe is just [a] consistent line that runs through the whole *Babylon 5*. Any reservations I've had about doing anything, I always said, "As long as Joe writes it, I'll read it." You know? Yeah. But those other series, when they pass on to the next writer and the other writer—

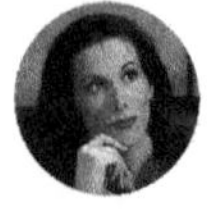

BROWN

It's watered down. The real [*Star Trek*] crew is really strong and really defined, and the races that came from [creator] Gene Roddenberry are really defined. Then you get all these ancillary races and you're saying, "How many non-aligned worlds can we have in one universe?" I've played a few of 'em. I just need to say, 'cause I love [when] they come up to me and a fan says to me, "You were Vekor in this episode, and where exactly did you come from?" I go, "Damn, I have no idea."

> Vekor, the character played by Brown in the two-part *Star Trek The Next Generation* episode "Gambit," still doesn't have a name for her species.

They don't give you little flashcards with that information, do they?

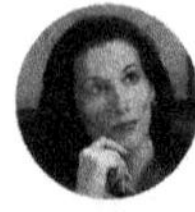

BROWN

No. They just look at you and say, "Well, you're kind of this alien and you're kind of this."

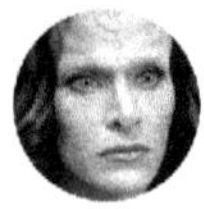

DOBRO

Joe does incredible research. [In] the bible on *Crusade*, my character alone was masses and masses of pages. I had a question— Since every series I do, "My world is dead"—that's absolutely true—I have to say it at least once an episode.

> On *Hypernauts*, Kulai—the role played by Dobro—was the last spiritual leader from a world destroyed by the treachery of one of her own species, played by recurring *Babylon 5* actor Ron Campbell. On *Crusade*, Dureena Nafeel's homeworld, Zander Prime, was destroyed by the Shadow Death Cloud.

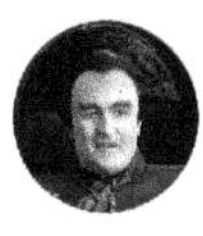

JURASIK
That's a possible title of your autobiography.

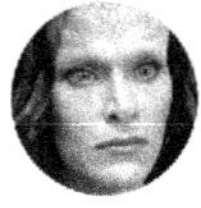

DOBRO
You'll be my ghost writer.

> Peter Jurasik had recently written *Diplomatic Act* (Baen Books, 1998) in collaboration with William H. Keith, Jr.

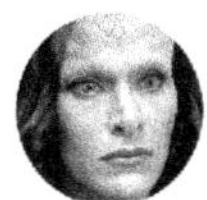

DOBRO
I asked some question. I always had tons of weapons and knives and all that stuff. I asked them something about the technology of my world since, you know, it was dead. They didn't know, and—I think it was [reference editor] Fiona [Avery]—went and did all this research and came back with like a ten-page synopsis about the entire industrial revolution on the planet.

> Fiona Avery's background on the history of Zander Prime was published in *Crusade: Other Voices*, Volume 2 (Published by B5Books.com).

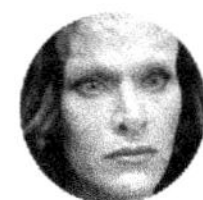

DOBRO
[The *Crusade* writers are] incredibly thorough and all this backstory—that you'll never know—it really helps define a character and why you make certain choices. The fun thing about Joe is he's very specific this is what it is. He's so open to thoughts on your character.

I always have a funny story about Joe. I didn't work with him all that long—obviously since [*Crusade*] got killed—but he took us to this small convention in L.A. when we had been shooting—I don't know—like a month or two.

> The convention was almost certainly LosCon 25, held 27–29 November 1998, at the Burbank Airport Hilton in Burbank, CA, but the editor has located no confirmation of the *Crusade* cast members in attendance. The event immediately followed the 25 November 1998 debut of "Sleeping in Light" on TNT. "The Path of Sorrows," *Crusade*'s ninth episode, also wrapped that day.]

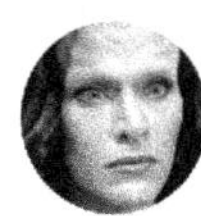

DOBRO
He took like four of us, and we had no idea what this whole sci-fi thing was, you know? Joe gets up there on the podium and he is fucking hilarious. He's cracking jokes. Everyone is laughing. We all walked up and we went, "Who was that?" He

said, "You'll never see him again. You'll never see him again. You'll never see him in the office." Because Joe at work was like serious. Do you know what I mean?

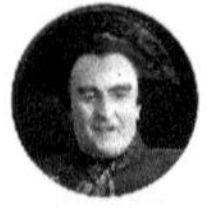

JURASIK
You actually piqued my interest when you said "the fun thing about Joe." You started that one sentence, I was like, "You gotta tell me! What's the fun thing about Joe?"

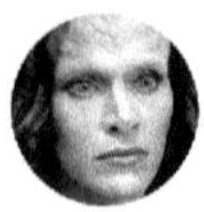

DOBRO
He's got this incredibly wonderful sense of humor and you never seen it at work where he was just like very serious.

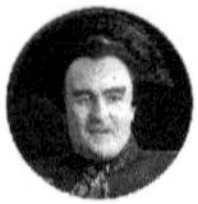

JURASIK
As a follow up to that, what's interesting is that's why it was so hard to get things changed in a script, because Joe had all this backstory that you talked about. That's true. He had so much stuff there. If you went to chat with him about it, you'd be there for three hours. You'd be there for three hours and he wouldn't change it. I'd go on for 20 minutes, and then he'd say, "Well, thank you Peter. No change."

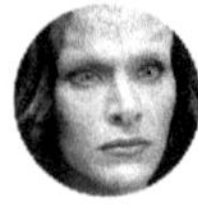

DOBRO
Then there was all this stuff that's in his head for episodes like two years from now. You can't change this because it won't make sense over there. But at least he was open to listening, which I thought was unusual.

So, as an actor, it would be a very difficult thing if you're trying to create your own actor's story, but the writer has the definitive story. He actually knows how your character is going to wind up in the end.

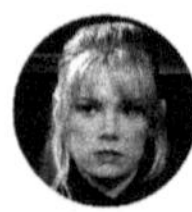

MONAGHAN
It depends on how you like to work. He didn't have a lot set up for my character. That's the first thing I did when I got the role. I said, "Joe, so what's going on?" I knew sort of what was going on, how I could serve the story, but I want to know that stuff.

If they know that, it's like, "Oh, thank you." Give me all this information. I like that when they know all this stuff, because instead of making it up by myself—because I can make up ancillary stuff—but if I know what's important to serve the story, then this is how I go and this is how I move and this is how I view the world, and stuff like that. I actually like it when writers can give me that, if you have good writers.

It must have been a cool thing for you. You opened up a script one day and you actually have a name for the character. You went from "Number One" to "Margaret Halloran," or whatever the hell her name was.

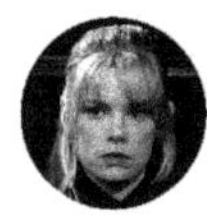
MONAGHAN
He actually let me change the name.

Oh, really?

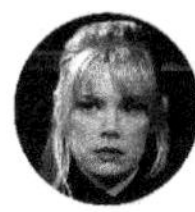
MONAGHAN
That was funny, because when we were shooting, I asked him, "So I just have one question for you: I know we don't have the name yet, but it's not—" What was his name? What was evil guy's name, the president who killed the former president?

Clark?

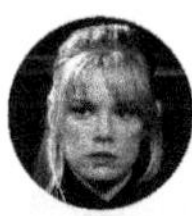
MONAGHAN
Clark.

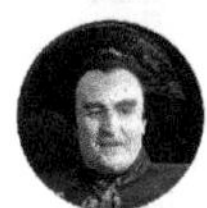
JURASIK
Is this one of those *Star Trek* things? Because I don't watch much *Star Trek*.

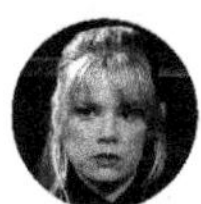
MONAGHAN
It's not Clark, is it?

He let me change the name because I didn't like the first one.

> In the 28 January 1997 Final Draft of "Objects in Motion," Number One's name was revealed to be Margaret Halloran. For the 4 March 1998 revision, a few days before production, the first name was altered to Theresa.

If Babylon 5 is actually coming back—possibly as a franchise, because I was talking to somebody at the Sci-Fi Channel and they have high hopes for this beyond a pilot—everybody sitting here in this room has a character who could conceivably come back at some point. Are you guys interested in that, or do you feel more that you've left these characters behind now?

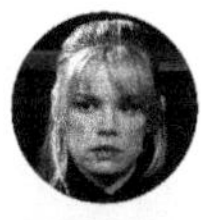
MONAGHAN
We're actors; we like to work.

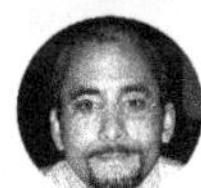
BIGGS
If Joe called me up today and said he wanted me to come and read for something, I'd be there in a minute. But I'm not like waiting by the phone, either. As more time goes and more things happen, and you get into other things— It was such a positive experience that if Joe called me, I'd definitely see what's going on.

Do you find that old cliché about time heals all wound is that, as actors, you forget all the crap that goes on in the series and all the bad stuff? Even the difficulty wearing makeup?

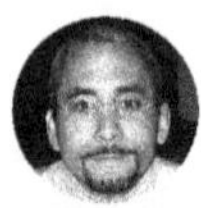

BIGGS
You're not forgetting it. It's still there.

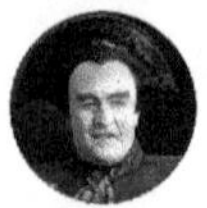

JURASIK
That's why they let a whole hiatus go before they negotiate the next year's salary—the cooling off period.

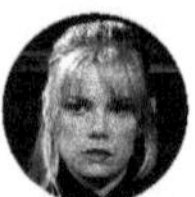

MONAGHAN
The edges get blunted.

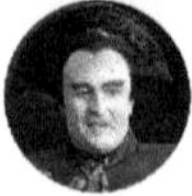

JURASIK
None of us really forget what a series is like. That's the question. You don't forget what a series is like to shoot.

I suppose you know that it's going on the Sci-Fi Channel, and I know that there were problems, which may well change, now with a negotiations for the Screen Actors Guild. When [Babylon 5] moved from syndication into cable, the money was not very good. I know that was a concern, and presumably this pilot is going to shoot before whatever contracts get renegotiated.

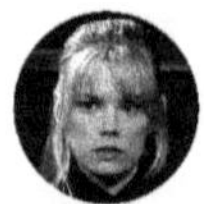

MONAGHAN
I think, with the negotiations, they're gonna have [the agreement be] retroactive.

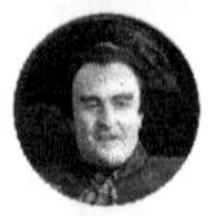

JURASIK
That's right.

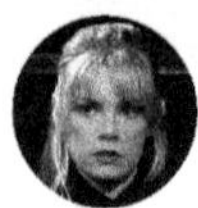

MONAGHAN
Whatever's negotiated now, I think will have to go along with the new guidelines. I could be wrong.

It could be a whole different ball game for this program than it was for Crusade, which got caught in the middle of that.

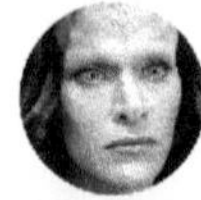

DOBRO
Probably so. I don't think it will be a strike, personally.

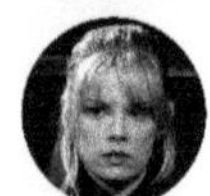

MONAGHAN
I hope not.

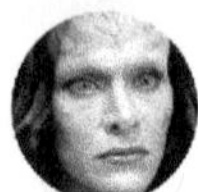

DOBRO
Do you guys?

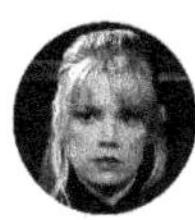
MONAGHAN
I don't know. I don't know.

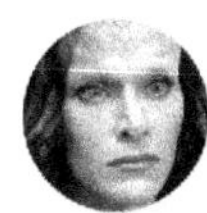
DOBRO
Everyone is pushing to not have it.

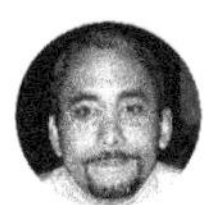
BIGGS
What have they got, four days, five days?

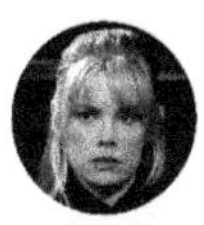
MONAGHAN
That's for the Writers [Guild].

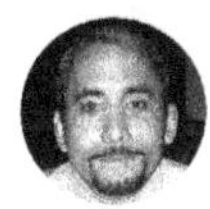
BIGGS
I don't think the actors are going to strike. I think the writers might.

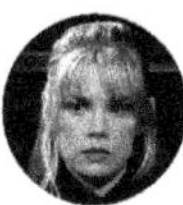
MONAGHAN
The writers are having a lot of the same issues as the Screen Actors Guild. So I think that they're gonna get some stuff worked out and it's because of that, the SAG will be...I hope. I don't know. I don't know.

The thing that worried me about the AFTRA strike—and I think the reason so many big-name people came out in support of the commercial actors, even though they obviously don't do commercials—is that it's like the producers are out to break the unions. If they're really serious about that, then there could be a strike. I don't know.

From what I understand, the amount of money sitting in the actors' coffers is not that much because they wiped a lot of it out during the commercial actors strike.

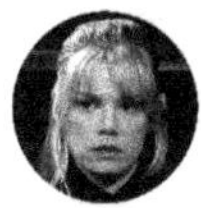
MONAGHAN
I couldn't tell you, but I wouldn't be surprised.

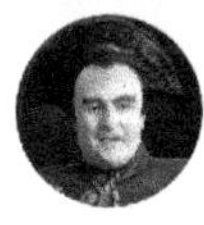
JURASIK
You guys know Armin Shimmerman? He's one of our negotiators. He's a buddy, and I chat with him—we have phones in North Carolina, so we actually talk, they're the wind-up ones, right—

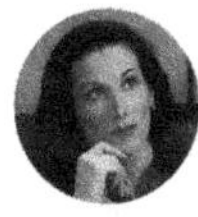
BROWN
Jerry is not in his room and he's not here. I don't know where Jerry be, unless he's taking a shower.

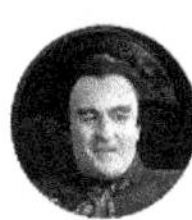
JURASIK
Armin says the real problem with it. He's very hopeful that there's gonna work out, but they're trying to get stats to bring to the producers and say, "Look, this is how much you guys make when you sell *Babylon 5*"—or any series—on cable, and

this is how much you're paying us, based on standards that you did in back in '82. Unless they have those compiled and put together— He said they're really behind on getting that together and having that stuff really, real ammunition to bring—

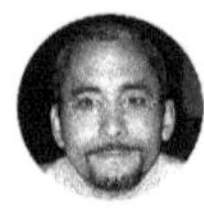

BIGGS
The writers or the actors?

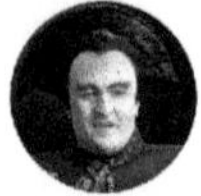

JURASIK
The actors, and the writers too.

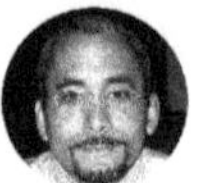

BIGGS
But aren't the actors the weakest of the unions as far as the writers, directors and —

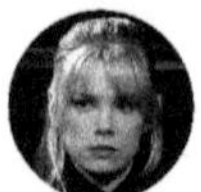

MONAGHAN
I don't think so, because if the actors walk, everything shuts down. Period.

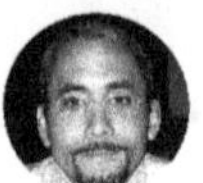

BIGGS
Well, weaker of the three. Don't you think we're the weaker of the three?

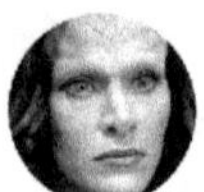

DOBRO
I think DGA is the strongest.

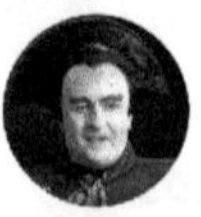

JURASIK
But aren't we the most charismatic? No one can dance like our union.

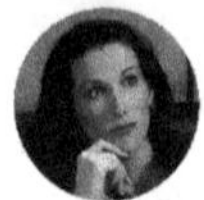

BROWN
It's 5:45, and this show opens at six. Since you got to ask a lot of questions of the ladies, and the boys just showed up, I'm going to see if they can be released to go downstairs. Could you turn [the recorder] off for a second?

> The interview continues with the female cast members gone and Jerry Doyle holding court.

Are you actually looking to get outta the business now, Jerry?

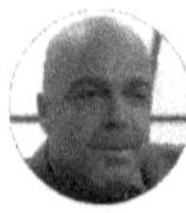

DOYLE
I dig politics, man. I love the business, don't get me wrong. You get to work with all these people we work with for six years, make good money, good friendships, travel around the world; that doesn't happen a lot. But the realities of the business are I'm not gonna sit around and wait for something to happen. Who was it that said, "I'm now too old for the parts I used to be too tall for?" [Laughs.]

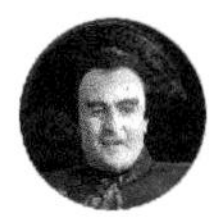

JURASIK
That's great.

It's funny because I was just saying to Julie last night, "When I met a couple of you guys when you're doing the Babylon 5 pilot—and you weren't in the business for very long at that point, you're sort of stockbroker-turned-actor—"

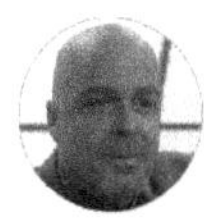

DOYLE
Yeah.

"—so are you becoming actor-turned-politician?"

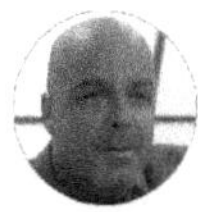

DOYLE
Yeah, yeah, yeah. I'm going for the hat trick. Wall Street was the money. Hollywood was the glamor. Washington is the power.

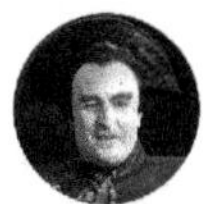

JURASIK
Whoa. He is going for it. He's got a plan.

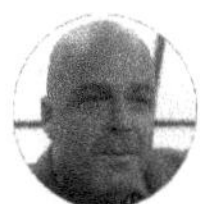

DOYLE
I want the hat trick. I just dig it. I like getting involved in stuff that I think really matters.

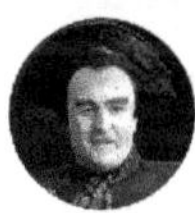

JURASIK
Joe, it's about—in terms of overall thing—staying happy, passionate, and excited about what you're doing.

All your priorities are changing because you've moved.

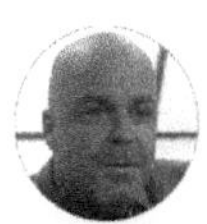

DOYLE
And he's working more than he did in town!

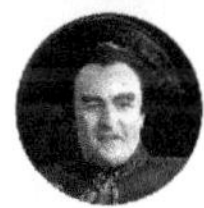

JURASIK
It's true.

Rick, you're becoming a family guy now. Do you find that your priorities in life are starting to shift now?

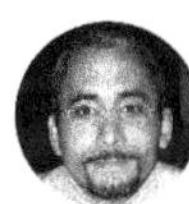

BIGGS
Sure. Yeah, I mean. It's not as important—the business—and the balance is more important to me now that I have other interests, and then I'm not like totally just consumed by myself and my career.

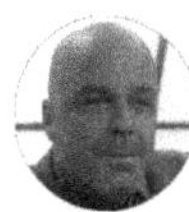

DOYLE
You don't judge your day by, "Did I get an audition or the call back?" You come

home and your son's there. You're like, boom, you know? And [Peter], with Ben, what a lucky kid Ben is. You guys wanted to have kids forever. It didn't happen. Finally, all of a sudden and he gets adopted into this totally cool—people who love him and don't beat him.

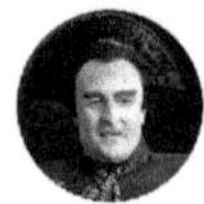

JURASIK
It sounds like I should adopt Jerry,

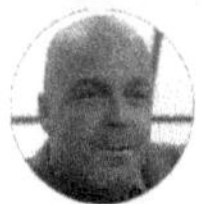

DOYLE
No. Being adopted, I appreciate that.

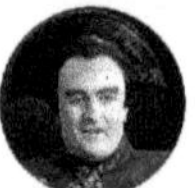

JURASIK
You know what, it's a completely mutual love.

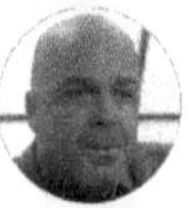

DOYLE
He could have gone a Rosie O'Donnell; then he'd be fucked.

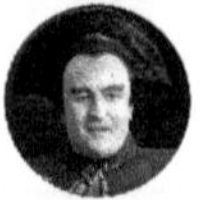

JURASIK
There's nothing I love better than being a dad, now. I really mean it. It just feels completely satisfying in every way.

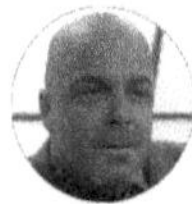

DOYLE
Plus you were smart enough to buy a place and put your money away. We saved a few bucks, but a lot of actors don't get the shots at building up a nest egg and having the ability to say, "Hey, I'm looking at other options."

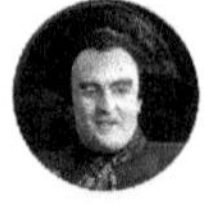

JURASIK
That's right.

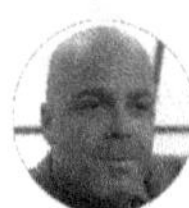

DOYLE
Because they're still waiting for that one option that gives 'em a bank of money. Then, maybe if we weren't comfortable and had other things in our lives that were exciting, maybe we'd still be going "I gotta get in and bust that door down." Maybe that part of it is gone and maybe a certain amount of happiness—

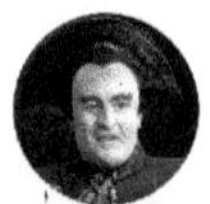

JURASIK
Who knows? Thank God we're living our lives. [Laugh.]

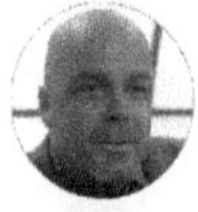

DOYLE
Would you wanna be Robert Downey, Jr? I don't care how talented he is.

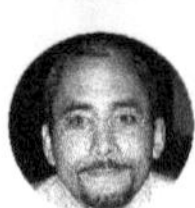

BIGGS
How miserable he must be—

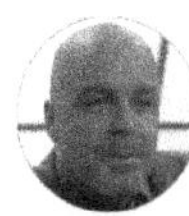
DOYLE
Yeah, exactly.

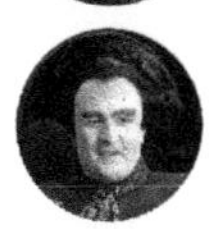
JURASIK
I read the last week he got busted walking around Culver City.

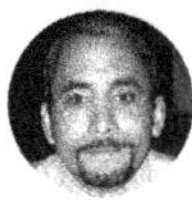
BIGGS
Yeah, it was right down the street from my house, on Washington with this drug addict guy who is his friend. No drugs were found on him, but I mean, god, it's an alley in Culver City. What was this? The Screen Actors Guild Award?

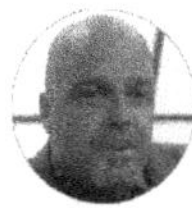
DOYLE
I think they were picketing something. [Laugh.] They, they were striking something.

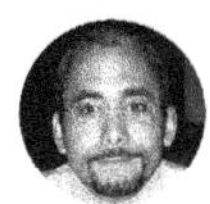
BIGGS
I mean, the guy's on one of the top ten comedies—

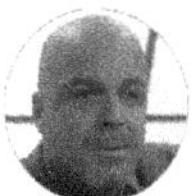
DOYLE
Coming outta prison.

> After being released from the California Substance Abuse Treatment Facility and State Prison, Robert Downey, Jr. was cast in *Ally McBeal* as the eponymous character's love interest, Larry Paul, earning an Emmy nomination and Golden Globe Award for his performance before being abruptly written out of the show, following the Culver City arrest in April 2001. Downey subsequently turned his life around, remaining sober since 2003 and becoming a major box-office attraction in movies based on Marvel Comics and the Sherlock Holmes stories of Arthur Conan Doyle, among others.

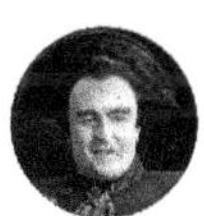
JURASIK
I know.

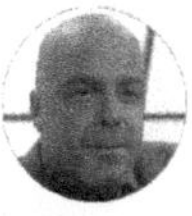
DOYLE
It wasn't like he was coming out of Stella Adler—

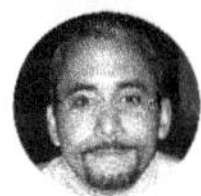
BIGGS
This is what I think we gotta do. We either gotta get on a reality show or we gotta get arrested. One of the two.

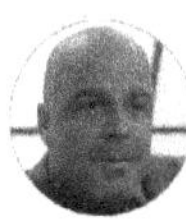
DOYLE
Look at the business.

I'd go for the reality show.

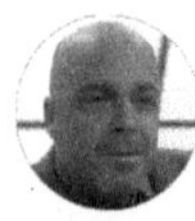

DOYLE
People are coming off reality shows and getting movies. I know actors that are trying out for reality shows—

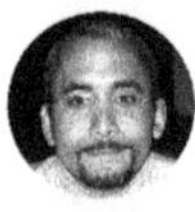

BIGGS
Right. Because they know that's—

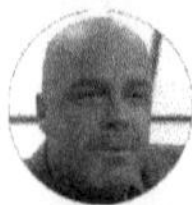

DOYLE
That's the way to get a gig.

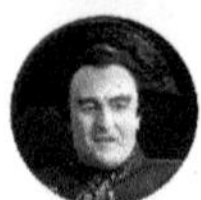

JURASIK
If you're on *Survivor*—

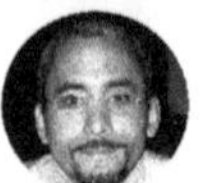

BIGGS
You're gonna see me—

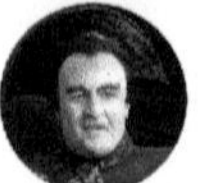

JURASIK
Richard Biggs, Accountant.

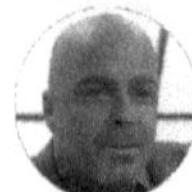

DOYLE
Community activist Richard Biggs on *Survivor 3*—

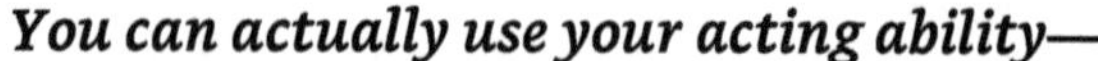

You can actually use your acting ability—

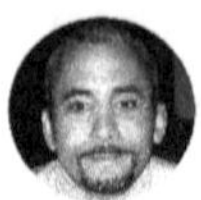

BIGGS
That's true. Hey, you know what happens when you get kicked off *Survivor*? You're on *The Today Show*. You know what it would take for me to get on *The Today Show*? You're on Letterman, too. That's what I'm saying. Either I go hang out with Robert Downey, Jr., or you get on a reality show. Either way, man, it's to the top.

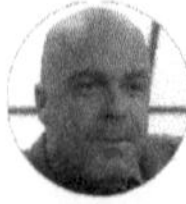

DOYLE
Boxleitner said the reason he's not working is because he has good parents.

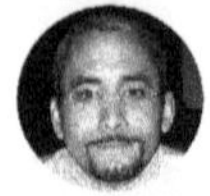

BIGGS
That's right. They didn't get him high at six years old.

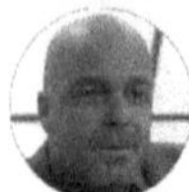

DOYLE
He doesn't come from a dysfunctional family.

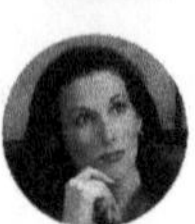

BROWN
He loves himself. He doesn't need all this shit.

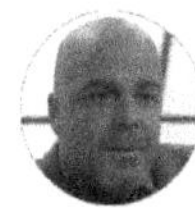
DOYLE
No. It's just amazing. It seems like all the lunatic fringe are getting work. Poor Matthew Perry trying to struggle by on $750,000 a week.

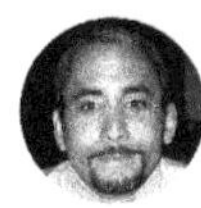
BIGGS
Guess he's gonna have to shoot another movie.

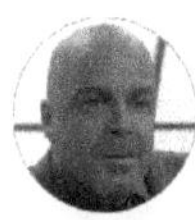
DOYLE
God. Yeah.

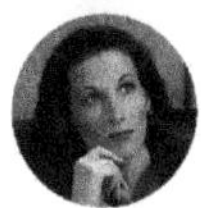
BROWN
But have you ever seen Matthew? I've met Matthew several times. I was at a party with Matthew, and after meeting him, he stood, I swear to god— There were 500 people at this party. It was a producer's house up in the Hollywood Hills, and it's all Christmas, everybody just really relaxed. It's not like your typical Hollywood party where everyone's checking everybody out. They're actually kind of cool, you know, and he's standing like this. If you were all the people, he was like this.

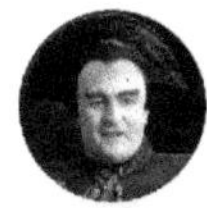
JURASIK
Against the wall nervous?

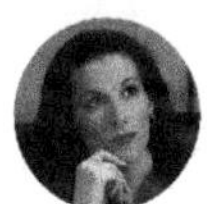
BROWN
He doesn't know what the hell to do with himself.

I was looking at my watch. I wanna get you guys down so you start making some money, but maybe we could sort of wrap this up this way.

What brings you guys back to these conventions? A couple of bucks in your pocket? I find it hard to believe that [Jerry and Rick] are gonna fly from L.A. to do a sci-fi convention, or [Peter's] gonna leave your family. What is it that actually brings you back to meet people who watched the show you did a couple of years ago? What's the attraction?

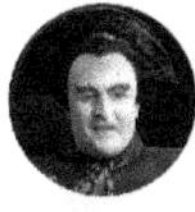
JURASIK
I came back because [Julie] offered me good money.

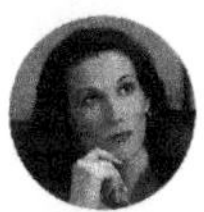
BROWN
I did.

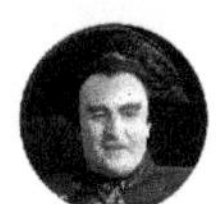
JURASIK
She set up a good deal, and I get to see these guys.

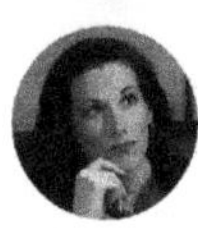
BROWN
That's part of it.

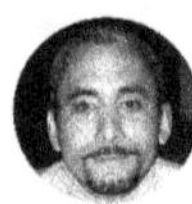

BIGGS
I know it's funny, we all live in the same city—most of us live in the same city—but we rarely see each other.

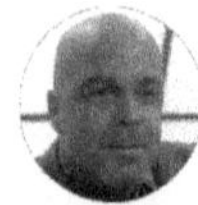

DOYLE
We never see each other.

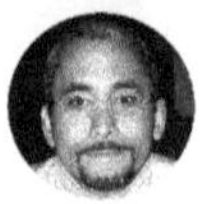

BIGGS
We know that we're gonna have a good time, we're gonna see each other, we're gonna talk like we do and laugh when we go to these conventions, and we're gonna make a little money.

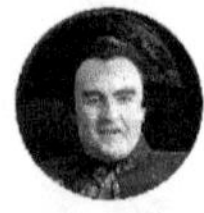

JURASIK
Why not?

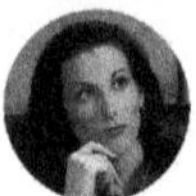

BROWN
There's some fun bennies of the fans. Sometimes, somebody will do something.

I remember when [Rick's] wife was pregnant and I went to a gig with him down in Virginia. My goodness, the man had to hire a U-Haul to get all the presents and gifts home for his new baby.

Jerry's running for office and you pump the flesh wherever you gotta, you know? This, it's just good.

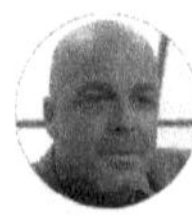

DOYLE
I have that thing called the internet. My website got 1.3 million hits in the last campaign. It didn't equate to the 73,000 votes, but people were typing and not voting. But now that's a way of getting the message out.

[To Peter] Actually, I was gonna file a claim with the Federal Elections Commission because Ben [Jurasik] pushed the plunger, right?

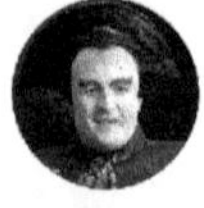

JURASIK
That's right.

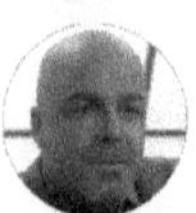

DOYLE
He's not legal to vote. Oh, that's right. I wanna recount.

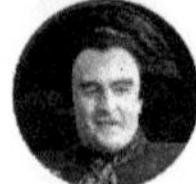

JURASIK
What am I saying? Ben pushed it.

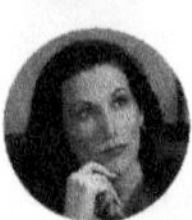

BROWN
So there's ancillary things going on here, for myself. I gotta tell you the whole idea. Peter moved to [North] Carolina. I moved up to Northern California, to be

with my son. If I didn't have these wonderful crazy people who trust me with their money and this convention circuit— I've got this whole other thing going on that gives me freedom. I can write, I can produce. I've sent something to Peter and to Richard—I've asked Jerry to read it—a script that I wrote, a new series.

It's about freedom. Conventions are also about freedom. They're walking away money. They're I don't have to take that part because. I bless the fans every day. I say, thank you god, Joe Straczynski, for putting me on a show that people want my autograph.

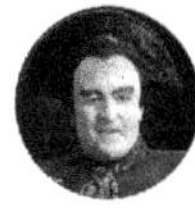

JURASIK
We were talking about different priorities with family, you know? It's true. You're hard pressed not to do it. I mean, my wife says, "What are they wanting you to do for two days? Go! Get out of the house! What are you sitting around here for?" I just hang around with Ben, you know. Let's play electric guitar, go fishing again tomorrow—

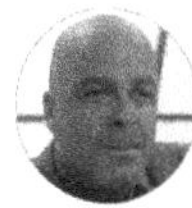

DOYLE
Ben's going, "Go!"

Audition for another series just so she can get you the hell out of the house.

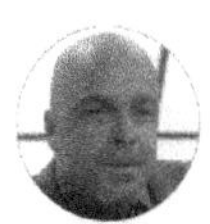

DOYLE
"I wanna hang with mom for a change. Dad, you smothering me here. Okay."

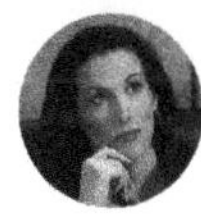

BROWN
You never know who you're gonna meet. I had [*Star Trek*'s] Leonard Nimoy on the phone the other day, you guys.

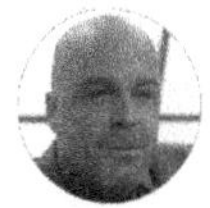

DOYLE
Oh, nice.

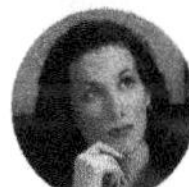

BROWN
I'm cooking a deal for Leonard Nimoy. I'm having a conversation with Leonard Nimoy. I was jazzed.

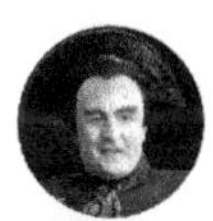

JURASIK
Good. Of course you should be.

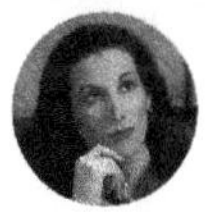

BROWN
Why not? 'Cause it's fun.

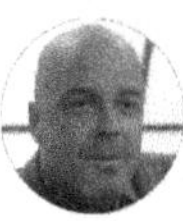

DOYLE
Live long and prosper.

But we're not talking Star Trek here, not 30-some-odd years you're doing conventions. It still must be strange because it's been a couple years now [since the show ended], and yet, every day there's somebody who turns on the Sci-Fi Channel and watches Babylon 5 for the first time. It must be weird because they might write to you or something, and it's brand new for them.

> Syfy began broadcasting in 1992 as the Sci-Fi Channel. In 1999, the cable channel dropped the hyphen and the word "channel" from its name to become "Sci Fi."
>
> Sci Fi financed the conversion of *Babylon 5* to widescreen and broadcast the series in 2000, taking over the show's strip syndication from TNT. Sci Fi subsequently re-broadcast *Crusade* (its first repeat after debuting on TNT) and commissioned *Babylon 5: The Legend of the Rangers.*
>
> In 2009, Sci Fi once again rebranded, becoming "Syfy."

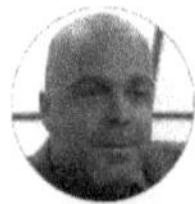

DOYLE
Different people are finding the show.

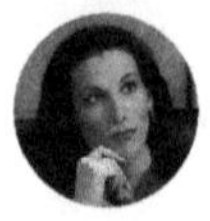

BROWN
Absolutely.

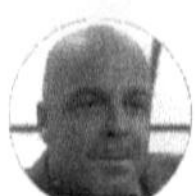

DOYLE
A different base is finding the show.

I didn't do conventions for a couple years, three. I stayed out of it. Then I saw this new 36-foot center console fishing/diving boat with twin 250 [Yamahas] hanging off the back.

Bang out eight conventions, he's got the boat. It's gonna be called *Thank you, next.* [Laughs.] You want this personalized?

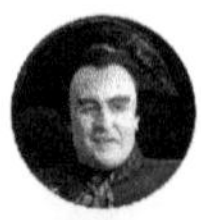

JURASIK
That's what it should be called.

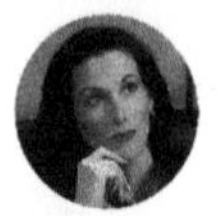

BROWN
It's good times. It's easy, and its better than digging a ditch. You know what I'm saying? I'm grateful for it.

Of all the people that I work with, booking shows, anybody looks at me and says, "Well, this doesn't really matter to me. It's just so little of my money," they can find another agent. I wanna work with people that when I call you up and say,

"Hey, man, you're going to Italy. Hey man, you're going to Australia," They go, "Cool."

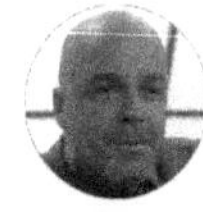
DOYLE
All over the world!

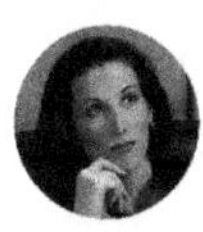
BROWN
Be happy. You know?

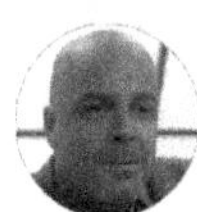
DOYLE
I can't name a person that's been in the *B5* universe that has gone to these things and treated the fans poorly. I think the people who go truly appreciate the fans for what they did for the show, what they did for us. We go there because it has a whole lot of benefits, but we go there knowing they're the reason that we are there. I think they come away from these things going, "Cool."

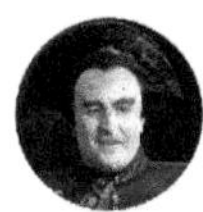
JURASIK
That is true about *B5*, too. Yeah.

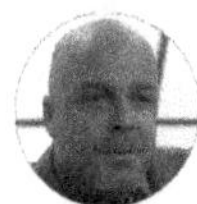
DOYLE
I've seen some other shows and other people and you just wanna go, "Hey, if you don't want to fucking be here, then don't come."

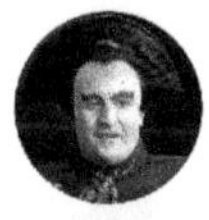
JURASIK
Exactly.

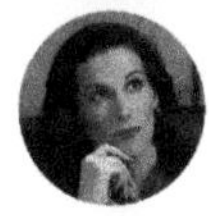
BROWN
Right. I don't have time.

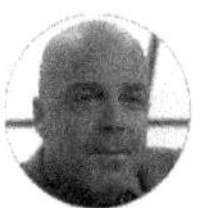
DOYLE
The fans don't deserve it.

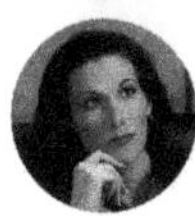
BROWN
I really don't have time to waste on people that are disdainful of the very people that are putting them on television.

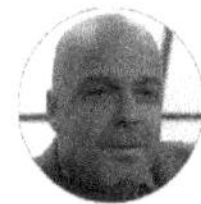
DOYLE
That's why I diss [William] Shatner every time I get a chance. He's a fucking asshole. [Laugh.] I tell the fans on stage, "Why do you let him treat you like this?"

[Impersonating Shatner's staccato delivery] "I don't. Sign. Autographs. For. Less than. Fifty grand." Please—

Fuck you. If he wasn't Captain Kirk, he couldn't get a job at making Whoppers.

All of a sudden Galaxy Quest is looking more and more biographical, isn't it?

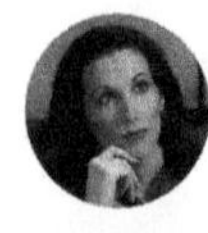

BROWN
They knew what they were writing.

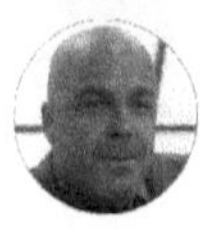

DOYLE
Absolutely. I saw myself in some places in that movie too. NASA calls their *Space Cowboys* their *Galaxy Quest*. *Galaxy Quest* is our *Galaxy Quest*. What a great movie. *Galaxy Quest* would be a great series.

Printed in the USA
CPSIA information can be obtained
at www.ICGtesting.com
LVHW050437270923
758146LV00004B/164